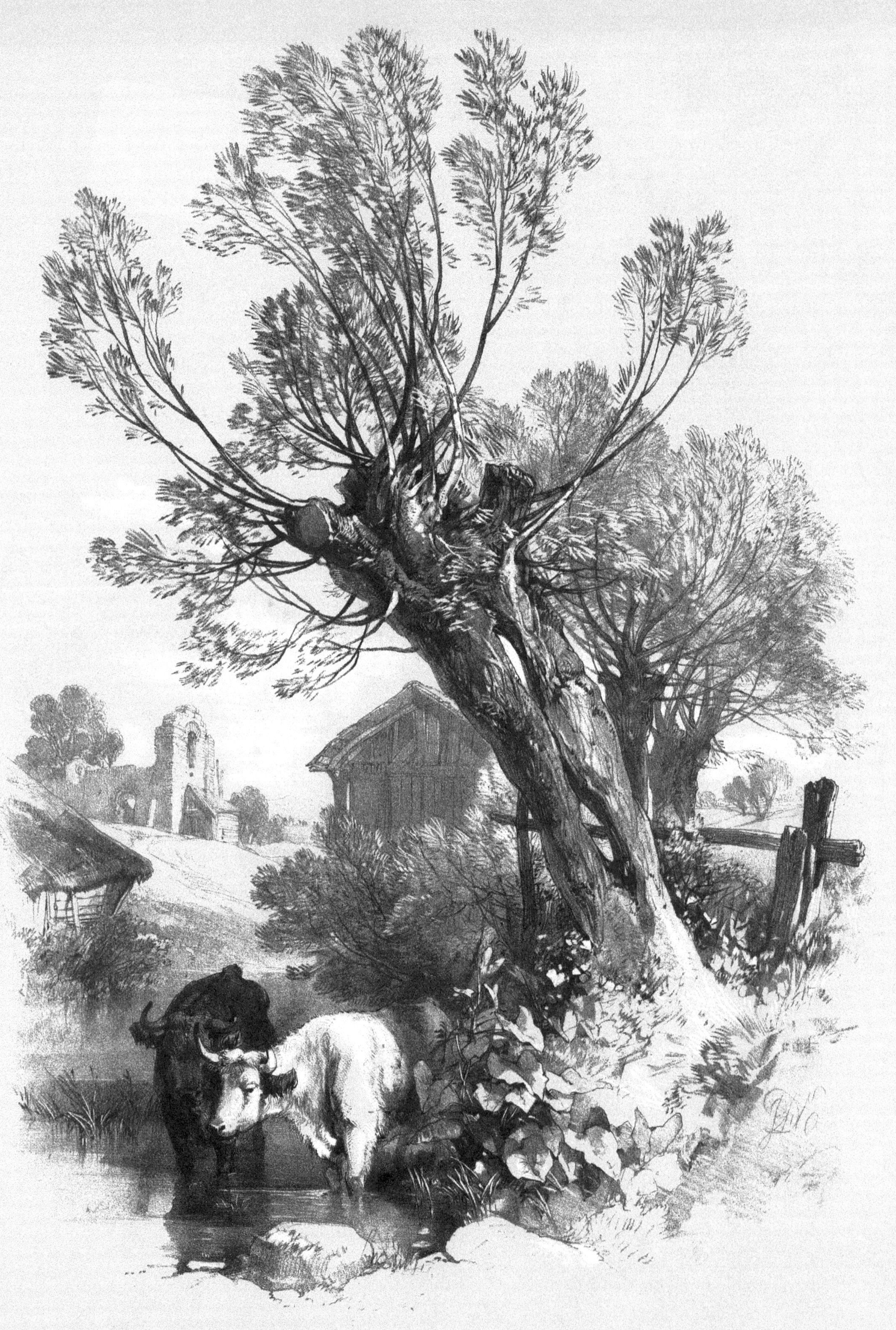

ON DRAWING TREES AND NATURE

A Classic Victorian Manual with Lessons and Examples

J. D. HARDING

DOVER PUBLICATIONS, INC.
Mineola, New York

Bibliographical Note

This Dover edition, first published in 2005, is an unabridged republication of the third edition of *Elementary Art: or, the Use of the Chalk and Lead Pencil Advocated and Explained,* originally published by David Bogue, London, 1846. The Dover edition also includes a supplement of 23 plates from the same author's *Lessons on Trees* (Day and Son, London, 1855). Plate 22 of the main section appears as the frontispiece in this edition.

Library of Congress Cataloging-in-Publication Data

Harding, James Duffield, 1798–1863.
    [Elementary art: or, The use of the chalk and lead pencil advocated and explained]
    On drawing trees and nature : a classic Victorian manual with lessons and examples / J. D. Harding.
      p. cm.
    Originally published: Elementary art: or, The use of the chalk and lead pencil advocated and explained. 3rd. ed. London : D. Bogue, 1846. Also includes a supplement of 23 plates from the author's Lessons on Trees.
    ISBN-13: 978-0-486-44293-8 (pbk.)
    ISBN-10: 0-486-44293-4 (pbk.)
    1. Blackboard drawing—Technique. Pencil drawing—Technique. I. Title.
NC865.H34 2005
741.2'3—dc22
                                       2005042848

Printed in Canada
44293407   2025
www.doverpublications.com

PREFACE.

THE sale of two large Editions of this Work, and its favourable reception, not only by the Public, but by the Profession,—from many distinguished Members of which the Author has received the most gratifying testimony of its usefulness,—afford not only a strong assurance of the truth of the Principles propounded, but also evince a decided approval of the method by which they are explained and practically illustrated. The Author, thus encouraged, has, in preparing a Third Edition of the Work, spared no pains to render it still more deserving of Public favour.

Among the improvements which have been made in the present Edition, the following may be enumerated as the most considerable.—The instructions, which, in the two former Editions were confined to the Use of the Lead Pencil, have in the present been rendered equally applicable to the Use of the Chalk. This extension seemed to be required in consequence of the more extended employment of the Chalk, as an Instrument of Art, since the appearance of the first Edition. Of late, indeed, since the manufacture of Tinted Paper has been so much improved, and its use, consequently, increased, the Chalk has almost entirely superseded the Lead Pencil for drawing on such paper. The whole work has been carefully revised; the Instructions have been, as much as possible, simplified, in order that they may be the more readily understood; and that the Student may be spared the trouble of so frequently turning to the Plates, Cuts have been introduced into the text in proximity to the passages to which they relate. With respect to the Plates, all the subjects are new except one; and every one, from the most simple to the most complicated, will be found to illustrate either directly or indirectly some important Principle in the practice of Art. In the execution of the Plates, the Author has availed himself of the most recent improvements in Lithography. Those on tinted paper—with the effect of Drawings touched with white—are in the same style as the Author's " Sketches at Home and Abroad," which appeared in 1837, and were among the first Examples of Lithographic Drawings executed in this manner in England.

To elucidate and inculcate the Elementary Principles of Art, founded on an observation of Nature, and to show how they can be most efficiently applied by such an instrument as the Chalk or Lead Pencil, has been the Author's aim in every portion of the Work. He recommends no maxims from his own individual practice; for though nearly all the Examples are drawn by himself, it is not on that account that the Student's attention is directed to them, but because they exemplify Principles, the truth of which may at all times be tested by a reference to Nature. He has endeavoured to show the Student the advantage of adhering to such Principles in every step of his progress; for those only can be said to study Art advantageously who, looking continually to Nature, apply the means and materials of Art, at their command, in conformity with her dictates. It has therefore been his desire to place before those who wish to study the art of Design, such simple rules for their guidance as will enable them, in the first place, to learn how to look at Nature, and then how to represent her by Art.

Some works on Design, though very ably written, are not sufficiently elementary or practical for beginners; while others present little more than a copious catalogue of materials, as if the method of rightly using them was so plain as to require no explanation. In others, again, the Authors seem to consider that exellence in Art is chiefly shown by a disregard of Nature; and the works of the greatest Artists are referred to in confirmation of the absurd proposition,—as if their chief merit consisted in their very faults and mannerisms; while, in truth, such Artists are only to be considered great, from their general adherence to Nature, and in spite of the defects resulting from a peculiar mode of practice. In this way, dogmas deduced, or, rather, extorted, from the capricious practice of particular Artists, are set forth as infallible rules for the Student's guidance, instead of philosophical principles, founded on the unchanging Laws of Nature.

It appeared to the Author, that the disadvantages above alluded to might be remedied by providing the Student with a Work, such as is here offered to him, explaining the Principles of Elementary Art by a reference to Nature, and showing, by Examples, how they are to be carried into Practice. He trusts that the Work will be of service, not only to those who intend to devote themselves to Art as a profession, but also to those who may be desirous of acquiring a practical knowledge of it, either as an elegant accomplishment, or as a useful aid in other pursuits.

With the view to promote this, and in order to furnish the Student with assistance to which he may continually refer, as well as to make his work more decidedly useful, the Author has increased the number of Plates, and the Pages of Illustration, much beyond what he originally thought would have been necessary. The course he has followed has been suggested to him by his experience in actual instruction; and he has endeavoured to show how, by so simple an instrument as THE CHALK or LEAD PENCIL, such a knowledge of Art may be acquired, as may lead to eventual success.

The chief object of this Work is, to explain the Principles of Elementary Art, and to teach the Student how to apply them by means of the CHALK or LEAD PENCIL. When he has sufficiently mastered what is here placed before him, he may then proceed to the study of Composition, Colour, and General Effect. These he will find explained and illustrated in "The Principles and Practice of Art," a work which the Author announced in the Preface to the second Edition of the " Elementary Art," and which he has recently published.

To his friends, E. LANDSEER, R. A., and W. P. FRITH, A. R. A., the Author is indebted for the subjects in Plates 2, 3, and 4. In reference to the other Plates, it is only necessary for him to add, that they are from his own Sketches, the subjects of which have all been taken from Nature.

4, GORDON SQUARE,
UNIVERSITY COLLEGE, LONDON.

CONTENTS.

INTRODUCTION.

Elementary Practice to be accompanied by the explanation of first principles, 1.—The faculty of observation and comparison to be exercised, 2.—How Nature may be best interpreted by Art, 3.—Importance of commencing the Study of Art on right principles, 4.—The usefulness of Art, 5.—Erroneous views of many persons on the subject, 6.—Causes of the want of success in the pursuit of Art, 7.—" Bold " and " Soft " Styles, 9.—Importance of practising with the Chalk or Pencil, 9.—Progressive Course of Study, 11.

CHAPTER I.
GENERAL REMARKS ON THE USE OF THE CHALK, OR LEAD PENCIL.

The evidence of the mechanical process by which a likeness to Nature is obtained, ought to be as much as possible concealed, 13.—Of Lines, their utility and defects, 14.—Of the application of Lines to indicate character or quality, 15.—Excellence in Art not a gift but an attainment, 16.

CHAPTER II.
ON FORM.

Importance of correct drawing, 17.—Applicability of the Chalk, or Pencil, to the delineation of Forms, 17.— Perfection of Form in each class of objects, 18.—Our judgment on the productions of Art influenced by our feelings, as well as by our knowledge, 19.—Of Selection, 19.—To clothe objects properly, a knowledge of their Forms requisite, 20.—Of the different Forms presented by objects, according to their position and the direction in which they are viewed, 21.—Disadvantage of commencing too early with Colours, 23.

CHAPTER III.
ON THE APPLICATION OF THE CHALK, OR PENCIL, TO THE DRAWING OF FORMS.

The effects of the hesitation felt by beginners, 25.—How confidence and precision are to be attained, 25.— Defects of a hard Outline, 25.—Mode of holding the Pencil, 27.—Of determining the inclination and position of Lines, 27.—Of drawing Curvilinear Figures, 28.—The different effects of Outlines of a different kind, 30.—Where Character should be chiefly displayed, 31.—Of the amount of Imitation required, 31.

CHAPTER IV.
ON COPYING, AS PREPARATORY TO THE STUDY OF NATURE.

Of the right intention of Copying, 33.—Drawing from Memory, 34.—Difficulties at first attendant on the attempt to draw from Nature, 35.—The habit of merely Copying, without regard to principles, an impediment to progress in Art, 36.—Mode of determining the relative situation of objects, 38.

CHAPTER V.
ON FOLIAGE.

The importance of Foliage in Landscape, and the apparent difficulty of its truthful imitation, 40.—The Artist not required to distinguish the leaves of trees with the precision of a Botanist, 41 —" Slight " and " Highly-finished " Drawings, 42.—The idea of Form conveyed not by the dark outline alone, but as it is viewed in connection with the space which it encloses, 42.—Shade suggestive of the rotundity of objects, and of the presence of Light, 43.—Property of Shade, 43.—The attention

CONTENTS.

attracted by the illuminated parts of objects, 44.—Nature *puts on* the *light*, the Artist, using the Chalk, or Pencil, *puts on* the *shade*, and leaves the light, 44.—General properties of Shade to be observed in depicting Foliage, 45.—Common errors in depicting Foliage pointed out, 46.—Of the Outlines, 46.—Relation between the form of the Leaf and the form of the Masses or Folds of Leaves, 47.—Arrangement of the Groups of Leaves, 48.—Flexibility and Rotundity, 49.—Requisites in the outline of Foliage, 51, 52.—Their exemplification, 54—57.

CHAPTER VI.

ON STEMS AND BRANCHES.

General properties of Stems and Branches, 58.—Mode of properly attaching the Branches to the Stem, 59.—Bark, 60.—Rotundity, 61.—Direction of Light, 62.—Mode of growth in Branches, 63.—Difficulty of tracing the Branches, 64.—Semi-transparency of Foliage and Opacity of Stems and Branches, 65.—Diligent practice, guided by knowledge, required to insure success, 65.—Forms of the Stems, Leading Branches, and Folds, 67.—Uselessness of copying the forms of Foliage minutely, 68.—Errors pointed out, 69.—Mode of study to be observed, 69.—Properties of the Beech, 70.—Importance of first acquiring the power to draw some one tree well, 72.

CHAPTER VII.

ON FOREGROUNDS.

Grass and Herbage, 74.—Evenness and unevenness of Ground, 75.—Mode of representing the blades and masses of Grass, 75.—Spaces between the masses, 75.—Manner of forming Leaves, 75.—Effect of various kinds of plants in Landscape, 76.—Similar lines expressive of different qualities, accordingly as they are employed, 76.—Knowledge of the separate parts requisite, 77.

CHAPTER VIII.

ON LIGHT AND SHADE.

Solidity indicated by Light and Shade, 79.—Character of Surface as seen through Shade, 80.—Difficulty of detecting the precise outline of objects, 81.—Forms rendered more distinct by contrast, 81.—Ideas of roundness and solidity suggested by Light and Shade, 82.—Natural Shade and Accidental Shadow, 82.—Mode of representing Shades and Shadows, 84.

CHAPTER IX.

ON THE USE OF THE BRUSH.

Different effects of the Chalk, or Pencil, and the Brush, 86.—Comparative advantages and disadvantages of each, 86—88.—Mode of attaching the several masses of foliage to each other, 89.—Shade and Local Colour to be kept distinct, 89.—Best mode of operation, 89.—Washes of Colour for Skies and Distances to be carried over the places of darker intervening objects, 91.—Advantages of a knowledge of the true principles of Art, 91.

APPENDIX.

ON THE MATERIALS.

Paper, smooth and rough, 93.—Chalk and Pencils, 94.—Coloured Paper, 95.—Use of the Stump, 96.—Mode of obliterating Chalk or Pencil Marks, 96.—Of fixing Drawings on the Paper, 97.—Of the facilities for Study and Practice afforded by Lithographic Drawings, 97.

SUPPLEMENTARY PLATES.

99.

ELEMENTARY ART.

INTRODUCTION.

IN the following pages are embodied the results of the Author's experience in imparting a knowledge of Elementary Art, accompanied by graphic examples, such as he has found to be best suited to impress its principles effectually on the mind. Having proved the usefulness of the precepts and the examples in communicating, with facility, both practical and theoretical knowledge, he has been induced to lay them before the Public. The wish, on his own part, to extend assistance, has been seconded by the entreaties of many, who have desired to be directed aright in their views of Art, and in their efforts to acquire skill in its practice, whether as an auxiliary to other pursuits, or for the purpose of cultivating it as a profession.

The invaluable Art of Lithography, by affording the greatest facilities for the publication of Books of Lessons, and Studies of all kinds, and for placing in the hands of the Public, at a very moderate cost, Original Drawings by accomplished Artists, has contributed not only to the more general dissemination of the productions of Pictorial Art, but also to increase the desire to become acquainted with its principles and practice. Such examples, however, are of comparatively small value as subjects of imitation merely, unless at the same time the Student receive instruction in the principles of Art, as well as in the manipulation of the materials.

To render such examples really profitable to the young in Art, for whom they are intended, some explanation of its first principles is necessary, in order that they may know what they are about; for without this knowledge they will never advance in Art beyond the rank of mere copyists of other people's works: however acute their sight may be, or ready their hand at fac-simile imitation, they will never be able, of themselves, to select and truthfully depict the beauties of Nature. After having copied any of those examples, they require something more than to be told that what they have done is either too large or too small, too wide or too narrow, too light or too dark,—all such mistakes might be self-evident, requiring no master to point them out; such information acquaints the pupil with what he probably very well knew, but affords him no real instruction in the principles of Art.

Some explanation is required of the various methods employed to characterise the various objects: whether certain modes of depicting their forms and qualities be in accordance with the principles of Nature as applied to the practice of Art; and whether an attractive result may have been a fortunate accident, or may have been intentionally worked out by the Artist. Something is required which shall exercise and cultivate the faculties of observation, comparison, and reflection, so that whilst the mind is thus acquiring more distinct ideas of forms and their relations, it may be prepared to perceive and appreciate the higher beauties with which Nature has surrounded us on all sides, and at the same time be rendered capable of more readily acquiring distinct ideas on other subjects.

It is not to those only who intend to study Art as a profession that I desire to address myself, but to those also who take it up as a pleasurable pursuit. There are many who regard it as of easy attainment; and if they discover in themselves an aptitude for imitation, at once decide on becoming either professional artists, or amateurs, concluding, though most erroneously, that they are in possession of an intuitive talent which will enable them to attain in " Six Easy Lessons," a thorough mastery over Art. Others, highly susceptible of its beauties, but unable to trace, in the works of the painter, effects to their causes, believe it to be a mystery, and that its charms are attributable to the power of innate genius, without which every attempt must be futile.

The chief object which the Author has ever kept in view in this undertaking, is to remove those erroneous and too generally prevalent notions, and to cultivate a just taste for a useful and intellectual pursuit. The difficulties which present themselves at the commencement, are such as are common to every other important pursuit; and are surmounted in proportion as a knowledge of correct principles is attained, and as intelligence becomes operative in guiding the hand.

Excellence is to be obtained, not in the practice of the style, or more correctly speaking, the manner of any model, but from a knowledge of the principles of Art and the truths of Nature, which alone should suggest the adoption of every style or manner. Unless the study of Art be based on such truths, its practice can only end in disappointment.

Art is the graphic interpretation of Nature; and every painter either expresses his ideas of her in his own idiomatic pictorial language; or, guided by his knowledge, and his own peculiar views, embodies, in his own style, the excellencies of another. Every student in Art must not only be furnished, in the first instance, with ideas, but with some graphic means of expressing them; and as the first difficulty to be overcome in Art is the attainment of signs for the expression of ideas, it is to this that the attention of the student will be chiefly directed throughout this volume.

Every original painter relies chiefly on himself for the characters, or graphic language, which he employs in his interpretation of Nature. He diligently studies her beauties, and investigates the various modes adopted by his predecessors and contemporaries in their imitations of her originals, deriving from each such aid as may be most subservient to his own views; and thus making their thoughts and practice conducive to the eventual attainment of a method both true and original. The amateur is differently placed; Art, with him, is but a secondary consideration, a part only of his education. Exempted from the necessity of becoming conspicuous for high and peculiar attainments, he is enabled to save himself much time, by at once adopting the ideas of others, without studying for himself their natural prototypes. He should be careful, however, to assure himself that the productions of Art which he selects for imitation have been wrought from a knowledge of Nature; for on his ability to make a right selection depends the profitable employment of his time.

Like language, Art also has its rules; and it is within its province not only to express some ideas more powerfully than written language, but also to distinctly represent others that are wholly inexpressible by its more arbitrary signs.

Those who would aspire to pourtray the creations of a vivid fancy, or to depict Nature, faithfully and forcibly in all her charming and endless variety, must consent to adopt such means as are employed in the acquisition of written language itself. None ever indulge a hope of learning a language unknown to them by merely tracing its characters, or transcribing a few passages from books written in it; none would be so unreasonable as to suppose that they could attain any degree of literary excellence by imitating the peculiar handwriting of some celebrated author. Why, then, should any one expect to attain excellence in Art by the mere mimicking of its characters, as employed by any particular master? The belief, however, is all but universal, that mechanical copying is the ready road to such excellence; and years of the most precious portion of life are but too frequently wasted in mind-less imitations of other people's modes of representing Nature. Those who copy, however accurately, may continue to do so through a long life with unabated zeal, and yet never be able to express by means of Art one original idea.

If the study of Art be commenced on right principles, and steadily pursued, skill in its practice may be attained by all in proportion to their general aptitude for other intellectual pursuits. Art, if properly viewed, should be esteemed an indispensable part of a liberal education ; for who is there amongst the many young men daily leaving our public schools and universities, with leisure and fortune at their command, that would not feel it to be an acquisition? It has, indeed, been called a new sense, from the gratification it affords, and the power it gives of fixing scenes, persons, and events, to which the memory can refer. Who is there to whom in future life such a pursuit would not be delightful, if not eminently useful? It would afford a delightful retrospect to the nobleman and gentleman who have sought foreign climes in order to extend their knowledge of the world, but whose recollections of scenes and places they have visited, perhaps for the first and last time, are every day becoming more and more indistinct. What a source of pleasurable interest to themselves, to be enabled, with the pencil, to recall them, both to the mind and the eye, with truth, freshness, and reality! The world has been greatly benefited by the valuable information derived from Pictorial Art. Without fatigue, all the ends of the earth, its inhabitants, its forms and features, organic and inorganic, are rendered familiar to us. It brings home to our hearths the reliques and vestiges of former ages ; it records what " Time's effacing fingers " are daily obliterating ; it enlarges on all sides our field of mental vision, and becomes daily a more indispensable coadjutor to the extension of knowledge. However desirable in other instances, skill in Art is highly important in the profession of Surgery; for it is an undeniable fact, that the Medical man may, within the compass of an ordinary volume, procure for himself more valuable and varied materials to refresh his memory, and apply to daily recurring cases, than he would be able either to gather or to retain in the shape of preparations; and this, too, without hazard or difficulty, and at a less cost of time and trouble: and many distinguished practitioners have most successfully availed themselves of Art, as a means of imparting information which could not otherwise be conveyed.* To how many of our Soldiers and Sailors are we not indebted for our knowledge by graphic representation of the scenes in which they have travelled and fought? The Lawyer who can draw, has thus an additional language to assist him in eliciting or affording explanations where every other language fails. To the Engineer and Mechanician, it is absolutely necessary:—in short, there are few conditions of life in which it would fail to prove a most useful auxiliary, applicable to many purposes not contemplated until its powers are tested. As an accomplishment, it is no small part of its recommendation that it has often proved a most valuable resource in the vicissitudes of fortune.

Seeing the general usefulness of Art, it seems truly astonishing that, as a branch of education, it should be so much neglected. This neglect appears the more striking, when it is considered that, under *proper* instruction, all might acquire sufficient knowledge for every practical purpose. The youthful and the least informed mind may be initiated into a knowledge of the principles of Art without more consideration of innate predisposition than is looked for in regard to other studies. Does any parent ask what degree of genius in youth is necessary to the acquirement of Latin and Greek, or of any other language? or for a natural inclination sufficiently marked towards any other branch of a general education? All who are required to receive what is termed a good or liberal education, are, without much reference to native talent, placed in circumstances favourable for its attainment. Yet, with reference to Art, it is

---

* If the Student derives much of his most valuable knowledge, during his attendance at the Lecture-Room and the Hospital, from a progressive series of Anatomical Plates, how much more would delineations, founded upon his own experience, in after life, with observations on the cases, form an invaluable storehouse of surgical facts, applicable to new accidents and presentations, and always at hand to assist the uncertainty of memory?

the reverse of all this: every parent first desires to discover in his children some demonstrations of natural inclination for it; and not until satisfied on this head does he venture to place them under instructors; and then only as an experiment to ascertain if his conjectures concerning their talents be correct. Not unfrequently, from his own ignorance of any benefits derivable from Art, he is led to look upon it merely as busy idleness—a pastime, occasionally filling up a few vacant hours; or, at best, merely affording—more especially from the hand of a daughter—some trifling ornaments for the drawing-room, whose appearance is not generally improved by such family decorations. These are the successors of the ancient family of samplers, and of the yet more ridiculous pretensions to pictures, wherein the Gentle Shepherdess, Charlotte at the Tomb of Werter, or some equally touching incident, was most elaborately set forth in gaudy silks and worsteds. Such tawdry inanities, in by-gone days, passed for taste, and occupied the place of that which now, in its turn, should be removed for what is better and more intellectual. From the boy is expected some glaring and ample display, and he is encouraged to attempt something *great*; which, when completed, by the finishing touches of an abler hand,—concealing the young artist's want of power, or correcting his mistakes,—is viewed by indulgent friends and relatives as an indisputable mark of his genius. The youths themselves, ungratified by the applause which they know to be undeserved, are happy for the time in gaining the box of colours (or *paints*, as they call them), with all the enticing paraphernalia so adapted to the waste for which their prolific ingenuity never fails to find ample scope. When older, they learn too late how little real knowledge they have acquired; and, disappointed with a practice in which much of their time has been irksomely, because fruitlessly, spent, they attach no real value to Art, but rather look on it with disdain.

Those who do not apply for instruction in Art until after their education in other respects has been completed, have, at this advanced period, to contend against many disadvantages. Their time is then no longer at their own disposal, on account of their being immersed in pursuits of profit or pleasure; and their matured minds enable them to comprehend the theory of Art so readily and so fully, that they have, in consequence, too little patience to apply it, and to overcome the mechanical difficulties necessarily attached to the practice. Disinclined to submit to the labour requisite to overcome the preliminary difficulties, and hoping to find some " easy style," they wander from one Artist to another, till, wearied with the fruitless search, and disappointed in their hopes of quickly attaining excellence, they abandon the pursuit of Art,—ending, as they begun, in error; for they ascribe their want of success to their want of *genius*,—whereas the true cause was their neglect of employing means within their power. Generally speaking, it is better not to enter upon the study of Art too early; for, as it is an appeal to the mind, and not, as commonly supposed, to the eye only, and requires reflection, discrimination, and judgment in the proper application of its means, it may be taken up with the best prospect of success by those who are sufficiently advanced to possess such qualifications.

These observations, though true as regards Amateurs, do not equally apply to those who would devote themselves to Art as a Profession; for as *their* business is to excel, and, if possible, to carry the pursuit beyond their predecessors (an arduous and difficult task), or to strike out some new objects for attainment, *they* should never take it up unless naturally predisposed to do so; but when once determined, they should devote themselves heart and soul to the undertaking the moment that circumstances will permit.

Success in the Artist or Amateur depends on the general powers of the mind, and on these being rightly directed. The method here presented, is intended to assist the Master to explain his Art in such a manner, that his time and talent may not be thrown away, nor the Pupil labour in vain. That this is too frequently the case, numbers of those who both give and receive Lessons can amply testify. And why is this? Because the Artist is called upon to explain how he paints his Pictures, or, in other words, to teach his " style;" for those who apply to him, but too frequently seek only to know the particular colours he uses, and how he compounds, and spreads them over a given surface. From want of the necessary previous information in his Pupil, he, indeed, can rarely attempt more: prepared for the opposition to his assurances that the Pupil is beginning at the wrong end, and, knowing or fearing that his endeavours to impart really valuable, because *rudimental*, instruction, would be unavailing, he yields, and makes a semblance of teaching an ambitious aspirant to write the language of Art, before he has mastered its alphabet. Let us watch the Lesson, and examine its results. All are struck by the readiness with which the Painter produces a pleasing effect in his Picture—it has been the business perhaps of a few hours; the Pupil has learned what colours are used—their mixture—and how applied; knows the peculiar qualities belonging to them—how, if wrong, they are to be removed; he has seen the mechanism of the work—but nothing more. All the complexity of thought necessary to its production must be going on at the same time, but the Painter cannot stop to explain the various reasons which influence his operations, still less to describe the elementary and progressive steps by which he at length acquired his enviable power. Unhappily, his Pupil can do no more than follow the mechanical progress of the work with his eye, without being able to follow the Artist in his mind. Thus he witnesses the completion of Picture after Picture, and, if he gains any information, it is of such a kind as he can rarely or never apply for himself. As yet, he has not learned the "knack" he sought; and, after a like trial of another and another Master, he at length discovers that he has indeed begun at the wrong end. He has not taken into consideration the years of previous study;—the thousand failures that preceded success;—the stores derived from the study of Nature and Art;—the materials collected;—the experience; though all these have been silently and invisibly operating, and the result is now seen concentrated in the Drawing or Picture before him. The ease, the freedom, the decision, at once surprise and delight; but the labour of years, not of hours, has been witnessed. Does the Pupil believe it possible that so much knowledge can be made available to him by the practice of a few hours?—knowledge, to gather and develop which, the Artist has brought into action all his enthusiasm and the most unwearying industry. It is enough, by way of answer, to recall the well known anecdote of Sir Joshua Reynolds, who, when one of his sitters paid for his picture, and observed it was for three hours' work, replied, " No, Sir, it is for the work of thirty years." How different is the plan pursued in regard to other Teachers, when imparting instruction in the various other branches of a liberal education! They are permitted to begin with the elements of the knowledge required. The Musician begins by teaching the value of the notes, their names, &c. The Linguist, from the alphabet, proceeds through the orthography of the words, their sounds and meaning, and from their grammatical agreement to the finished sentence. The Artist, however, strange to say, is almost invariably required to begin with the end, and to deceive his Pupil by pretending to impart in a few hours that which he has devoted a life to acquire. I lay particular stress on these mistakes, as they are the real impediments to a more general diffusion of a sound knowledge of Art.

There are other errors equally fatal to the acquisition of Art. Some persons, whose ambition does not tempt them beyond the use of the Chalk or Pencil, choose their models according to their natural dispositions, selecting such as are "bold" or "soft." Indeed, all works of Art are distinguished by them under one or other of these appellations, and are estimated accordingly. By such mis-bestowed admiration, they unfortunately betray their own want of knowledge; for surely nothing can be more absurd than the delight too commonly expressed at seeing Rocks and Trees, Stocks and Stones, "so attractively soft,"—a quality at variance with their very nature. There are also many who appreciate the merits of an Artist by the amount of labour visible in his works; and who dwell with admiration on the numberless times it has been necessary for him to retouch a Picture. In other pursuits, such tests rather make the want of ability the more apparent. The admiration bestowed on others for their "boldness and dash" (the usual expressions) is equally mistaken, where the boldness consists in the reckless freedom with which every principle of Art and Nature is violated; where every particle of resemblance is unheeded, nay, almost avoided, for the sake of exhibiting an appearance of power, when, in reality, ignorance is rendered the more apparent from the assumed disguise. For examples of the *bold* style (and bold it truly is so to outrage Nature), and of the *highly finished* or *soft* style, see Plates 14 and 15. The general errors relative to instruction in Art, and in the selection of "bold" or "soft" examples as models, are my apologies for noticing them.

These prevalent, and even fashionable, errors, are not only fatal to the development of real talent, but are directly opposed to the acquirement of that knowledge which can alone give to Amateurs the power to appreciate Art, or the ability to practise it with success.

Amateurs and Students will do well to attend to the advice of the Artist who urges them to use the Chalk or Pencil; for both, though simple, are yet effective instruments in the practice of elementary Art: indeed, the true foundation of Art is to be laid in the mastery over one or the other. There is no "royal road" for either Artist or Amateur, and there are not two different roads respectively adapted to each; consequently, if in this work the road be shortened, or in any manner smoothened, it is as imperative on the one as on the other to adopt it.   Whatever may be their expectations, I can confidently assure them, that, unless they will devote their time to a right pursuit of Art, they can never hope to succeed in any respect, much less to become Painters of Pictures.   Can it be denied, that it would be much more desirable, to devote sufficient time to acquire sound information, and the power to skilfully use the Chalk or Pencil, and to be alive to all the charms of Nature and Art, rather than to libel and outrage both by unmeaning "boldness" or "softness?"   This is but too frequently done by those who endeavour to reach at once a degree of excellence, which can only be attained by a long course of unremitted study and constant practice.

It has been the ordinary fate of Art in these days, notwithstanding the advantages which it offers, to be looked upon as little better than a plaything. This arises from a want of perception of the importance of Art, and from an opinion of its not being within the reach of regular instruction.   Works of Art are indeed looked upon as the result of some especial gift, with which Artists are endowed by Nature.   There can, however, be no greater mistake.   Can persons be great in Art, and yet be in all other respects without talent? Or, do the most highly gifted in other respects, understand Art without the aid of observation and reflection?   Without these they can neither justly appreciate its merits, nor derive true pleasure from its beauties; and, in consequence, much of the Book of Nature is sealed to them.   All her grand and graceful combinations are lost on those who refuse to study properly the only means which can open their eyes to behold, and their minds to receive, the varied impressions of her grandeur and beauty.

The study of the Chalk or Pencil, unaided by Colour, the one grand object of most Amateurs, offers little to attract their attention.   Without troubling themselves to reflect on what may be the advantages derivable from the use of those simple instruments of Art, they at once despise them as unworthy of consideration.   Captivated by the charms of Colour, they neglect the preliminary study of Form and Composition, and thus involve themselves in inextricable diffi- culties.   These they generally ascribe to a want of natural talents, though with as much reason as the mariner, who had never studied the science of Navigation, would attribute *his* shipwreck to a want of genius.   Sir Joshua Reynolds has remarked, that " those who have never observed the gradation by which Art is acquired, who only see what is the full result of long labour and application, of an infinite number and infinite variety of acts (and such is the progress towards the power of painting Pictures), are naturally apt to conclude, from their inability to do the same, that it is not only inaccessible to them, but can be reached by those only who have some gift of inspiration."   When, however, it can be shown that, by the use of simple instruments, such as the Chalk or Pencil, all persons may attain the great essentials in Art,—correct and striking delineation of Form and Character,—they deservedly claim more consideration before being hastily rejected.

From the very commencement, truths are to be learned, and their relative values ascertained.   All such as relate to the form of objects, their character, arrangement, mutual influence, and their light and shadow, may be learned by the use of the Chalk or Pencil; and, when the mind is familiar with the truth in these respects, and when practice has enabled us to display it with facility and effect, we are then in a condition to advantageously avail ourselves of the more powerful means of Colour,—but not till then.   What are the natural steps which conduct to it?   At first in possession of but few ideas, a simple instrument is all we can require to express them; they increase in number and in force, and exceed our power to depict them satisfactorily with our previous simple means. We are then naturally led to adopt such as are more efficient; perhaps we first take up one colour, such as sepia, and, when this in its turn is found too feeble and limited, we then take up various colours; being prompted by a desire to express ideas only within their especial province, and to find in their more extended capabilities, ample means for the display of our more extended knowledge and feeling in all their force.   Any other course, which presents us with means, far in advance of our knowledge or necessities, must be fallacious.   There must always be a relation between our ideas and the means we employ to express them.   Comprehensive means do not bring comprehensive ideas; but comprehensive ideas will always suggest the search for the means most capable of expressing them: indeed, they give increased capacity to the most feeble.   Hence, then, Colours, the most comprehensive of all the means of Art, if sought at first, lead to inextricable difficulties, and have the effect of discouraging natural aptitude, by presenting to it obstacles which appear insurmountable.

The principles which I have endeavoured to explain in the following pages, are such as have guided my own judgment and practice; and, should they be proved to be erroneous, I shall at least suffer as much as those whom I propose to assist.   If, on the contrary, they be founded on Nature, the only true basis of Art, and be proved to be essential, they should be as valuable in time to come as they now are.   If they will stand this test, they are unquestionably entitled to be received, and ought not to be rejected, however they may vary from previously entertained and widely circulated opinions.

The contents of these pages I hope may tend to correct the erroneous views of Art too generally entertained ; exemplify the value of well-founded principles ; and render useful service both to those who teach, and to those who are learning, the Elements of Pictorial Art.

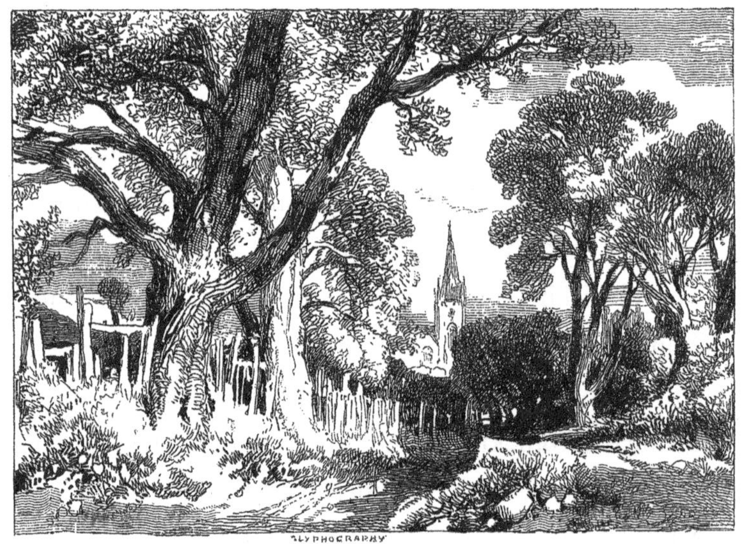

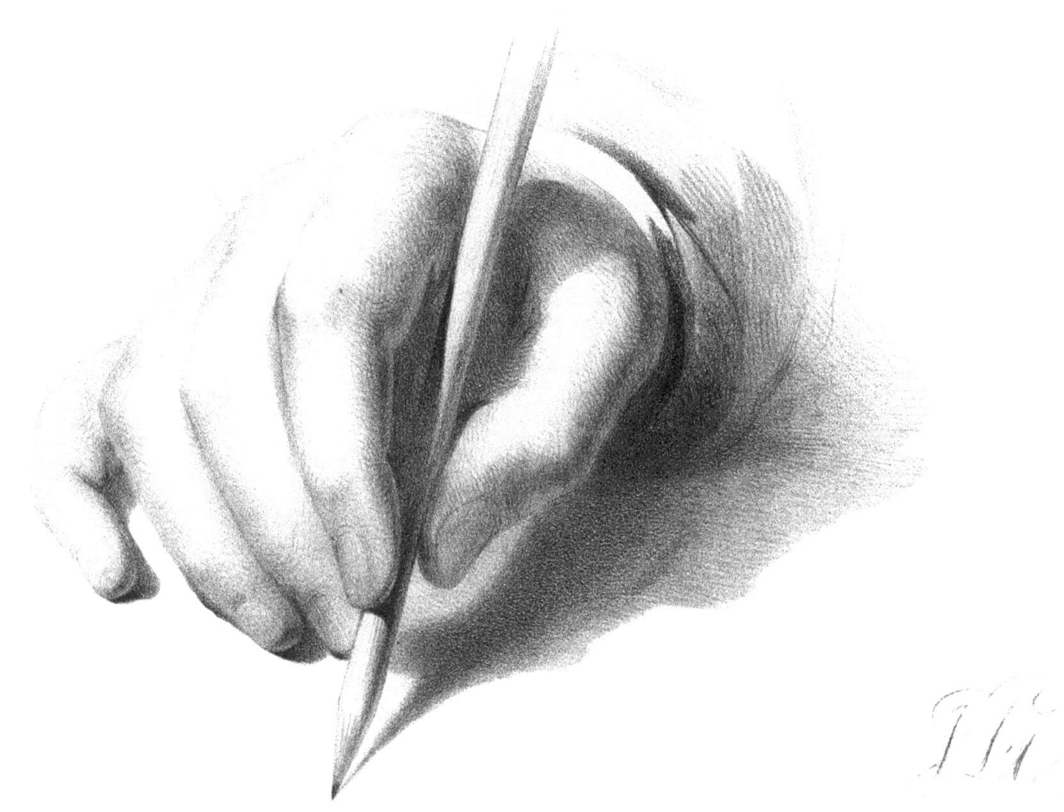

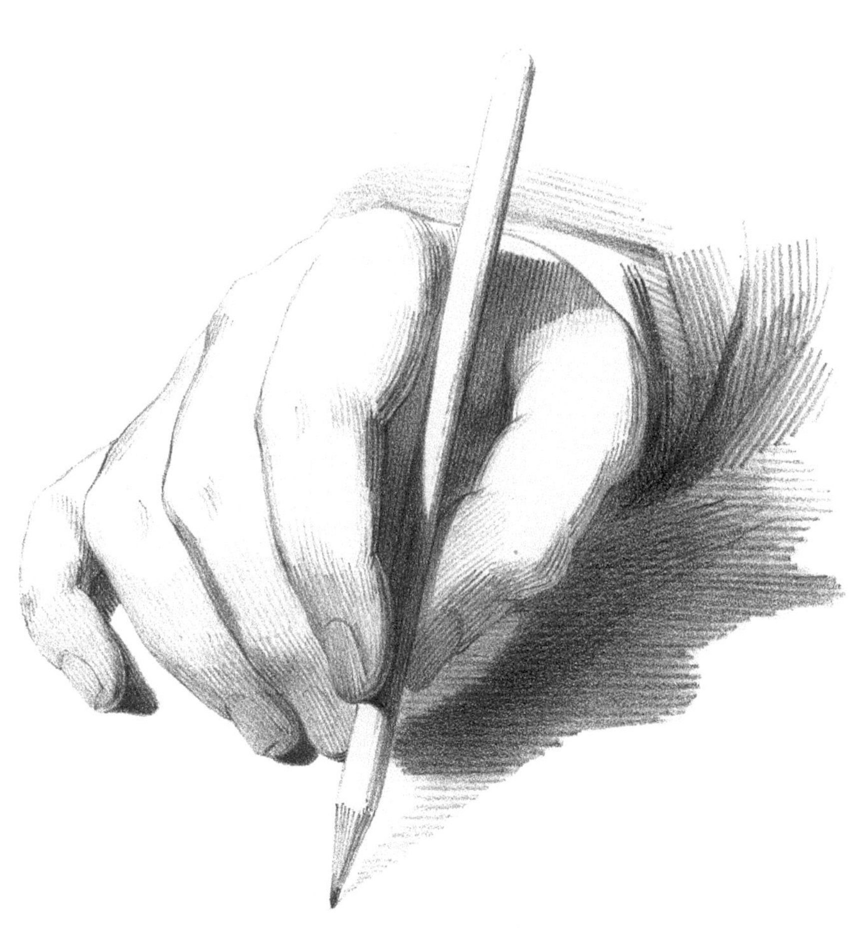

Plate 1

CHAPTER I.

GENERAL REMARKS ON THE USE OF THE CHALK, OR THE LEAD PENCIL.

TO insure success in the use of instruments of any kind, it is necessary that their nature, qualities, and adaptation for the purposes to which they are to be applied, should be perfectly understood. The instruments here treated of are, the Chalk, or Lead Pencil; and the end to be accomplished by their use, an imitation of Nature. I shall first endeavour to explain their properties, how far they are adapted to attain the object proposed by their application, and what circumstances in nature, many or few, lie within their capacity to imitate.

It is, or ought to be, the object of all Art to produce as near a likeness to Nature, in every respect, as the instrument, or material employed, will admit of; not so much by a laborious copy addressed to the eye only, as by reviving in the mind those ideas which are awakened by a contemplation of Nature. In proportion to the vividness with which the pleasing features of Nature, under every circumstance and variety, of form, light, and shade, and colour, are revived and aided by the pictorial influences of Art, will be the merit of the picture. The renewal of the feelings originally excited by, or associated with, such features, constitutes the true purpose of Art; while the exhibition of the mechanical processes, or the operations of the instrument by which this is effected, should, as in the sister arts, be kept, as much as possible, out of sight: and since all materials and instruments are, more or less, adapted to this purpose, it is obviously important that we should study in what degree each is likely to succeed in accomplishing this important end.*

* See " Principles and Practice of Art," Chap. II. " On Imitation."

As the Chalk and the Pencil are simple instruments, they are, consequently, more fitted for expressing the first and simplest ideas of Art. But as all their operations are carried on by lines, it is evident, that though in tracing the great variety of forms, or in giving the characters of objects, they are very effective; yet, as distinct *lines* are not often found in Nature, either on the contour, or on the surfaces, of objects, they are, for these reasons, not always adapted for exactly imitating her. Were not their operations, indeed, carried on with judgment, advantage taken of their occasional fitness, and their general unfitness either concealed or avoided, nothing really satisfactory could ever be gained from their use. All imitations to be obtained by them are, first, with a line for the form, and with multiplied lines for the shades; and these lines should be so distributed and arranged, that the eye may be as little as possible offended by their obtrusion; and their distinctness, as mere lines, should be either totally or partially got rid of, as the case may demand. " The more unpretending, quiet, and retiring the means, the more impressive their effect. Any attempt to render lines attractive, at the expense of their meaning, is a vice." * Refer to Plates 2 and 3. In these we may see, that in the hair of the heads lines are not only useful but indispensable, and also in the drapery, where they assist in explaining its varied surface. On the other hand, for the flesh of the faces, and for the backgrounds of sky and trees, it is equally imperative there should be, as in these Plates, either no appearance of lines whatever, or that, as in the upper example of Plate 1, they should be so much subdued as to be unobtrusive. Though the absence of lines serves, in some cases, to give this character of smoothness; yet their presence is, in others, desirable, to indicate the rotundity, or sinuosity, of any surface,—such as of draperies. The distinctness of lines must be regulated, of course, by the character of the imitation in the other parts. Notwithstanding lines are, for the most part, contrary to Nature, these Examples may serve to show that they have power in conveying certain ideas; for generally, according to their direction, on surfaces, such as drapery, where it is evident they may be the least positively like Nature, our notions of the form or direction of those surfaces, are from them in a great measure received and confirmed.

---

* " Modern Painters," by a Graduate of Oxford.

Let us take, as an example, the Roof of a House covered with tiles, and proceed to shade it, or exhibit its surface, by merely placing lines upon it, as in Ex. A., without reference to its slope or direction. It will be seen that the perpendicular lines suggest the idea of its being upright, in complete contradiction

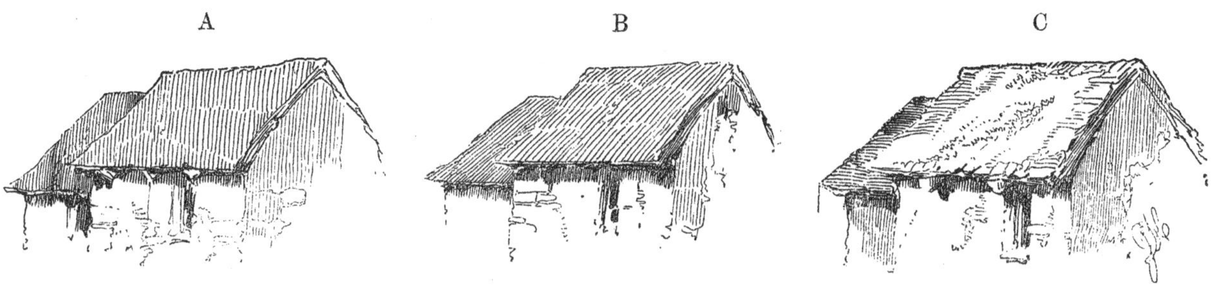

A   B   C

to the outline, which shows it to be oblique. Though more is done in Ex. B. by making the lines oblique, having the same inclination as the ends of the roof, yet as the nature of the covering is still not expressed, consequently some other arrangement must be adopted, which shall at the same time effect both. As tiles lie in horizontal lines, by such they will best be represented; and so, by terminating them in oblique rows, parallel to the ends of the roof, the double purpose will be gained, as in Ex. C. For the perpendicular wall in each Example, perpendicular lines are employed, and are left visible—although in themselves unlike Nature—because they convey an impression of truth by showing the wall to be upright.

Again, in the drawing of the Hand, Plate 1, where every part is more or less round, lines placed parallel to the outline, as in the lower example, do not give that roundness effectively; even though the proper degree of intensity in the the shadow be observed, the means obtrude : whereas, when carried in the direction of the surface, as in the upper example, its precise undulation is readily explained; but here the means do not obtrude. Again, it must be observed, that as no lines in this instance, and others of a like kind, are to be found in Nature, the lines used are crossed in many directions, to neutralize their unavoidable dissimilarity in this respect, always leaving those most wanted to express the surface the most distinct; and, as in both these cases of the Roof and the Hand, the impression of Nature is more truly obtained, we become, in consequence, affected only with the primary ideas sought to be conveyed, and are not annoyed with the means, which, considered abstractedly, are in all equally unlike Nature. These examples, though simple (for it must not be forgotten, that beginners are here meant to be addressed), will be sufficient to show to those who think on Art for the first time, that whenever a work of Art affords pleasure, it is because it is founded on some facts and principles in Nature, and not on means fortuitously or arbitrarily applied; for though chance should once succeed, yet, unless the reason of its success be discovered, the same success cannot again be insured.

In this way we first study Nature, and on the principles deduced from what we observe in her, we found such application of the means at our disposal, as may imitate her effectively. This ingenuity of the Artist, excited by and based on his knowledge, is commonly attributed to innate Genius, instead of being ascribed, as it ought, to an acquired habit of close observation and just comparison.

The Student should, from the beginning, be encouraged in this way to take a philosophical view of Art, to reason on it well, that he may be able to practise it with effect; to depend on the knowledge of principles, and not absurdly to rely "on some especial gift in themselves, some specific quality in the materials, or some false aptitude in their use, requiring no exertion of the mind to produce it, and making no appeal to the mind when done." "It is not the eye, it is the mind," says Sir Joshua Reynolds, "which the painter of genius desires to impress; nor will he waste a moment on smaller objects, which only catch the sense to divide the attention and counteract the great design of speaking to the heart." Were such consistent and enlarged views of Art more generally entertained among Amateurs, many would be added to the few whom we may be justly proud of possessing.

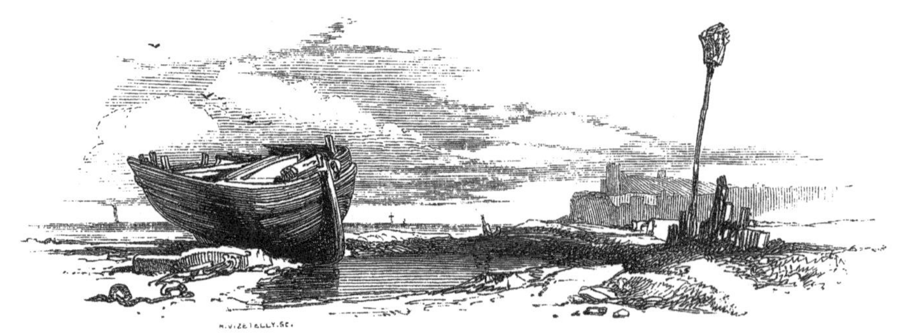

CHAPTER II.

ON FORM.

PERHAPS there is no branch of Art so important as correct Drawing. It is the sure foundation of every excellence, short of colour; and yet there is no branch so very much neglected, not only by those who merely take up Art as an amusement, but also by those studying for the future exercise of the Profession. All are too eager to use the brush, believing that colour and effect, in light-and-shade, comprise all that is necessary to be known; not considering that these alone, however good they may be, cannot afford satisfaction to the mind, if the Form of an object be incorrect. Incorrect Drawing is an offence to the eye, for which no excellence in other respects can compensate.

Our first impressions with reference to Art, are derived from the forms of objects; it is by their shapes that we distinguish them from each other, and not by their light-and-shade, or colour: for, deprived of these, we can distinguish them, were we to grasp them in the dark, or blindfolded. Neither colour, nor light-and-shade, has any influence over their forms; objects might change their colours, and yet retain their shape in all its integrity.

For the purpose of drawing Forms simply, without regard to their peculiar or proper colours, the Chalk or Pencil is especially adapted. The knowledge of Forms is so very important, and the power to draw them well, is a qualification so indispensable to the Amateur, as well as to the Artist, that I think I may assert without fear of contradiction, that it would be impossible for any one, not possessing such knowledge and power, to attain any degree of excellence in Art, or to produce any work of great merit when viewed as a whole. Correct drawing, or delineation of Form, is the only sure foundation for Art; and with its unaided power many works have stood the test of ages, and excited the admiration of every generation, and every individual who has seen them. Witness the wonderful and almost magic statues of the ancient Sculptors, which yet look as if they came breathing from the hands of a Praxiteles, a Phidias, or a Michael Angelo.   Form is the Sculptor's only sphere of effect; and yet what beauties he displays!   To him colour is valueless; the beauty of his outline not only compensates amply for its absence, but so little is the want of it felt, that there are few, with the smallest portion of good taste, whose feelings would not be outraged by its presence; and there are equally few who would not prefer the beauty of well-proportioned and finely-formed features, to deformity bedecked in the richest colours.

Form is the grand essential—the " prima materia" of Art; and over this the Artist can obtain entire control.   In this he may be perfect, and obtain a mastery even over Nature: for, by combining in a whole the separate perfections selected from a great number of individuals, he may produce a more perfect form than she bestows on any one; whilst in Light-and-Shade, and Colour, he must ever feel his inferiority.   There lives no man, nor perhaps has there ever lived one, so perfect in form as the Apollo Belvidere; though from among the varied instances in Nature the parts have been collected which, in this sublime statue, are united into one perfect and transcendent whole.

Among the other productions of Nature, there is a degree of perfection prevalent in the forms of each kind respectively; and he who is best acquainted with the greater beauties of the human form, her most perfect work, will be more sensible of this fact, and will have an eye more keenly alive to observe all her other beauties, under all the properties and relations of form, quantity, symmetry, proportion, and variety.   He becomes more ingenious in discovering the pictorial merits of every work of Man, and more skilful in directing the hand to aid the beauties, or correct the deformities, which he may find in the works of Nature.

Though much gratification is not generally expected from the study of Form, yet much more may be received from it than is commonly imagined.   Form has a decided influence on all minds; and to various forms belong various sensations and associations: the Venus, or the Hercules—the Greek Temple, or the Gothic Cathedral—the Tree, full grown, or the Sapling—the sturdy Oak, or the pliant Birch,—each affects the mind with a different feeling; and if this be perceptible in the broad differences marking one from the other, it is no less so in the more minute varieties incidental to each object of the same kind. This, then, constitutes

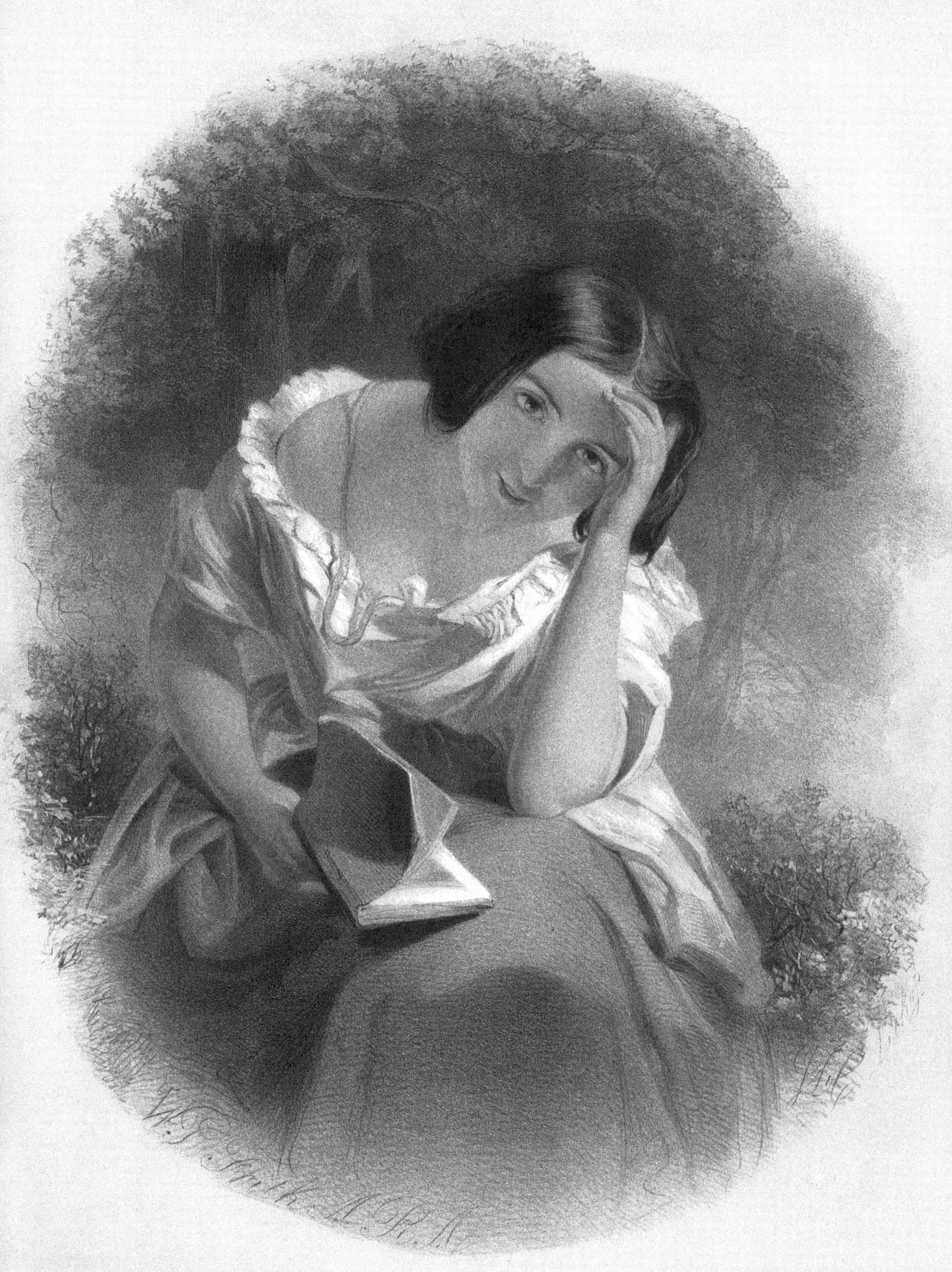

Plate 2

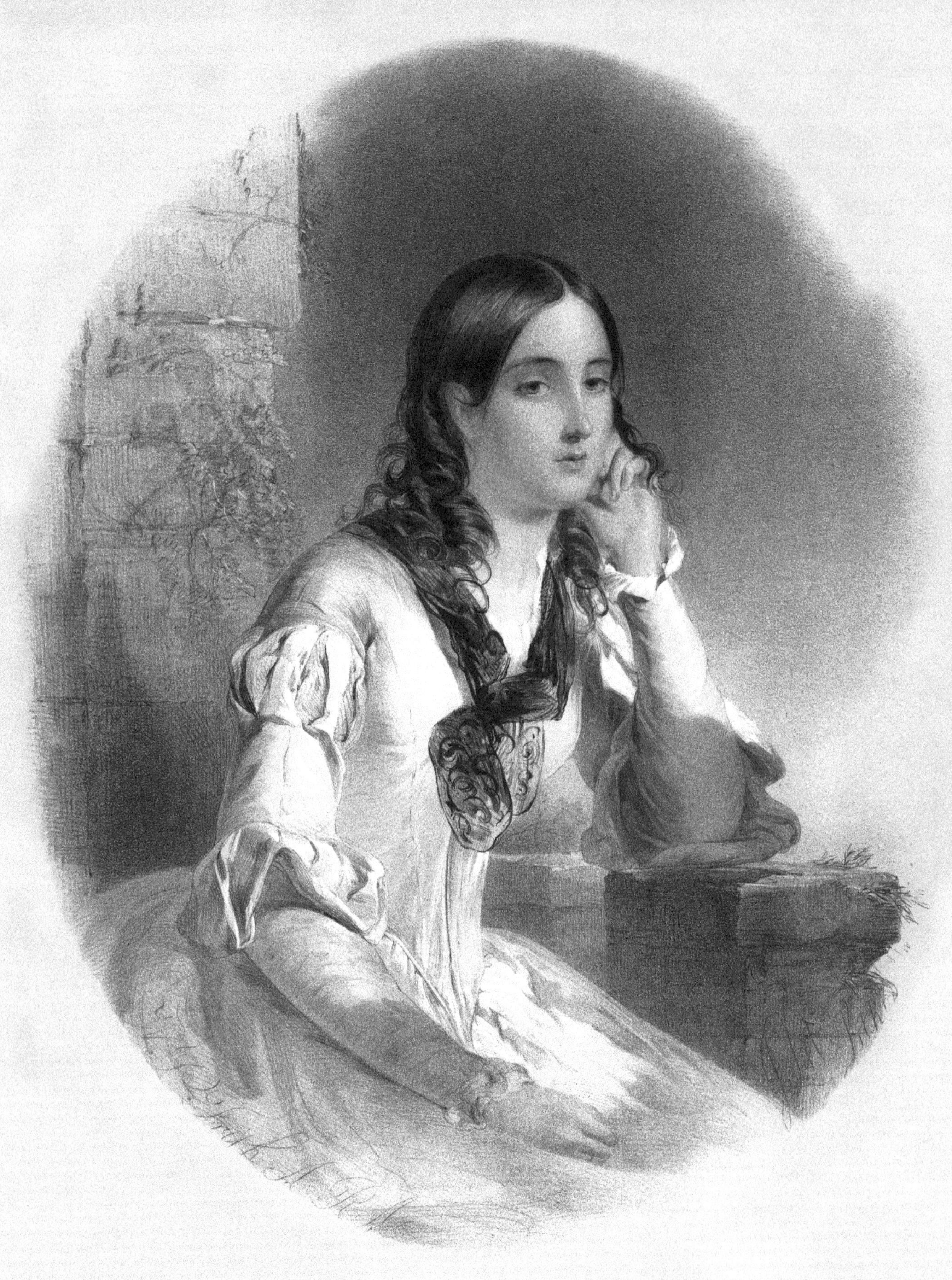

IL PENSEROSO.

Plate 3

the necessity of being acquainted not only with Form generally, but for distinguishing the greatest beauty of which each object is susceptible; its beauty, of course, being in proportion to its capacity to raise in the mind all those feelings naturally connected with it. This is the *beau ideal* of Form.

Infancy and Maturity affect us differently, and all examples of either unequally. In order, then, that each may be influential in the greatest degree possible, from many examples in each must be selected the most beautiful parts, which being skilfully combined, will enable us to awaken most powerfully those sensations individually and separately belonging to and associated with the different ages.

But it is not circumstance of age alone, or the mere beauty peculiar to it, which affects us. Judging always of the merit of Art by its effect upon us, and by our dispositions, as well as by our knowledge, we cannot fail to admire most whatever we find most, accordant with our own particular feelings. This may be made quite evident by Plates 2 and 3; it would be less easy to prefer one to the other, according to our judgment, than it would be to prefer, according to our feelings, either the serious or the mirthful,—either the individual who appears to have been influenced by aristocratic associations, or the more simple child of Nature; and both may fascinate and excite pleasing emotions in the same mind, according as it is at one moment disposed to be grave, or at another gay.

By observation and comparison, the patient investigator of Nature discovers beauties lying scattered and veiled amidst her blemishes; beauties which are assembled and concentrated in the works of those whose abundant excellencies make them worthy of imitation and study; helping the eye to become sensible of those accidental defects in Nature everywhere mixed up with her beauties, completing the knowledge whereby the former is separated from the latter, and accomplishing a form "more perfect than any *one* original." At the same time that the exact form of all objects are learned, a desire is induced to express that knowledge correctly and tastefully, and the surest foundation is laid for that good taste and refinement, so necessary to direct the impulses of true genius.

Some appropriate means by which the Student may acquire the ability to represent objects in all their differences of form and characteristics, constitute the elementary steps in Art; and are here presented to him, coupled with an exposition of the laws common to them all. The end which he is to look forward to is that nice perception of the superiority of one form of an object over another in point of beauty; and, more especially, when the distinction is so delicate as to be felt, rather than seen.*

To a correct Outline, all the beauties of expression and character may be superadded to a degree so powerful, as, in their combination, to leave little more to be desired for mental gratification.

If the power to exhibit the refinement of beauty in any one object, other than the human form, were the Artist's only object, it would not be worth toiling for; but it must be remembered, that his perception of the true and the beautiful in one thing, is a great step towards his perception of them in every other; and having become alive to beauty, and sensible of its influence, refinement and grace, in proportion, pervade his works: they then not only present a true delineation of objects, but a faithful expression of all the accessory beauties of which they are susceptible.

A thorough knowledge of the Human Form is required to enable us to clothe it well and consistently, since it never is, or never should be, so enveloped in Drapery, as entirely to hide its proportions; and again, in Animals, where their hairy covering will not admit of being represented by continuous lines, such as are used in depicting other objects, the lines, or strokes, besides distinguishing the nature of that covering, should be so arranged as perfectly to suggest the true Form underneath (See F, in Plate 4). This Example also serves to corroborate what is said in pages 14 and 15.

To become acquainted with the forms of objects under every variety of action, position, and place, and to acquire the power to draw them well, without fear and without failure, it is necessary to draw them repeatedly. This power is best attained with an instrument like the Chalk, or Pencil, the operations of which, if incorrect, can be easily and repeatedly effaced, and with equal readiness renewed. In its firmness, the yet trembling, because unskilful, hand finds a rest or stay, till, assured by practice, and guided by knowledge, it gradually becomes independent of support, and is enabled to trace forms correctly, rapidly, and *boldly*. Then, with the certain prospect of success, the Chalk, or Pencil, may be laid aside for the Brush, the operations of which require great

---

* See " Principles and Practice of Art," Chap. IV., On Beauty of Form.

dexterity and rapidity, particularly in Water-Colours, where the difference between all that is good or all that is intolerable (I speak only of the mechanism) depends on using it without that hesitation which at first is generally felt when using a Brush, whose operations are known to be indelible, or nearly so. For though various devices may be had recourse to for removing faults and failings, it is not easy to hide them when they have been once committed; and if devices be used in one part, they are almost rendered necessary throughout the Drawing, so that mistakes may not be more obvious in one part than in another, and also that their detection may thus be made difficult. How vastly superior in many essential and valuable qualities of Art are the works of those whose skill and decision mark a perfect acquaintance with, and mastery over their subject, compared with the timid and uncertain productions of others, who, notwithstanding their patient toil and unwearied labour in correcting, or rather in overlaying their failures, can hardly coax a spiritless and unmeaning picture into being ! *

In Drawing forms readily and accurately, the eye requires as much practice to see truly, as the hand to execute: those nice shades of difference, which distinguish one thing from another, of a like kind, or one position of it from another, are neither seen, nor depicted, intuitively. Even the simplest forms assume complicated shapes where they are viewed in the direction of their planes; and although it may be very easy to perceive that a circle is a circle, when the eye is immediately over its centre, it is not equally easy to depict the degree of its approximation towards an oval, in proportion as the eye is removed from the centre, and as the visual ray becomes parallel with its plane. If we take any simple and single figure, which must always be made up of at least two lines, such as a leaf of any kind; so long as the visual ray is at right angles to its surface we distinctly see its form, and it is comparatively easy to adapt the lines to each other, so as to represent it truly; but if the object be seen obliquely, that is, if the visual

---

* "We have little doubt that almost all such failures arise from the Artist's neglecting the use of the Chalk; and supposing that either the power of drawing Forms, or the sense of Beauty, can be maintained unweakened or unblunted, without constant and laborious studies in simple Light and Shade, of Form only. The Brush is at once the Artist's greatest aid and enemy; it enables him to make his power available, but at the same time it undermines his power; and unless it be constantly rejected for the Pencil, never can be rightly used."—" Modern Painters," by a Graduate of Oxford, page 236, second Edition.

ray be not at a right angle with the surface, but inclining towards its plane, then we no longer see the true figure, and have to represent it by two lines, both of which vary considerably from the true form, and yet adequately suggest it to the mind.

We may take a cube, each side of which is a square, and can be readily represented by four straight lines of equal length, and at right angles with 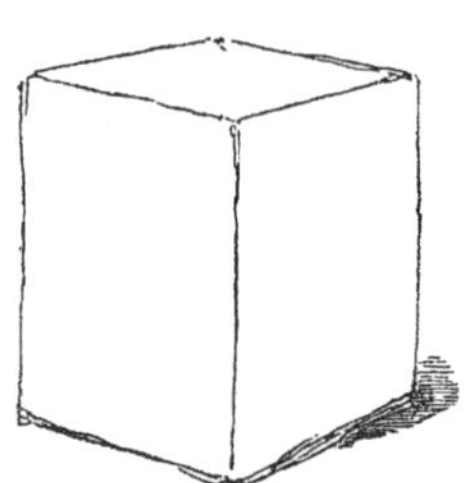 each other : when viewing this body, it may be so placed that the visual ray may be more or less in the direction of the three sides which may be seen at the same time ; it then would assume the form here given, where each side is represented by a form quite different from a square, and each angle, instead of being a right angle, as it is in Nature, is here either acute or obtuse. Although the lines describing it vary from the actual truth, they still convey to the mind a correct idea of the actual figure.

Now, if this be the case with a figure so comparatively simple as a cube, and if to represent it truly requires a practised eye and hand, much more knowledge and skill must be required to represent the human form, or any portion of it, in all its various aspects, when seen from different points of view and in different positions ; to adapt and adjust the ovoid curves of which it consists, and that so truly as to present a complete embodiment of a perfect form, though every line be at variance with the form as it actually exists in Nature.

An egg, viewed with its longer axis perpendicular to the visual ray, takes the form by which we generally recognise it ; if viewed from either end, directly in a line with its longer axis, it is then of a circular form ; both these forms may be easily understood and represented : but when viewed as it lies on a table, and when its longer axis is not immediately presented to us, its form then differs essentially from those alluded to, but withal, by such nice shades of difference, as to require great practice, either to see, or to trace, them truly.

I hope I have said enough to convince the lover of Art how much is to be gained by the study of Form ;—that he ought to devote his first labours to correct Drawing, enthusiastically and *exclusively,* as the best means of attaining the end to which he aspires, rather than vainly to waste his time in seeking, by application to this or that Master, to be put at once into possession of a power which has excited his ambition. If he fancies that he can obtain by purchase, a

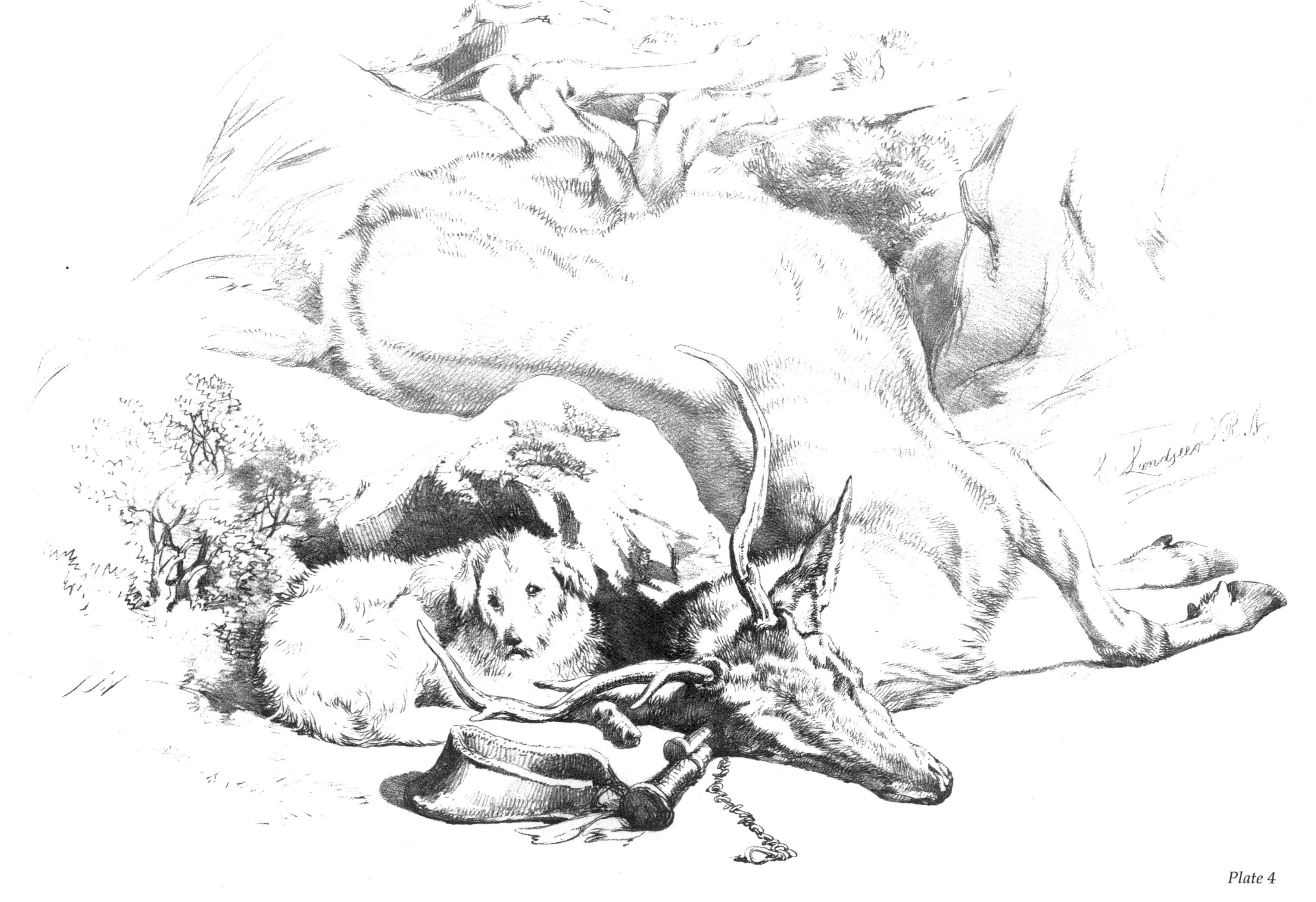

Plate 4

talent which is only to be acquired by diligent and well-directed study, he will most certainly be disappointed.

At the commencement, the Student is surrounded by difficulties, which he should attempt to surmount one by one; to overcome many, or all, at a time, would be impossible. When this is expected, or attempted, by commencing at first, or too early, with Colour, disappointment is inevitable. There can be no doubt that to this cause may be attributed, in many instances, the want of success, and in many more the relinquishment of the pursuit altogether : whereas, by the contrary course, the difficulties unavoidably attending the practice of Art, gradually yield to his assiduity; while a consciousness of improvement cheers him in his pursuit, and encourages him to continue his labours. He may rest assured that, though the practice of the Chalk or Pencil, may appear dry and unprofitable, he is most certainly taking the best and surest road, and is laying the foundation for a positive and speedy mastery over those difficulties which are peculiar to Light-and-Shade, and Colour; for unless he have the knowledge and practice of Form, he cannot give his unfettered energies to the other great branches of Art.

A knowledge of Perspective is a great aid to correct delineation ; but it does not go beyond this, and does not enable us to convey one particle of sentiment. The principles of Perspective it would be unnecessary here to lay down, as so many excellent works on the subject have already been published, and the required knowledge can be obtained from all or most of them.

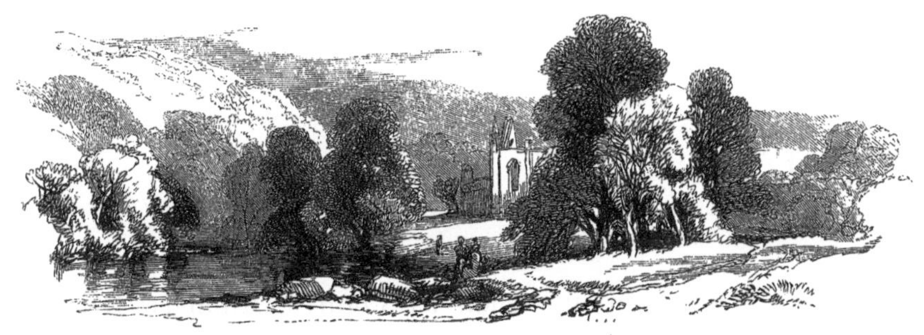

CHAPTER III.

ON THE APPLICATION OF THE CHALK, OR PENCIL, TO THE DRAWING OF FORMS.

THE three grand divisions of Art,—Form, Light-and-Shade, and Colour,—are entirely independent of each other, so that the merits of one cannot compensate for the defects of any of the others. The form of an object remains the same from whatever side it may be lighted; nor would a change of colour effect any change in its shape.

Where so much depends on manual dexterity, it is important to practise in such a way as shall render the Hand most obedient to the Will; because, when sketching from Nature, many objects require to be drawn rapidly, from their

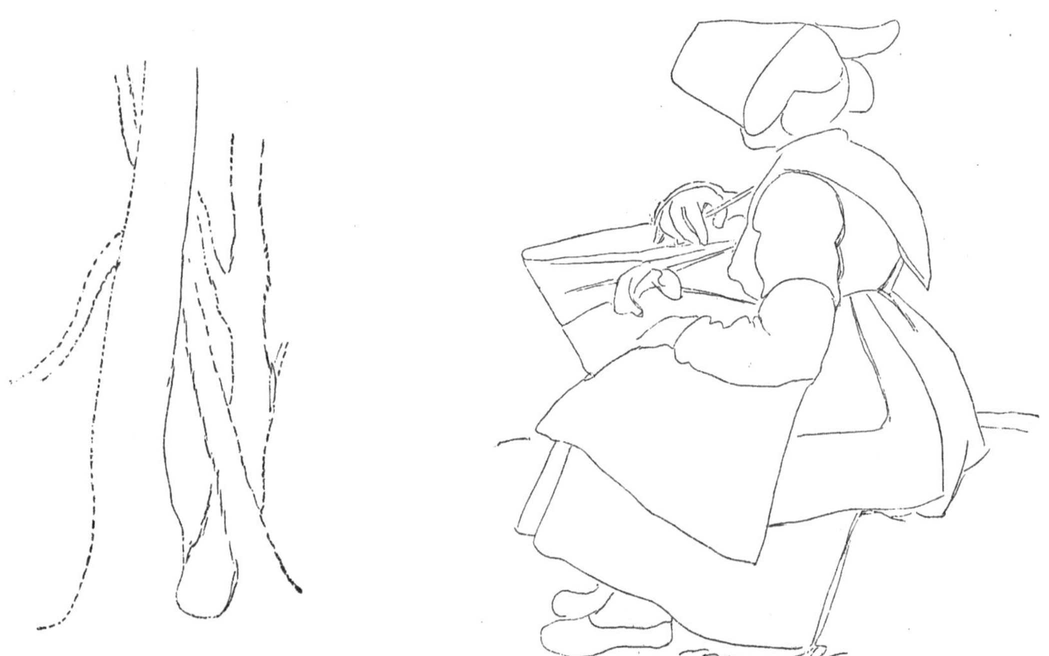

liability to change their position,—such as Figures, Animals, Boats, &c. It is highly important, under such circumstances, that the forms and relations of objects should be arrested while their first impressions on the mind—always the strongest—are yet fresh and vivid.

Ignorance chiefly occasions the hesitation at first felt; and Forms of all kinds are timidly and inaccurately drawn, either by a series of dots, or by continuous lines void of character, as in the examples on the opposite page, or in some other way equally feeble and indeterminate. The same result also occurs when too much attention has been paid to the means, or when an effort has been made to throw off fear altogether.

The method most likely to succeed is to first consider the direction of a Line, and then, having determined its two extremes, to mark both by a dot: whilst the hand commences from the upper one, the eye should regard the lower, and thus the mind is best assisted to comprehend what the hand is about to execute. If the Line be not too long, it should be drawn boldly and lightly, and at once: and though the first and second attempts, or more, should be unsuccessful, they ought not to be immediately effaced, as is the ordinary practice; on the contrary, if they be lightly drawn, as they ought, and left on the paper, the Student, by having them before him, will be the better able to judge how far they are right or wrong, as compared with the object he is drawing from; and be thus guided in leaving what is right, or in correcting what is wrong.

When any object has been satisfactorily sketched in this manner, the true Line should be selected from the others. It should be marked here and there emphatically; not left continuous, lonely, and unbroken, even though made lighter or darker, by way of giving some idea of the Light-and-Shade, as in the annexed example: because, however well drawn and executed in such a way, violence is, nevertheless, done to our feelings, by forcing on our attention the falsehood of a hard boundary Line, in connexion with the truth of Form, and thus enfeebling its effect on us, by the mode of presenting it. The better plan is, rather to suggest the actual Form

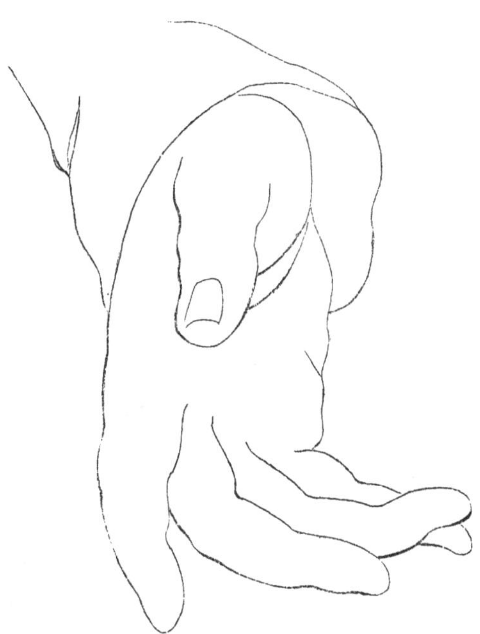

by approximating lines, than to define it absolutely by one; because at the same time that we are by such means made sensible of the true Form, and of the Light-

and-Shade, we gain also some idea of the character of the surface, whether rotund or concave, such as the boles of trees and the sinuosities of draperies, as may be seen by the annexed Examples.

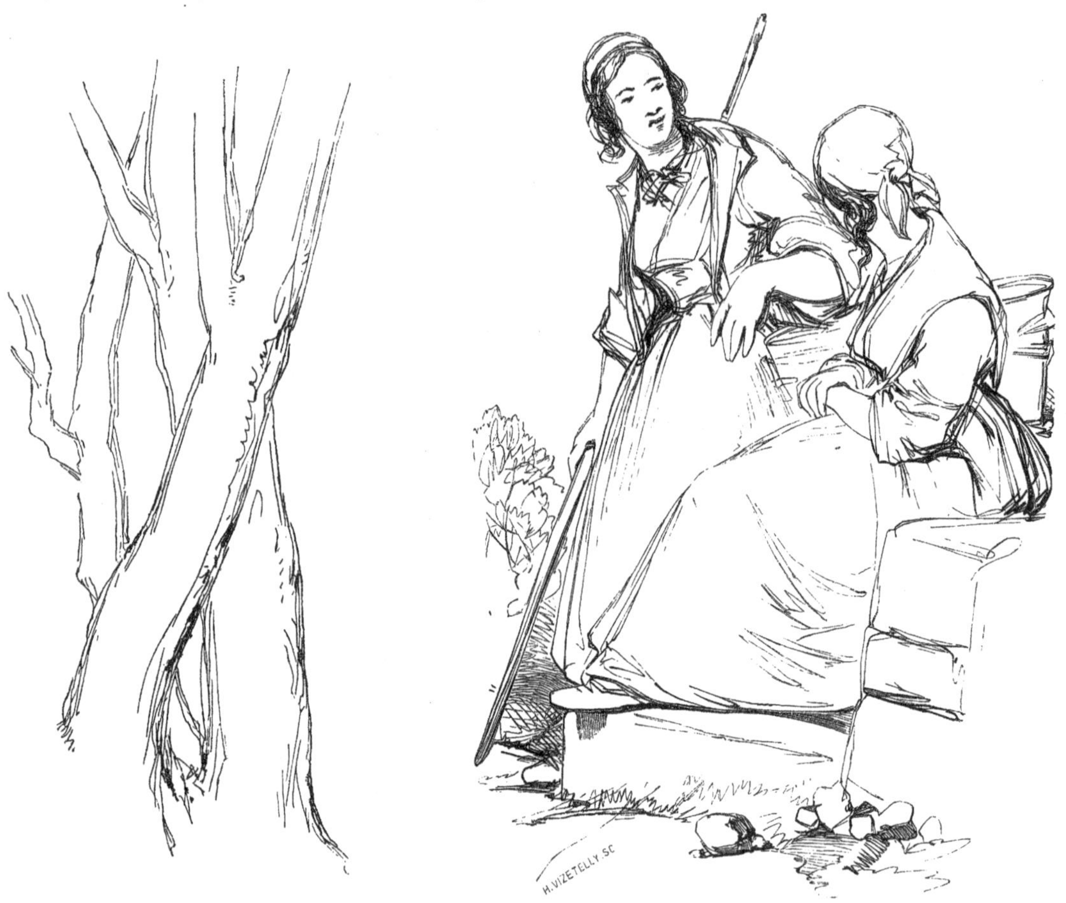

This method is superior to the dry and cold precision of a single line, and would seem to deserve the preference for the following reason :—there are no lines in Nature, as has been before remarked; consequently, in Art none should be distinctly apparent. By this means, as two or three lines are given, and are only here and there emphatically marked; and as from their sometimes uniting, and sometimes separating, it would be very difficult, if not impossible, to say which line had been the first, or which the second, or to trace the course of either definitely; and as the true line belongs entirely neither to one nor another, and sometimes even would be found between two of them,—it must then be an imaginary one, existing only in the mind : the perfect truth being adequately suggested by what is done, the attention does not become fixed on the defect of lines as representatives of Nature.

Before proceeding farther, it may be as well to observe that, when first sketching the objects, the Pencil should be held so as to have the point about an inch and a half, or two inches from the ends of the fingers, and the thumb brought so low down as to be nearly opposite to them; and all should be rather bent, as shown in the upper Example of Plate 1, so that their flexibility may be entirely at command. When sketching, particularly on a large scale, instead of working from the joints of the fingers or the wrist, the whole arm should be at liberty from the shoulder joint, and support should be obtained only from the tip of the little finger. It is a common habit to hold the Pencil like the Pen—a great fault;

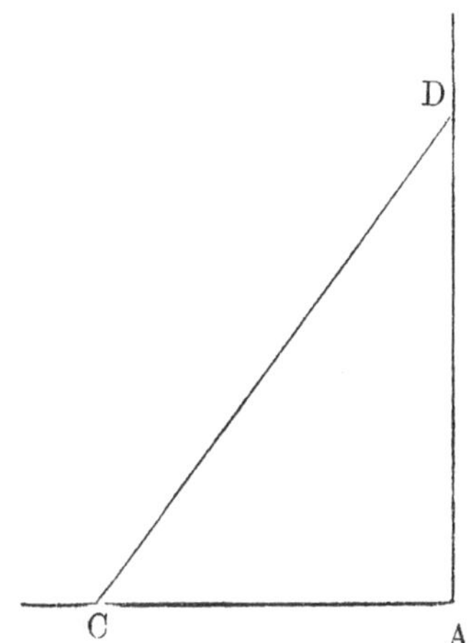

for the Hand, being thus confined, is able only to make with facility lines in the direction necessary for writing; whereas, in drawing, they are required in every possible direction, and of every form: it is of the utmost consequence, therefore, that all the pliability of which the Hand is capable, should be brought into action.

All inclined lines will be most accurately drawn, by comparing them with lines forming a right angle, either by actually drawing the right angle against the line required, or by supposing it. The former is the better plan in the first instance. Upon the horizontal line A C, it will be easily seen how far the point C is from the angle A, and how high up on the perpendicular line the point D is from A: the two points decide the inclination of the line D C.

Again, in the Gable-end of the House, in the annexed example:—first draw the perpendicular line A B, and the line D C at right angles with it; and having ascertained how far up the line A B, the apex of the Gable I is to be, and how far

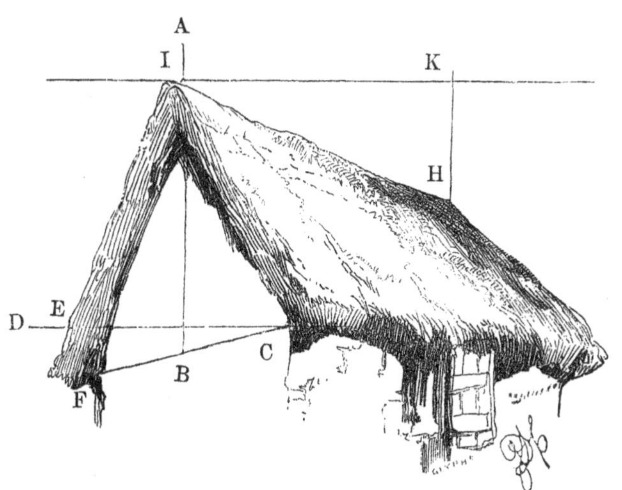

from B, on the line D C, are the ends E and C of the sloping lines of the roof, which form the Gable, place the two points, E and C, and draw the lines I C and I E, observing to continue the latter to the point F, below the line D C, and the true inclination of the roof will be obtained. It will be easily seen where the point F is to be, by drawing the line F B C forming an acute angle with D C. Then again, for the perspective line of the roof I H, first draw the horizontal line I K indefinitely; and having determined how far on that line, as at K, as well as how much below K, the point H would come, the direction of the line H I is gained. This being done, the further corner to the right, nearly in a line with C at the opposite extremity of the roof, the lower line of the roof may be determined by the direction of the line D C produced, considering how far the required point ought to be below this line, and how far it would extend beyond where the perpendicular line, continued downward from H, would cross it; next let fall perpendicular lines from the points F and C, for the angles of the wall: thus, unaided by any knowledge of Perspective, the whole is drawn with sufficient accuracy.

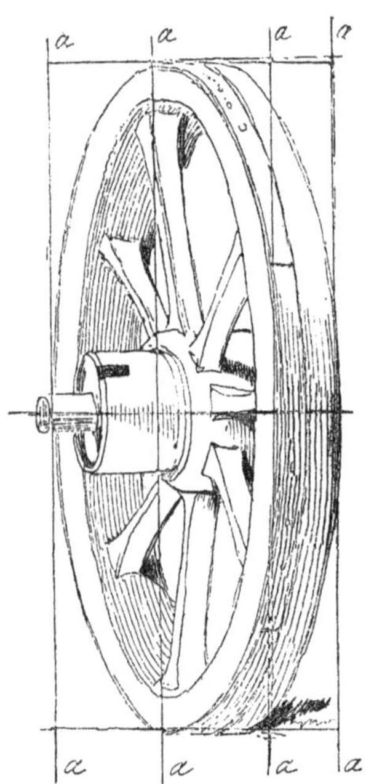

Gothic arches, or any other figure composed of curved lines, may also be accurately drawn, by first setting up a framework of right lines, such as the perpendicular lines *a a a a*, and the three horizontal lines, in the annexed example. The original, or model, is either to be divided, or conceived to be divided, by straight lines in the same manner and proportion. The curves may thus be precisely determined by observing their relation to the straight lines as they approach, come in contact with, or recede from them. The most complicated forms, whether curved or angular, may be accurately, though mechanically, drawn by means of a frame-work of lines, at right angles with each other, forming a number of squares. The practice, however, here recommended is intended only as an aid to the eye in the beginning; if carried beyond this, the Student would acquire the habit of determining on the accuracy of his drawing, not by comparing, as he ought, one line with another, and judging of the adaptation of all by their significancy and power in conveying a clear and correct idea of the object, regardless of the union of all in a perfect whole; he would take part by part, and judge of every line by comparison with those artificially employed ;—and thus, instead of deciding on the merits of his copy by its general significance as compared with the original, he would estimate it by its correspondence in detail with the means employed to obtain accuracy mechanically.

The curved lines in the Human Figure may be obtained in a similar manner, by first drawing straight lines, inclining, according to the intended direction of the curves, as in the annexed Example, and forming a continued series of angles.

Then, by merely cutting off the positive angles more or less abruptly, by lines of greater or smaller curvature, as may be required, we thus obtain more perfect and delicately varied curves, than could be obtained by drawing continuous curved lines at first.

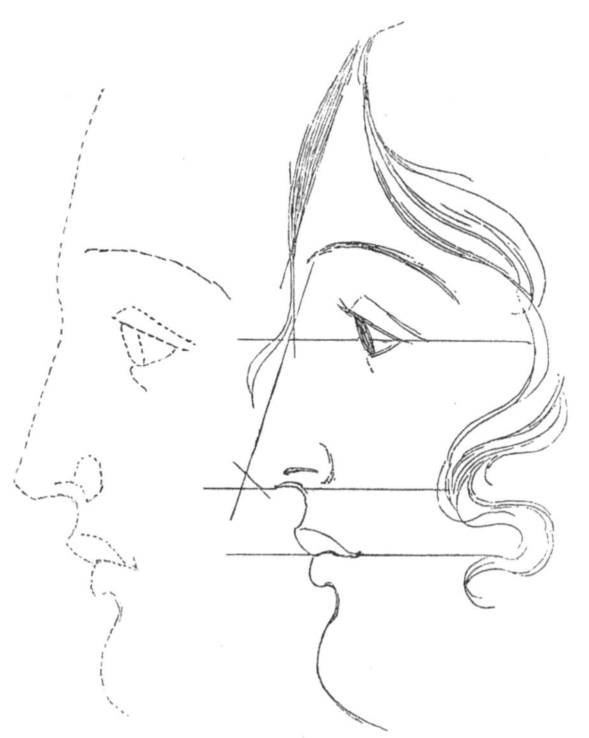

This method of comparing sloping and curved lines with such as are perpendicular or horizontal, is not confined to copying. It is also of great use in drawing from material objects, whether natural or artificial; the Port-crayon, or Pencil, will serve where comparison is required with horizontal lines; and a string with a small weight at one end, and used as a plumb line, will serve for such parts as require to be compared with a perpendicular line. By such simple methods the relations of the lines,—whether straight or curved, or both,—of the most complicated forms, may be accurately compared and estimated, which is the first step towards their being accurately drawn.

These Examples, well studied, will, it is hoped, be sufficient to show the intelligent Pupil the necessary application of this method; experience only can teach him how far it may be extended. In drawing Forms, it is almost universally applicable.

At first, it is more than probable that the difference between the merit of two methods employed in drawing the Examples, given in pages 24 and 26, will not strike the Student's eye, especially the hard outline of the Hand; for as it has the great essential of correct drawing, the meagreness of the single line used is the less likely to be felt. The difference between this and the other and better Examples, at page 26, is also less likely to be noticed; because in the latter, the outline, not being single, is not so manifest as he is at first always prone to make it. The different Outlines are, however, very dissimilar in their effect. In the one, where the Outline is single and positive, the eye unavoidably follows it; in the other, where the Outline is not single nor positive, the eye is unable to detect it without an effort, and, therefore, rests on the surface, as it does in Nature; and whilst the Form is perfectly understood, some idea is also obtained of the texture and roundness of the surface. But when, to the frigidity of a single line, incorrect drawing is added, its defects, as a representation of the natural boundary of an object, become more obvious. For reasons, previously alluded to, it is possible that the Student may discover no great difference between Plates 14 and 15, or between those and all the others given in this work. Unless his knowledge of Nature and of the purposes of Art should have corrected his judgment, he may even find himself joining in the popular error of admiring what is false and unnatural. Such admiration is the more to be guarded against, since Art is generally so little understood, that the Learner is in constant danger of being led away by the indiscriminate praises he hears bestowed on that which only pity spares from the severest criticism.

In order, then, to avoid this liability of the Student to err, by mistaking the wrong for the right, which would leave him for ever in ignorance, he must make the improvement of the Hand depend on the correctness of his Judgment, and never allow himself to practise with the one, without having previously exercised the other.

Though it might be admitted that the principles propounded and explained in this Work are correct, and beyond refutation, yet still objections might be be raised to the methods of working them out; and it might be said that the processes are tedious, and likely to chill the ardour of genius. To this it may be replied that it is the same with all rules, whether of Science or Art—all are slowly acquired. Few, however, think that the true principles of language—so irksome to youth—destroy genius, and mar the future Scholar. All those rules and precepts which are at first acquired with so much difficulty and reluctance, at length become familiar, and are habitually applied in practice without an effort. The Orator speaks correctly and fluently without reference to the rules of his grammar; and the Artist, in like manner, at last draws without thinking of the rules which mechanically guided his early steps,—rules without which neither of them could bring his genius into full play, or refine and improve his feelings. The Student in language at first labours over his rules, and finds it difficult to express a simple idea, because his attention is distracted and divided between the idea and the language in which it is to be conveyed: but when he has learned his rules thoroughly, he then, unembarrassed and at ease, bestows his attention on the choice of words; applies them with facility in their precise signification; and at length feels, to the fullest extent, the force and spirit of the language, and conveys his ideas in it with proportionate power, taste, and feeling. By the same order of progression only can the Student in Art be made to learn and feel, and to impart his knowledge and feeling to others effectively.

The first sketch having been made, and the required forms, and their relative sizes, obtained by lines slightly traced, as in Plate 5; those lines should be partially removed, and the whole should be completed, by giving such character as will best convey a just idea of the nature of the object as well as of its form. The lines on the limits of the shadowed sides and parts are to be made darker and more evident, where they are more evident in Nature; carefully comparing, moreover, the different parts with each other, and preserving in each its relative degree of intensity. The open windows, and the spaces between the piers, on which the building rests, are marked with darker lines; and the stones of the piers with wider or narrower lines, accordingly as their separations would be found in Nature. It will also be seen, that besides the outline, much is necessary on the surface to characterise it properly;—those parts only being depicted which in Nature are most evidently marked.

All that can ever be effected with buildings, or, indeed, any other objects, is to convey distinctly an idea of Nature. In a Building, whether it be old or new,—whether the stones composing it be of regular or irregular shapes,—when sufficient is pourtrayed to show this, enough is done; the likeness is not improved by exhibiting the portraiture of every stone, since the Spectator only recognises the circumstances above alluded to in connection with the general form: the number of stones contained in it being as little known to him as to the Painter, the exact representation of all is not felt as essential to a satisfactory resemblance.

What is required in individual portraiture is, that the qualities and nature of the object should be so represented as to recall to the mind of another those features, circumstances, and ideas, by which it is remembered; and these are entirely independent of the number of lines employed.

We should acknowledge no greater degree of likeness in a Portrait, were the hairs of the head to be numbered, and every part elaborated with a Dutch-like patience. Much time, which might have been usefully employed in a more comprehensive view of Nature, is thus often thrown away on insignificant details. Gerard Dow and Teniers painted Heads like Nature, and so did Vandyke and Titian; but what a different effect is produced by each on the mind! In Landscape, Titian and Hobbima each adopted a manner varying from the other, and yet each was true to Nature. By the one, our ideas of Nature are exalted and improved, because he has selected her most striking and most imposing features, —her rarest combinations,—and has intellectually set them before us in works which engross our minds and feelings by a sense of what is impressive and beautiful. Not so by the other; he has taken Nature as he found her—in her every-day dress,—and has given us little more than the most unimaginative observer might see. By the one we learn to feel and to appreciate the sublime and the beautiful; in the works of the other, we see that a laborious and mechanical effort has been made to obtain an exact copy of Nature, without regard to selection—without arrangement, sentiment, or beauty. Persons who are unacquainted with Art admire the works of Hobbima, because they are painted on a level with their capacities; but the works of Titian, from being of a higher order, require that the mind of the Spectator should be cultivated before it can perceive the fulness of their merits, and justly appreciate the talent of the Artist.

I have thought it advisable, nay indispensable, to urge, as I have done, the study of Form, not only as the best possible beginning of Art, whether for Amateur or Artist, but because it is so immediately connected with my particular subject,—THE USE OF THE CHALK, OR LEAD PENCIL.

CHAPTER IV.

ON COPYING, AS PREPARATORY TO THE STUDY OF NATURE.

"The mechanical practice of Art is learned by Copying."—SIR J. REYNOLDS.

TO draw from Nature well, and to be able to select her most beautiful features, should be the ultimate aim of all who study Art; and Art should be studied so as to obtain not only the most complete power over the means and appliances wherewith Nature may be imitated, but also a knowledge of what is within the proper province of Art to imitate. To attain the mechanical power, Copying of Examples is indispensable,—but not with a view of merely producing a fac-simile of any. A just idea of the subject intended to be worked out ought to be first acquired, and then the examples should be looked to for the mode of execution, bearing in mind the reasons for its adoption. When the copy is completed, comparison should be made with the original; not to determine the exactness of the resemblance between that and the copy, as regards the mere lines and strokes, but to see if the ideas intended to be conveyed are expressed with the same significance and power in the copy as in the original.

Copying necessarily implies a certain amount of imitation, and a general adherence to the style, or mode of execution, of the original; but lest this should degenerate into mere servile imitation, without anything like exercise of the mind, the Student, after having satisfied himself with the correctness of his copy, should then lay aside the original, and endeavour to re-produce the same subjects, with the same results, from MEMORY. This, though at first difficult, is nevertheless a most important practice, as it is the first step towards originality, and towards that independence which all must possess, who, ere they can draw well from Nature, or do anything at all, and do it well, must depend on, and act for, themselves.

The Student must start with the intention of Drawing from Memory; and when he is able to make an accurate, and an intellectual copy, he should commence the practice. He should begin by taking single objects, or the separate parts of such as are complicated, and having drawn them twice or thrice, should note to what extent his memory has been faithful. It is with Drawing as with Music: the first step towards playing a passage correctly is made when it has been played a sufficient number of times to fix it on the memory.

This practice of Drawing from Memory cannot be too much insisted on, as it best shows to what extent Copying is necessary; since some require the practice more, and others less, according to the degree of facility with which ideas are acquired and retained. The great art of teaching ourselves or others is to adopt such means as shall make our own errors and the merits of our Example most sensibly felt. No measures can be taken to correct errors that are neither seen nor felt; and nothing can lead the Student so surely to detect them as the comparison which he makes between his own productions from memory and the original before him.

Drawing from Memory is moreover calculated to fix not only precise ideas of objects in the mind, but also the process of embodying them. By this practice the Student learns to detect with more precision what his deficiency consists in, and is by degrees induced to rely more on himself and less on his model. By thus early practising from memory, he lays the foundation for his future independence, when, emancipated from the trammels of imitation, he can turn to Nature for himself. But before he can do this, he must, by studying from good models, have his mind enlightened, know what there is in Nature, and be prepared to look for and enabled to perceive her beauties.

Many believe that they cannot too soon study from Nature, as affording the best models. It is, indeed, true that she does; but of what utility are they to those who know little or nothing of their positive or relative merits; to whom the good, the indifferent, or the bad—for Nature has her deformities as well as her beauties—are all equally pleasing or unimpressive?

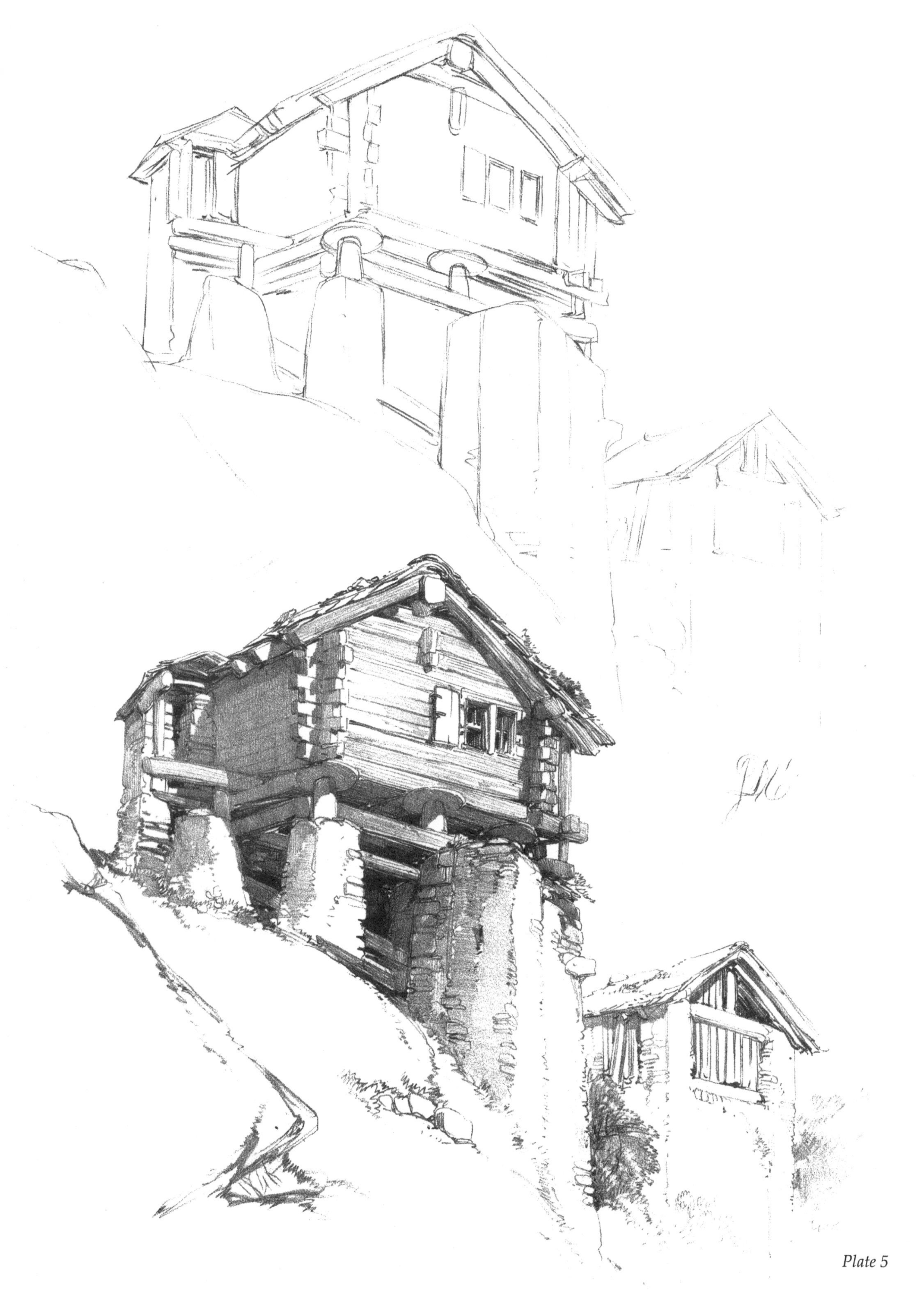

Plate 5

It is erroneous to suppose that we should go to Nature before we have acquired some knowledge, and cultivated and improved our taste, in some degree, by studying the works of those who have shown what is to be obtained there. The knowledge and experience of others ought to be the foundation on which we are to build, and on which we may expect to raise a superstructure of our own; otherwise there could be no progression in Art. Until we have learned the principles of Art, and can carry them into operation, we are not in a condition to study Nature with advantage, or to depict her so satisfactorily that we may be encouraged to go on.

That Student can hardly fail to draw well from Nature who, whilst copying the works of others, learns the principles of Nature therein displayed, and how they may be exhibited by means of Art; and he must first satisfy himself that he has acquired this preliminary knowledge and skill, before he practises from her.

When many objects in juxta-position, and of all forms, simple and complicated, at different distances, are to be drawn—and when, besides the true form of each, its relative size and peculiar characteristics must be known to be represented,—it is evident that to achieve this is an accomplishment which requires preparatory education, both in the knowledge of the objects themselves, and the capabilities of the instrument or instruments with which they are to be represented.

All are greatly embarrassed, and inevitably so, in their early efforts to draw from Nature; nor is this surprising, when we consider that the matchless original which they desire to imitate—complete, substantial, real—appears at once before them. When they find the apparently inappropriate materials from which her likeness is to spring, presenting, in their hands, every opposition to their task, it is no wonder they soon deem it hopeless. The work must of necessity have its various stages; and little similitude can be seen until it approaches completion, although each step may bring it nearer. The imitation in its early stages is so dissimilar to Nature, that ultimate success seems impossible, even where the course most likely to insure it has been adopted. The Student must first carry into operation the materials of his Art by copying works of Art—be familiar with the likeness to Nature, in kind and degree, produced by the different stages of his work—be able to anticipate the result of each, from the beginning to the conclusion,—before he can see his way clearly in drawing from Nature, or fix on a method of using the materials with such skill as to attain the desired object. But if he have studied good examples, and not merely imitated them, and tried the information he may have gained from them by what his memory retains, he will then look for no more likeness in the first stage of his Drawing, than should at first be expected; he will plainly see in what respects that which he is doing resembles Nature, or in what it is deficient; he will be in no danger of obliterating what he has done well, nor of neglecting to obliterate what he has done badly; and in this way, from the commencement of his work to its termination, he will be able to form a right judgment of its different conditions, and exercise that judgment without fear.

The memory, as before observed, must, from the first, be exercised on simple objects or parts of such as are complicated, gradually learning to attach them to each other and to form a whole. Drawing from Memory is, indeed, at first attended with difficulties; but these difficulties vanish, like all others, before practice, and the memory at length retains the impression of an entire subject with as much ease as it does any part of it. This exercise of the memory, in studying Landscape, is the more important, as it is constantly necessary to refer to it. Nature's effects are fleeting and incessantly changing; she is clad in her loveliest attire but for a short season, and her radiant autumn dress almost disappears as she puts it on. The Sun speeds with regular progression along his course; when rising he prepares to set, and while setting, sinks. It is not always practicable to delineate the charms of Nature at the moment we observe them; a variety of insurmountable obstacles frequently present themselves; and the Artist is compelled to gather much from the resources which his recollection and his knowledge supply. This constitutes the great difficulty of Landscape Painting.

To copy well is the beginning and the end of many an Amateur's hopes and expectations. To draw without an example appears so unattainable, that few aim at it, and fewer still expect to succeed; yet the ordinary ambition of most to draw from Nature is to draw originally; and for this purpose they should be early exercised in drawing from recollection.

When much time has been devoted to Copying, and so much gained by it that a good copy can be made at last without the trouble of constantly reverting to either the principles of Nature or of Art, or of practising their development, it then becomes more difficult to draw from Nature; and the Student is mortified to find how defective his own direct imitation of her is, as compared with his Copies of works of Art where the hand, without knowledge, has succeeded in gaining a kind of resemblance of her by a second-hand mimicry. The powerful conviction of this difference often represses all the hope of ultimate success in depicting Nature; and, disappointed and annoyed, the Student returns again to his former pursuit, unable to summon courage for the task he sees before him, precisely because his too great devotion to Copying, without study, has increased the difficulty of relying on himself, which he must do when he goes to Nature: his difficulties have been thus aggravated in a ten-fold degree by the very practice which, properly followed, should have tended to diminish, if not to remove them altogether. His ability to copy with ease and tolerable accuracy has led him to believe himself to be in possession of more talent than he really has; and he does not discover how greatly he has over-estimated his powers, till Nature puts them to the test.

As it is more easy to follow what another has done than to create for themselves, Students, both professional and amateur, are apt to devote themselves so entirely to copying, as to find it difficult to rid themselves of the trammels in which they have thus become involved. Instead of copying, to this degree, Drawing from Memory should be frequently practised. This gradually brings the Student within sight of that object which formerly appeared so distant, namely, the ability to produce an original Drawing; and his ardour increases with his increasing power. He finds himself following his own thoughts, his own way; and thus he loosens his fetters, and finally disengages himself from them altogether, and takes less and less pleasure in Copying, because he can act for himself. His power both to combine, and to create, increases; and, last of all, he looks only for hints from others to assist him in the delineation of any given subject from Nature, finding himself possessed of the power which he had so long envied and emulated in others.

This is precisely such exercise as belongs to other branches of knowledge. We first learn the ideas of others by reading; when those ideas are perfectly understood and well impressed on the memory, we express them in our own way, always adhering to the principles of the language used, until both the ideas and the language conveying them become equally original.

Were language itself invested with the imaginary difficulties which, to the uninstructed, appear to encompass Art, how many would be able even to write a letter? What is this but an original production, resulting from a knowledge of language and the principles of composition?

Though some Examples of characteristic outline are given in this Work, it is not pretended to give all that may be useful or necessary, either for this or any other subject, in the various stages of the Student's progress. He must look for them elsewhere,—and here only for a guide to their use. He will most probably find what he needs either in my Lithographic Examples, already before the public, or, perhaps, in his Tutor's portfolio.

Before the eye can become accurate, or the hand firm, some mechanical contrivance is requisite, particularly in the outset, to aid the learner in determining the relative situation of the parts, and the direction of the principal lines. It is a good method, and perhaps one of the best, to draw diagonal lines, from opposite corners, across the model, and the like on the paper on which the copy is to be made. By this the Student will discover that object, or the part of it, the nearest

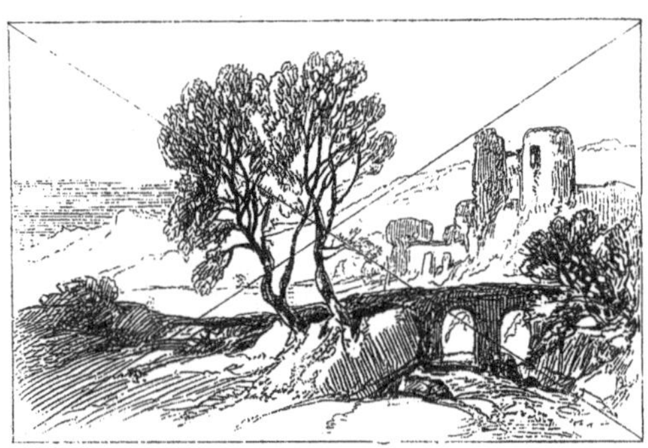 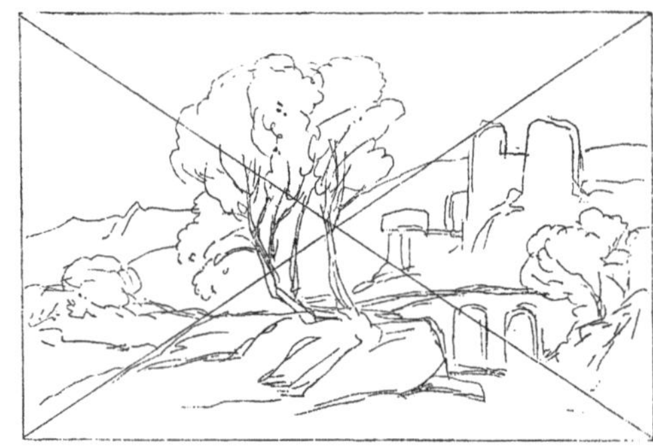

to the centre of the subject, from which he should commence, gradually attaching the other objects on all sides, until the subject fills the paper to its limits. The diagonal lines will assist very much in showing the relative heights and sizes of the objects. By such contrivances, the necessity for much erasing is avoided,—a thing often found disheartening to beginners. It is a common practice, however, to begin at one corner of the subject, and work to the one opposite; and the inevitable consequence is, that when nearly all has been drawn in, it is found that the parts, both individually and collectively, are either too large or too small, and that all must be erased. The same disasters result from beginning at various parts; it is found equally difficult to determine separately the size of each, both with relation to each other, and to the given limits of the whole subject; but by adopting the means above recommended, the Student, from the first, will obtain some distinct idea of the approaches he is making towards correctness. When practice has rendered these and similar contrivances no longer necessary, it is desirable that Copies should be made smaller or larger than the Original, to exercise the Student in judging of the proportions of objects, and to enable him so to adjust them to each other as to explain their relative magnitude. Without this power to explain objects in their proper and relative proportions, he could do little when drawing from Nature; and every lesson he learns should tend, directly or indirectly, to that all-important object. He should make it his business to learn from Copies those principles, which will enable him justly and fully to appreciate her varied beauties, and that practice in the use of the materials of Art, which will enable him to depict them correctly and vividly.

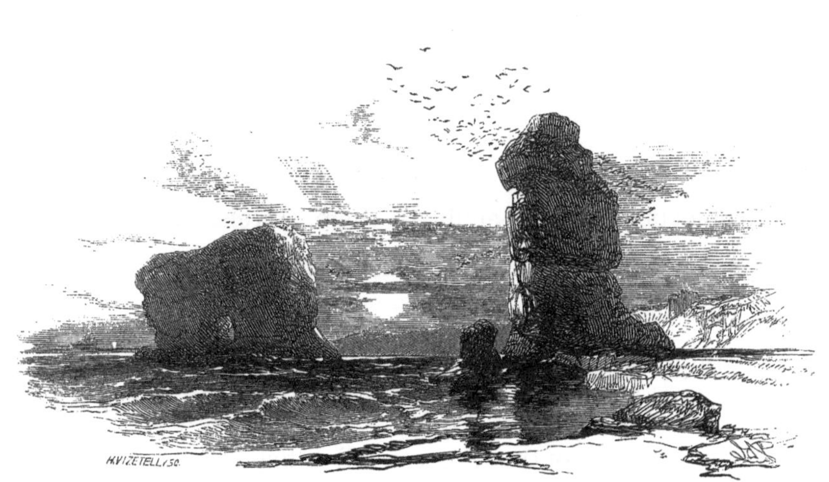

CHAPTER V.

FOLIAGE is a feature in Landscape so very striking, that we can scarcely say we possess *Landscape* without it; and those who intend to follow that department of Art, must look on the study of Foliage as of the first importance.

Owing to the difficulties apparently belonging to the truthful imitation of Foliage, very many are deterred from attempting it at all; and hitherto, though the Public have had many examples of Trees placed before them, no practical system of studying them has ever yet, as far as I am aware, been presented or explained. Yet this is the more demanded, because Trees, except in their Stems and leading Branches, do not stand before the spectator as objects so completely definable as most others, nor so much within the reach of the materials of Art: their peculiar *qualities* only can be attempted,—their height, their flexibility, their roundness, &c.; they cannot, in their forms, be copied with rigid accuracy: and for these reasons, the skill acquired in the practice of drawing other objects does not apply to them. Hence arises the necessity for studying, in regard to them, another application of the means of Art to their representation.

When the importance of Trees in Landscape is considered—how their infinitely varied and graceful forms, separate and combined, and their colours, contribute to augment, or, by contrast, to set off, other combinations—how all that is lovely in the face of Nature, or grateful in her brighter seasons, is associated with Foliage—and how much command the Artist has over it in every composition of Landscape, in the arrangement of Trees collectively, and over their forms individually—how much range they afford his fancy,—it will readily be admitted that they demand his best and most strenuous efforts, to obtain the mastery over what may be truly called the best and most tractable auxiliary of the Landscape Painter.*

Perhaps, to the difficulty of obtaining excellence in Foliage by such an imitation as readily conveys to the mind the likeness of other objects, and to its appearing to be so little within the reach of those rules which guide us in the accomplishment of other things, may be ascribed the commonly received notion, that to depict Trees well, depends more on the Artist's genius than on any rules which could be laid down; the more so, because the lines from the Chalk, or Pencil, seem less appropriate to the delineation of Foliage than to most other things; whereas, when well employed upon the perfect knowledge of it, they afford the most favourable means of giving the forms, the details, and the general characteristics of Trees, with great truth and freedom.

·In this work the Student will not find Examples of all the rich variety of Trees adorning the Park or Forest, and of all that are available in landscape composition. This would be unnecessary; he is never called upon to substitute botanical delineation for *pictorial effect*. In drawing from Nature he is usually too far removed from Trees, even the nearest, to be aware of any delicate *minutiæ*; he can only trace the more obvious and broader distinctions, such as exist between the Beech and the Elm, or the Elm and the Oak, &c. It is not his purpose to distinguish between Trees that are much like each other; he is not a painter of leaves in detail; but deals with the masses, the common forms, and their great distinguishing features: and would but waste his time in prosecuting a study more within the province of the Botanist or the Gardener, than the Painter.

The remarks that have been previously made on " The Use of the Chalk, or Pencil," are peculiarly applicable to their employment in the delineation of Foliage and Herbage.

When setting out, the attention of all Students is more or less directed to the operations of the instrument in their hands: they watch the lines made by

---

* In striking out a new track, all are apt to cling too tenaciously to ideas originating with themselves; and if my Reader should think that I have fallen into this error, and, in the yet untrodden path here pointed out, have advanced new views which may not appear to him to be always well founded, I invite him to carry these considerations to Nature, and test their correctness or incorrectness there; and to accept or reject them, according as they shall be found to be consistent with, or contradicted by, her.

the Chalk, or Pencil, instead of the effect produced by them, as if the imitation of Nature existed in them abstractedly. Hence some persons labour with the utmost patience to copy exactly, choosing a Line Engraving as the most captivating model; imitating every line in it—striving to produce softness and smoothness; concluding that in so doing they are making a *highly-finished drawing* (such as Plate 15): while others, not disposed to such labour, endeavour to effect their object with broader strokes (such as in Plate 14), and apologise for their want of patience, by giving the preference to what they denominate a *bold sketch*. Still all are looking to the means, and call a drawing "slight," or "highly-finished," according to the quantity of labour bestowed,—the number of lines serving as the index. This is very erroneous; for the labour, little or much, may have been mis-applied, as both the Examples referred to clearly testify.

In neither of them is there the least evidence of thought; the one displays rashness, the other inanity. At first sight, one of them may please by a semblance of power; but it is a power of the fingers, not of the mind; it is dexterity without truth or judgment; it is *power* mis-applied. The other has not even this low recommendation; the only idea that it forcibly impresses on the mind is that of *time* wasted. As a production of Art it is purposeless, idealess, and powerless. There is neither distinct form nor character in any one object it contains. The only utility of such examples consists in their exhibition of a collection of errors and deformities to be avoided. In neither can we avoid noticing the means employed, which are the more peculiarly obtrusive, because there is nothing else offered to the attention.

The Student must bear in mind what has already been observed, that the Chalk or Pencil produces its effect by a line for the Forms of objects, and by multiplied lines for the Shade; and also that every line is, in fact, a contradiction of Nature, however true to her it may be in effect.

No object in Nature has a line round it, which the Chalk or Pencil must necessarily give, to exhibit the shape of any object; neither are the shades on any object in Nature made up of a multitude of lines: here, then, are the contradictions which the mind must be made to lose sight of in all cases; but above all in Foliage. It is not in the outline alone, but in the outline viewed in connexion with the space it contains, that we acknowledge a likeness, as in the three first Examples on the opposite page; for if they were deprived of the outline by being cut out, we still should have as clear an idea of their different forms: and so of all solid and unbroken forms. These remarks, however, do not apply to Foliage,

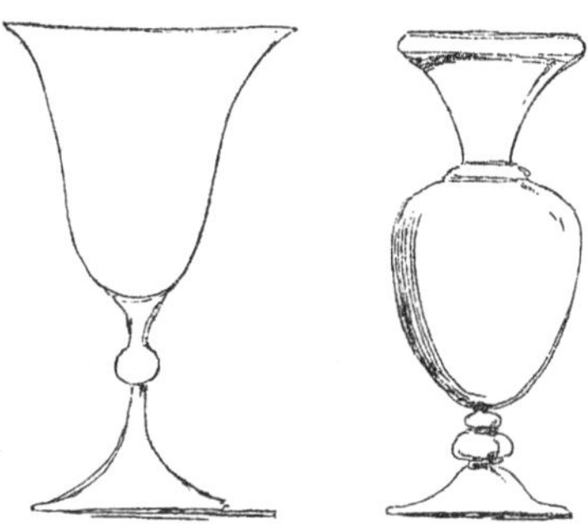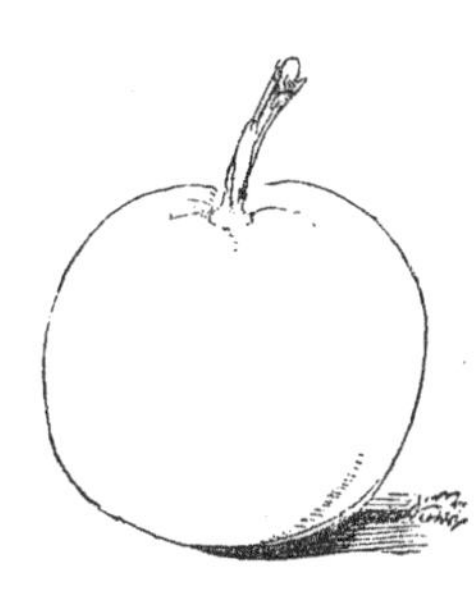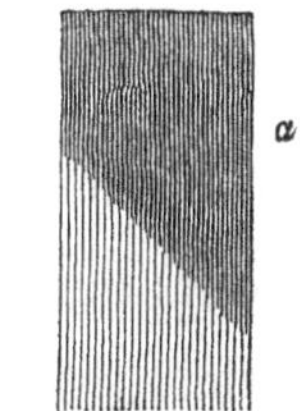

and we shall presently see why. To be sensible of the rotundity of objects, we must also be able to apply Shade to them, so that we may know the nature of the surface as well as the Form. The addition of the Shade is also suggestive of the presence of Light. Thus, then, with the Chalk or Pencil, we may convey ideas of Form, and Light-and-Shade; and to these may be added the character of the surface.

Already instructions have been given in reference to the drawing of Forms; and now we have to learn what are the properties of Shades, and how they may be represented. In the first place, they are even—alike in depth of colour every-where; or if they be darker in one part than in another, it is by imperceptible gradation from lighter to darker, and not by sudden transition. In the second place, Shade is retiring; that is, it appears to recede. In the Example *a*, the Shade, as there represented, is even: and whether it be desirable to produce it by lines at all, or by lines in any direction, it still ought to be *even ;* so far this is one step towards being like Nature. It must now be made to appear as if it retired, like Example *b ;* that is, it must suggest to the mind that idea. In Example *a* the Shade appears to lie on the surface of the paper; but in Ex-ample *b*, it appears to sink below it : here, then, are the two distinguishing facts with regard to Shade, irrespective

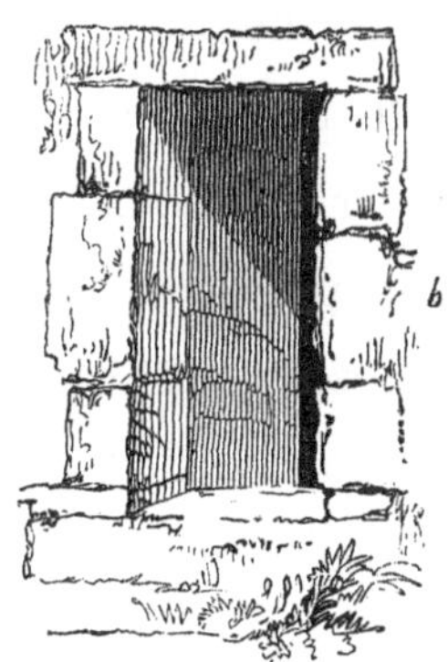

of its depth. We must experience sensations analogous to those we receive from Nature, ere we can pronounce the imitation true. In Nature we can put our hands *into* the Shades, but we put them upon the Lights.

The light, or illuminated parts of objects, are the most attractive, in proportion to their brightness ; and it is in the light parts of objects that we see their character and peculiarities. When an object, or any part of it, is obscured by shade, it is then difficult for the eye, without an effort, to clearly distinguish it; and as the light parts serve to make those in shade understood, the eye refuses to labour unnecessarily on the shades. For these reasons it is important to bear in mind, that as in Nature it is the illumined parts of objects which attract our attention, so must they be attractive in Art. On this consideration,—the attraction of all bright parts of objects,—hinges one of the great difficulties to be overcome. Light parts, also, must appear to come forward in contradistinction to Shades; and unless these effects be produced in all cases, nothing satisfactory is done.

We will consider the Lights and Shades separately, beginning with the Shade. In imitating Nature, it is always desirable that the operations of Art should, if possible, follow her course; but with the Chalk or Pencil this is impossible. Nature *puts on* the *Light* and *leaves* the *Shade;* whereas the Chalk or Pencil *puts on* the Shade, and *leaves* the Light (the white paper). Consequently as the Form of an object, being obtained by an outline, requires less labour and less evidence of material than the Shades, the attention of the Student is attracted to the Shade, and the Light is partially or altogether forgotten. Thus the influence of Art with the Chalk or Pencil is perpetually liable to be lost, because its operations are directly the reverse of Nature.

While, therefore, the hand is busy in putting on the Shades, the eye should watch the influence of its operations on the Lights; for, without Shade, the white paper is not Light, wanting the contrast of shade, which alone can make it appear luminous and attractive. We shall now endeavour to prove and exemplify these positions, by the attempt to draw a Tree, or, what will answer the same purpose, a part of one.

In the first place, then, it is important to know what belongs to Foliage generally, in order that what constitutes the peculiarities of each Tree may be the more easily superadded.

The shaded sides of Trees are gradually darker from the top towards the bottom, and from the extremities on either side to the centre, not by any sudden and violent transition, but by *imperceptible gradation.*

In depicting Foliage it is best to begin with the Shades and with horizontal lines, passing the Pencil from right to left, and from left to right, leaning rather more heavily on those lines passing from left to right, as the surer way of keeping them horizontal, making them also of equal length and breadth, and of equal strength, so that the entire tone of colour may be *equal,* as in Example 6, Plate 6; and in passing downwards, so terminating them as to leave crooked forms, as shown separately in Example 2. This is a very important part of the operation.

When sets of lines can with certainty be placed on the paper in this manner, the Student should unite them to each other, so as to form a body of Shade of any required quantity and intensity. In doing this, he must particularly observe to make each *set* of lines, as well as each individual line, of the same strength, so as to preserve the most perfect evenness in the Shade; giving to each set of lines also variety of form and size, and never allowing them to be seen following each other, as in Examples 3 and 5, but sometimes barely attaching, and sometimes separating, so that numerous interstices may be left, of various sizes. The sets of lines must, at the same time, be so united as to prevent the eye, as much as possible, from detecting their unnatural forms, or their number. See, again, Example 6.

The principal points to be remembered with respect to Shade in Foliage, may be thus summed up :—

    1st. The general evenness of the Shade. This is dependent on each line, and each set of lines, being of equal strength.

    2nd. Making the Shade gradually darker towards the centre, and towards the lower part.

    3rd. Leaving numerous insterstices.

    4th. In uniting the sets of lines, so that neither their precise forms nor their number may be apparent.

The inclination of the sets of lines must be towards the left, on the left hand side, at *d,* of the general mass of Shade; and towards the right, on the right hand side, at *e,* of the mass; each set of lines as they approach the middle of the mass, at *c,* gradually becoming less oblique.

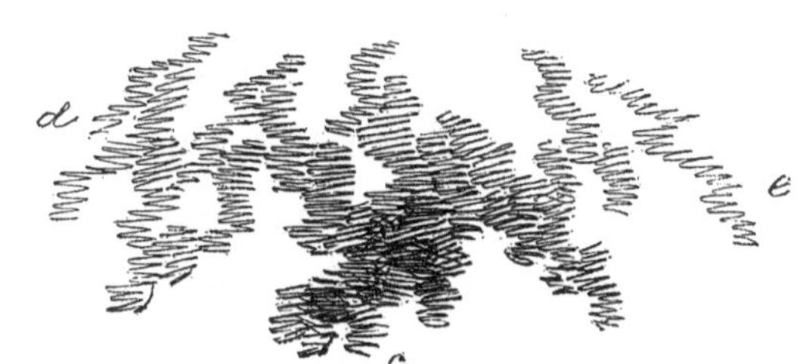

These are important considerations which must be remembered, and carried out with every set of lines.

To carry into effect the preceding instructions, which are in accordance with what we observe in Nature, it would hardly seem possible to choose any

instruments of Art more inappropriate than the Chalk or Pencil; the glaring
dissimilarity to Nature presented by the shape of each set of lines separately,
is even repulsive, and so totally unlike anything we see in Foliage, that if it were
not from the convictions of our judgment, we could never suppose we had advanced one step towards an imitation of Nature.

This may be sufficient to convince the Student how little is to be obtained from
any inherent properties in the materials or the instruments of Art, be they what
they may; and how indispensably necessary it is to have a clear idea of what is to
be effected at every step, that he may surmount the difficulties which attend
every stage of his work, and know not only how, but when to grapple with them.

The lines should be kept at regular distances from each other, not so as to
show alternately light spaces of white paper and dark lines of the Pencil, but so
as to be even, and still show that the shade has been produced by lines.   On
this depends the possibility of making the shaded parts of Foliage appear semi-
transparent; for if the lines be placed so close together as to be no longer
separately visible, this effect, as well as all appearance of leafing, is entirely lost
(see the Shades in the Trees of Plate 15); and if they be too widely separated,
they will become too obvious, and not only will they not look like shade, but
their own positive dissimilarity to Foliage will become too apparent to be
tolerable, as in Plate 14.

Before proceeding farther, it will be requisite to show how the Shaded side of
Foliage is commonly done, and the natural consequences of it (see Example 3,
Plate 6). Here all the strokes slope from right to left, falsely giving the idea of
some sloping surface; they are made darkest at one end, and joined at the other,
effectually preventing the shade from being *even:* they are wrong individually, and
more so collectively, by being passed over each other at the extremities. The
form of each set is obvious, and all their faults are increased and multiplied. So
also are those of Example 4, where the lines, though horizontal, are, from being
unequal in colour, and at various distances, still quite as wrong as those seen
in Example 3, if not altogether from the same causes. Again, in Example 5,
each set is following the other, and so representing a flat surface in shade, not
an even shade over an irregular object.

We come now to consider the outline, its peculiarities, properties, and effects.
By the outline, the peculiar character of the Tree is pourtrayed in the form of

the leaf; but though this characteristic outline may give the form of the leaf, it yet cannot pourtray all the leaves. By the Examples given below we may see that more than a certain quantity is not required. The outlines give us a clear idea, not only of there being leaves where they are thus positively represented, but we have also an impression on our minds of the existence of leaves in the white paper included within these outlines. If that impression be clearly conveyed to the mind by the general representation, any attempt to depict leaves individually would be unnecessary, nay, more, it would be useless. The Artist is not a painter of leaves of Trees, but of their broader and more general features; he cannot therefore pretend to depict them precisely and minutely, because he cannot see them either on the *masses* of Light or of Shade. In the body of the light parts, the leaves are overlapping, and breaking the out-line of each other, so that the eye cannot follow them; and to the same circum-stances, in the shade, obscurity is added, rendering the shaded parts of all Trees so very similar, that looking at some isolated portion of the shaded part of any one, it would be difficult to name it.

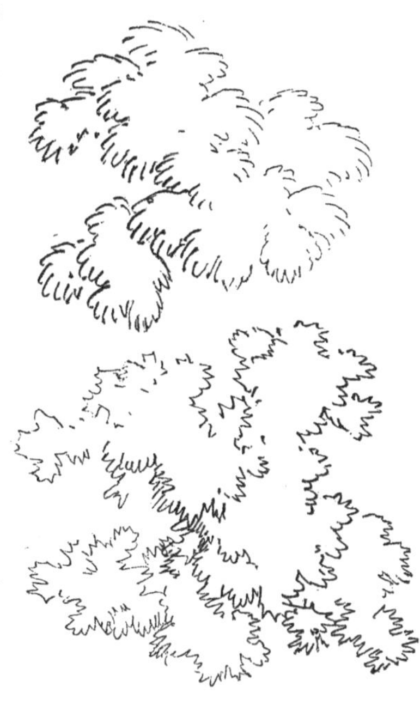

It is the peculiar form of the leaf of a Tree which must suggest the character of the outline to be adopted: whether it is to be irregular, like the Oak; round, like the Elm; or long and oval, like the Ash. It may also be here remarked, that the folds, or masses of leaves, sometimes take the form of the leaf: in the Oak they are irregular; in the Elm, round; in the Ash, long and oval; and in the Willow, of a still more elongated oval than the Ash.

In Example 4, Plate 7, the forms of the leaves of the Ash, and the way in which they grow on the branch will be seen. The leaves are composed of two curved lines; and the group radiates from a centre. If a line be drawn so as to touch the outer extremity of each leaf, we should have a large oval of this form; by carefully preserving this general form, we obtain, in a great degree, expression of another characteristic of Foliage,—Flexibility.

We come now to consider what kind of outline will best exhibit the form of the leaves, and their general arrangement in groups of an oval form.

It is best, at first, to draw the general form of the groups of leaves, and their masses, with very light curved lines, according to the kind of Tree intended, as in Example 1, Plate 6. Whilst an effort is afterwards made to pourtray the leaf by the characteristic outline, the general form of these masses serves to guide the hand in obtaining the general roundness, and the mind has, consequently, less to claim its attention at each step.

When Foliage is first traced by a very light characteristic outline, like Example 7, Plate 6—a method frequently employed, and when, in completing the Tree, it is found necessary to make the outline darker, the first cannot be rubbed out entirely, for then it might as well not have been drawn; and it being too tedious to follow *exactly* the first line, so as to make it as dark as required, a fresh outline is necessarily made, which, by sometimes doubling the line first made, and sometimes accidentally agreeing with it, causes both to be wrong, though each separately might have been right; the one effectually defeats the intention of the other, and both are spoiled.

When the general forms are traced as recommended, the characteristic outline may be added; and this is best obtained, by drawing at first only those lines on which the emphasis is to be laid (as in Example 7, Plate 7): these are all the upper lines of each leaf; and they should be always drawn from the centre of the Tree—where they should be light—towards the extremity, where they should be leaned on heavily, and be there made darker, and more emphatic. Unless the articulation be gained on the proper line, and also on the right part of it (the extreme end outwards, as at *a a a a*), it is quite impossible either to draw the leaves of a Tree, or any fold of it, of their true form, or to turn them in their natural position, especially on the right hand side of the Tree. Those who are not accustomed to place lines in these directions are always embarrassed; and often, when attempting the practice of turning them on the right-hand side, feel as if they were drawing left-handed, though, so far from it, it is allowing the hand its most natural motion.

These lines should be long practised in this way, singly; and it is desirable, whether drawing those on the right, or those on the left, to commence with the lines in an upward direction, as those at *a* and *e*, in the Example on the opposite

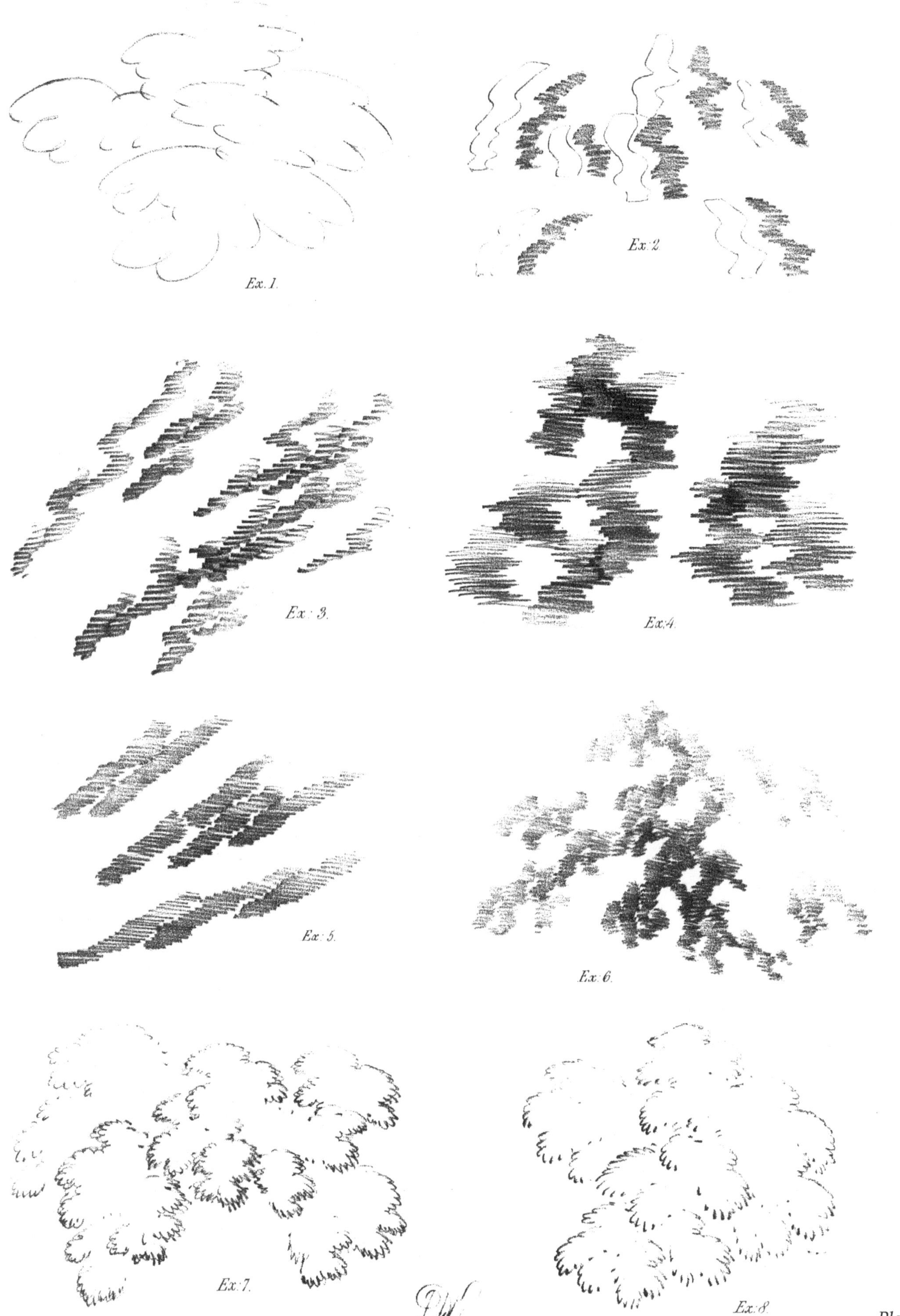

Ex. 1.
Ex. 2.
Ex. 3.
Ex. 4.
Ex. 5.
Ex. 6.
Ex. 7.
Ex. 8.

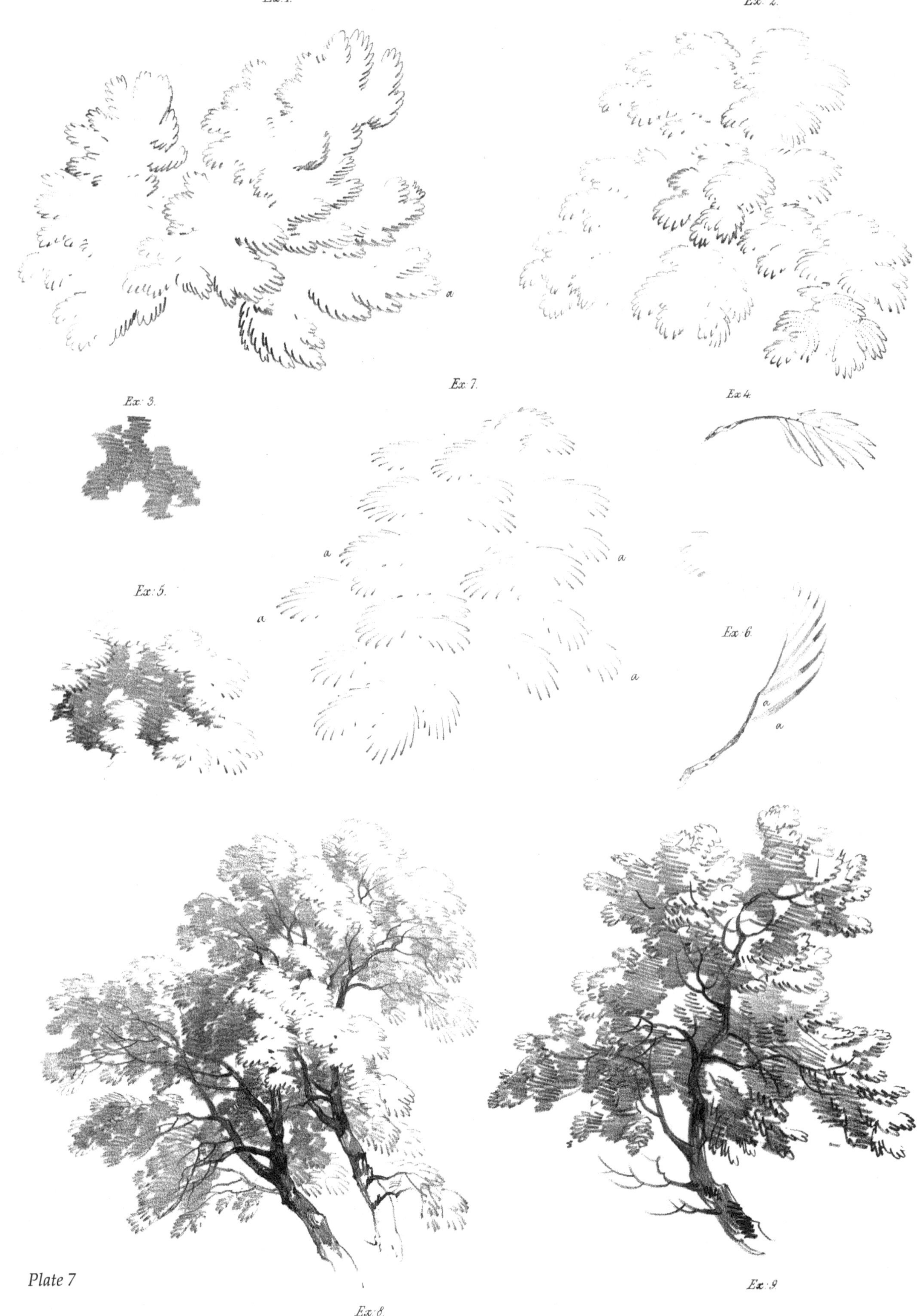

Plate 7.
Ex:1.
Ex:2.
Ex:3.
Ex:7.
Ex:4.
Ex:5.
Ex:6.
Plate 7
Ex:8.
Ex:9.

page, so as to form, at first, the groups, like *c c*, and afterwards bending down-wards in the manner of *d*. They should also be drawn of various sizes, gra-dually increasing, so that the power may be acquired of drawing them perfectly, and with facility, either by the motion of the fingers and wrist, or of the arm from the elbow and shoulder.

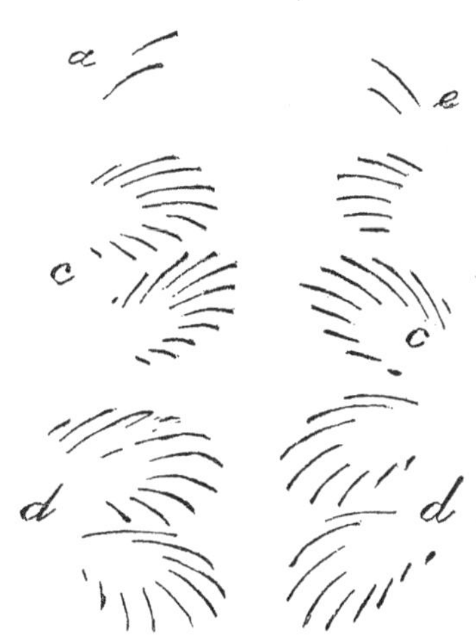

The appearance of Flexibility in the leaves con-tributes much to give the idea of roundness in the individual folds of a Tree ; and this is obtained by making the first lines incline a little upwards, and sloping them more as they gradually proceed down-wards, making them, at last, perpendicular, where the true shape of the leaf would be more clearly seen; the other leaves being seen in perspective, and overlapping each other wholly or partially, cannot, of course, be seen so plainly. Though no leaf be individually and entirely drawn, or attempted to be drawn, so much is done as to suggest the rest, and the eye and the mind are better satisfied.

The emphasis being secured on the strokes outwards, they are united by merely keeping the Pencil on the paper till it reaches the point, whence again the stroke starts outwards, and the outline is made complete, as in Example 2, Plate 7. The result thus obtained is more natural than that seen in Example 1,* where the emphasis being laid on the line passing inwards, and increased on the ex-treme end inwards, as shown at *a a*, in Example 6, it is impossible to turn round either naturally or freely ; and the leaves on the right hand side of the Tree appear to turn upwards, whilst those of the left turn downwards. What is thus done is done badly, awkwardly, and with great effort ; the leaves are neither natural in their shapes, nor in their position on the branches ; and, besides, they do not seem pliant. The defects of this method may be more evident on examining Example 6 ; where a portion of the character of Example 1 is drawn at large, with the lines extended by a paler colour, so as to show that if such as are drawn in Example 1 were continued, they would never unite in such a way as to give the true form of a leaf ; they also fail to give the least idea of the proper attachment of leaves to a branch.

---

* This is the most prevalent and erroneous mode of drawing Foliage, and I notice it for those reasons.

The contrast between these Examples is striking. The very defects and errors of Example 1, are rendered more conspicuous by the effort which has been made to turn round on the right-hand side. It is evident that this must be done with great difficulty; and that it is quite impossible by such means to give the least likeness to Nature in the form of the leaf, or to gain the least appearance either of roundness or Flexibility. Though, in any case, it would be a waste of time to delineate the shape of leaves of Trees with precise exactness; still the shape must be so far obtained, that the mind may have a perfect cognizance of the whole truth, from the amount of truth exhibited.

Again, in the illumined masses of Trees, to which we principally confine the representation of the leaves, we are conscious of their roundness from their contrast with the shade, where they appear almost flat, because shade prevents our seeing the roundness of the masses of leaves, or folds, as they are called; and the expression of roundness depends on the arrangement of the outline.

By examining Example 2, Plate 7, it will be seen that the paper encompassed by the outline appears round, and very different from Example 1, of the same Plate; because each turn of the lines on the right hand side of Example 2 corresponds and appears to be connected with, and to become the counterpart of, those on the left hand side, their connexion being carried on by the imagination, in such a manner as is shown by the dotted lines at the left hand and lower corner of the Example at *a*. No such appearance of rotundity is to be seen in Example 1, one of the most common methods employed; on the contrary, the whole appears perfectly flat.

There is another mode by which Flexibility may be still more perfectly expressed in the outline, and this is by occasionally separating the lines which represent the groups of leaves, and doing only just so much as may assist the imagination to perfectly comprehend the general form, without depicting it entire.

The Examples on the opposite page will make this understood. In one we have a continuous and unbroken line, exhibiting indeed the character of the Tree, and the groups of leaves, but scarcely indicating any Flexibility. In the other, the groups being separated by spaces, as at *a a*, a more forcible expression of Flexibility is thus obtained.

To the production of the characteristic outline of Foliage there are four considerations to be borne in mind :—

    1st. The form of the leaves, and their radiation in groups.

    2nd. The emphasis on each leaf at the outer extremity.

    3rd. Their arrangement, so that the portion of space they inclose may appear rotund.

    4th. The Flexibility; which first depends on the general curved form of each group of leaves; and secondly, on these groups being separated occasionally, and not represented by one continuous and unbroken line.

The Outline, therefore, as well as the Shade, must be practised separately, until the hand can execute each with facility and certainty. The Student must observe that he is not to imitate his examples by servilely copying them; but must endeavour to express their character and meaning as preparatory to an imitation of what he will find in Nature. In this manner he must practice within doors, before he attempts to draw from Nature out-of-doors.

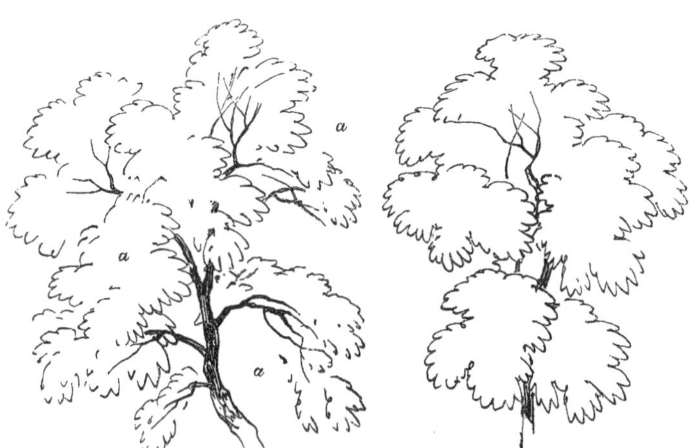

When the Student has made himself master of the Outline and the Shade, by practising them separately, and in the manner which I have endeavoured to explain, he should next proceed to attach them to each other. If each separately be right, and effect its purpose truly, they will, in connexion, aid and augment the merits of each other.

In combining the Outline and Shade, the principal points to be considered are the position of the characteristic Outline, and its effect upon the Shade.

This characteristic Outline requires to be placed where we most plainly see the leaves of the trees in Nature,—namely, on the extreme and outer edge, either of the Light or Dark side, where it separates from the sky, or any other object; and on the extreme edge of the masses of leaves in Light, where they separate from the Shade. The retirement of the Shade depends on the Outline, representing the leaves, being placed immediately on its edge, and being made a little darker than the Shade; and thus we shall have the same effect as has already been spoken of in page 43. Looking at Example 3, Plate 7, the Shade there, from being alone, lies *on* the paper, and appears to come *forward*, and all that is seen is a connected set of horizontal lines without meaning; and the eye also sees their form, which is unnatural, but inevitable. In Example 5, however, where the outline is attached to the Shade, the paper representing the Lights appears to come forward, and the Shade to retire. The Shade, here, appears to sink below the surface of the paper, and gives the idea of a space between, and beyond the surrounding folds, into which it would seem possible to pass; and this *retirement* of the Shade acts again on the Lights, by making them appear proportionably *nearer*, more *brilliant*, and more *attractive:* here, in the imitation, we are attracted by those parts which we are attracted by in Nature, namely, the Lights; and the attention which was given to the Shade in Example 3, is given to the Lights in Example 5.

The general roundness of the Tree depends on the Outline being made tender at the top and at the extremities, and becoming gradually darker, and exhibiting the leaves larger, towards the middle and lower part of the Tree; and displaying the greatest degree of strength on the Foliage of the nearest branches, that is, on those which come forward towards the spectator, where the leaves would, of course, be more plainly seen. In proof of these positions, see Example 8, Plate 7, in which the instructions so far given have been carried out. If this Example be preferred to Example 9, of the same Plate, that preference can be explained and justified. We can there trace effects to their causes; we can see the appliances of Art based on a knowledge of certain forms and properties of Foliage. In Example 9 the erroneous outline, such as Example 1, has here been applied to Shade falsely done, like Example 3, Plate 6; each is wrong separately, and when combined the errors are still more obvious: every important consideration has been neglected.

In Example 9, sometimes the Outline is seen on the edge of the Shade, and sometimes passing beyond, or lost in confusion amongst it,—now with leaves that are oval, then round,—now angular and small, the next instance large and pointed; and thus are drawn forms of every size and kind, each contradicting the other, and none perhaps agreeing with Nature, evidently showing that there was no contemplated intention, and no design when setting out. All the hopes and expectations were confined to seeing how it would look when done : and what could be expected from the effect of so many strokes, heaped on each other, or so promiscuously connected, but a mass of confusion ? Here has been no adaptation of means to an end.

Nothing can be more displeasing to the eye, or more repulsive to a correct judgment, than contradictions like these. Where is the roundness,—where the flexibility of the Foliage ? Where the evenness of the Shade ?—and does it retire as it ought ? Where is there any truth of Nature displayed ? Here the mechanism is most evident; every stroke may be counted, or nearly so. Can it be said that Nature is the better imitated in consequence ? And yet in this, or the like manner, thousands attempt to draw Trees. In Example 8, the means employed are much less obvious; and to count the strokes, individually, would be difficult, if not impossible. Is the imitation, therefore, less true to Nature ? The answer in this, as in the former case, must be—No. The strokes, without regard to what they are intended to express, should never be distinctly apparent; for in proportion as the means used, become evident, the likeness to Nature becomes less and less, and the poverty of the imitation more apparent. A comparison of these Examples may serve to show that there is no inherent merit in the materials : the same materials have been employed in both, and yet how different is the effect of each on the mind!

The Student must be reminded to practice from Memory; and he should have recourse to the original, merely that, by comparison, he may satisfy himself that he has followed the same principles, and, as effectually, as they are there illustrated. This practice from Memory is a *sine quâ non* in drawing Trees, because the mechanism of the model is not, or ought not to be seen; and because, in copying Trees from a Drawing, it is no more necessary to have exactly the same number of strokes, than in drawing from Nature to give the exact number of leaves on an individual tree. What is wanted is, that it should distinctly convey the idea of there being few, or many leaves, and of what kind.

Although it has been asserted that all that is required in the Shade is *evenness* of colour, and that no further approach to Nature need there be attempted, still if the Student be sufficiently skilled to do what has already been put before him, he will find that, by another adaptation of the lines on the Shades (such as in the annexed Example), he may obtain a greater likeness of Nature. He will here see that the lines are not horizontal, as he was first

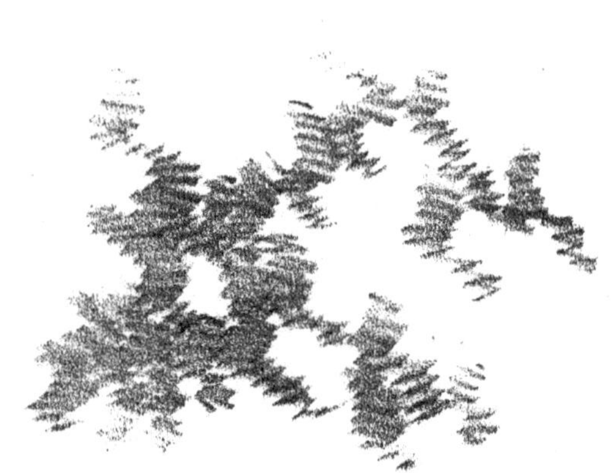

taught to make them, but that each separate line has a different inclination, so as to represent the various positions of the leaves in Shade, while the *evenness* of the Shade is still rigidly preserved. To do this well requires some practice ; and it should not by any means be attempted until the previous and more simple process, already detailed, be well learned. When attempting this, the kind of Tree must be first considered,—whether it has broad or narrow, long or short, leaves ; and appropriate lines must accordingly be adopted and distributed, as in Examples 1 and 2, Plate 8, where it will be seen that the instructions already given have been strictly attended to. One of the most important advantages to be gained by the adoption of this method is, that as the means by which the desired end is effected are less distinctly perceptible, the attention of the spectator is more exclusively confined to the character and spirit of the imitation.

There are also other important advantages attached to this method. By thus giving the lines every variety of inclination, they are perpetually presented at right angles, or nearly so, with the outline of the illumined folds of the Tree, as at *a a a a;* and by these means so much character is at once gained on the edges or extremities, that if a representation of the Oak be intended, a Characteristic Outline will hardly be required. For any other Tree,—although its

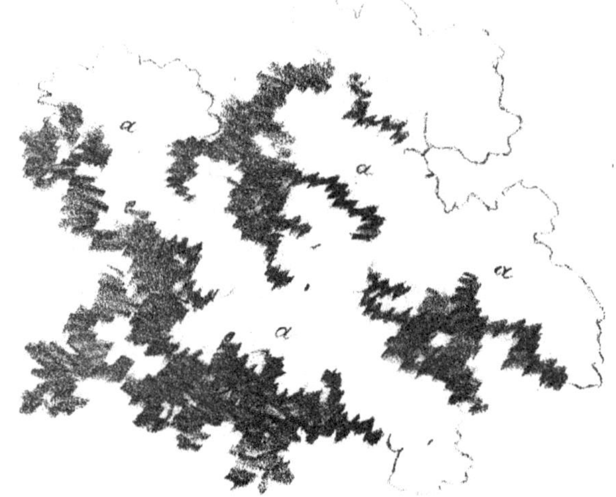

character may not be so nearly, nor so exactly given, as that of the Oak,—very trifling additions will change the present angular forms into such as are more oval, like the leaves of the Ash; or the character may be at once obtained by adopting longer and thinner lines for the Shade.

By these means, we also get rid of a great defect which attends the mode of placing the lines of the Shade horizontally, as explained in pages 44 and 45 ; for

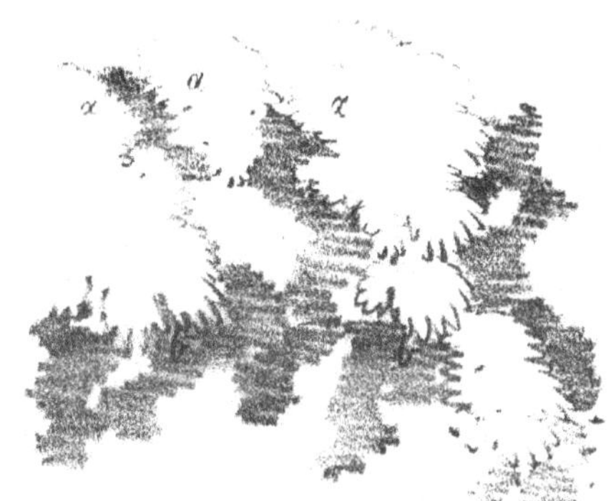

though character in some degree be thus given to the sides of the folds, as at *a a*, it is never given to their lower parts, *b b*, where, in Nature, the leaves are most plainly seen. The addition of a Characteristic Outline to the defective parts is consequently imperative; but as this cannot be perfectly adjusted to the Shade, some bare space is inevitably left between the Shade and the Outline.

By the method which I have explained, the character of the Tree is marked on the extremities of the shaded side, so that there also a definite Outline is dispensed with; and this is done by simply indicating the general form of the leaves, by such lines as *a a*, with the same broad point of the Chalk or Pencil, as was employed for the Shade. By these means, the character is added to the body of Shade, as at *b b* at the extremities; while both the Character and Shade unite and harmonise in such a way as to

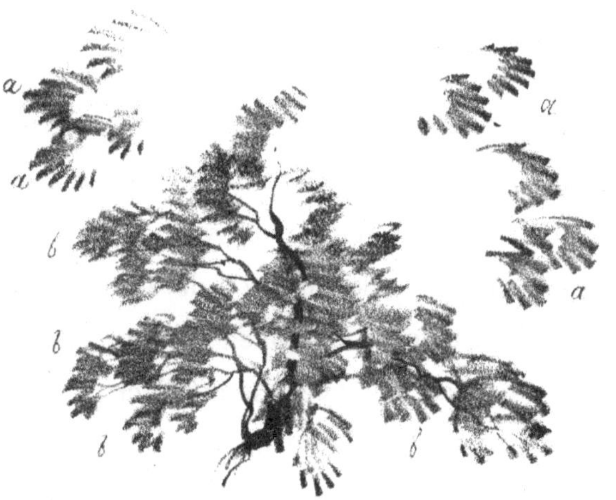

produce a nearer likeness to Nature. This may be seen by comparing Example 2, Plate 9, with Example 7, Plate 6. The Student, by carefully examining the branches of the Oak and Ash, in Plate 9, and comparing them in this their complete state, with their first stage, as shown in Plate 8, will perceive how very little has been added, in the shape of Outline, on the extremities of the folds in Light where they separate from the Shade, or on the extremities of the Shade where they would separate from the sky, or any other object beyond them. By an attentive examination he will also not fail to discover where, and to what extent, additions have been made, because the Examples in Plate 9 are those of Plate 8 completed.

Plates 8 and 9 are not only exemplifications of the methods pointed out, but also evidences of their efficiency. Examples 1 and 2, of Plate 8, are, respectively, preparations for an Oak and an Ash, or a portion of each, the Shade only being done, yet with all its properties; so that in this respect there may be no necessity for subsequent additions. Were the eye only to determine, it could find nothing satisfactory in either of these Examples, in their first stage, but rather the reverse. It is the mind, however, which in this stage of the drawing is the judge; and being enabled, from previously acquired knowledge, to perceive the truth amidst the apparent contradictions and deformities, it decides that what has been done so far is right. In Plate 9 these same preparations of Shade have the Characteristic Outline belonging to each attached. So great is now the change —so much more is there of likeness to Nature—so little to be traced of the unnatural and repulsive forms of the sets of lines composing the Shades—indeed, so great is the change in all respects,—that it is scarcely possible to believe that the first stages of these Examples were, or ever could have been, precisely those of Examples 1 and 2, in Plate 8. Yet such they were. If the Student be satisfied with the results, let him remember that every step has been guided by knowledge; that what has been done was not fortuitously done, but premeditated and pre-determined; not suggested by the eye or the feelings accidentally, during the progress of the work, but by a determination of the judgment to adapt the powers of the instrument employed to the exhibition of a series of truths, from a conviction that the eye, the intellect, and the feelings could only be gratified by the contemplation of what is true.

In Plate 9 another Example of the effects of the Outline is given, in the Stem of the Tree, where the Example 3 of Plate 8, has been finished by its addition; and its importance and its power will be felt by comparing this Example in its different states. Should this be not enough to produce conviction, the Student need only turn to Example 4, Plate 8, where he will find that that which appears to have neither definite shape nor meaning in the state he there sees it, may be made to assume any form. There, much more of the first state is left obvious than is desirable, but it is required for the Student's information.

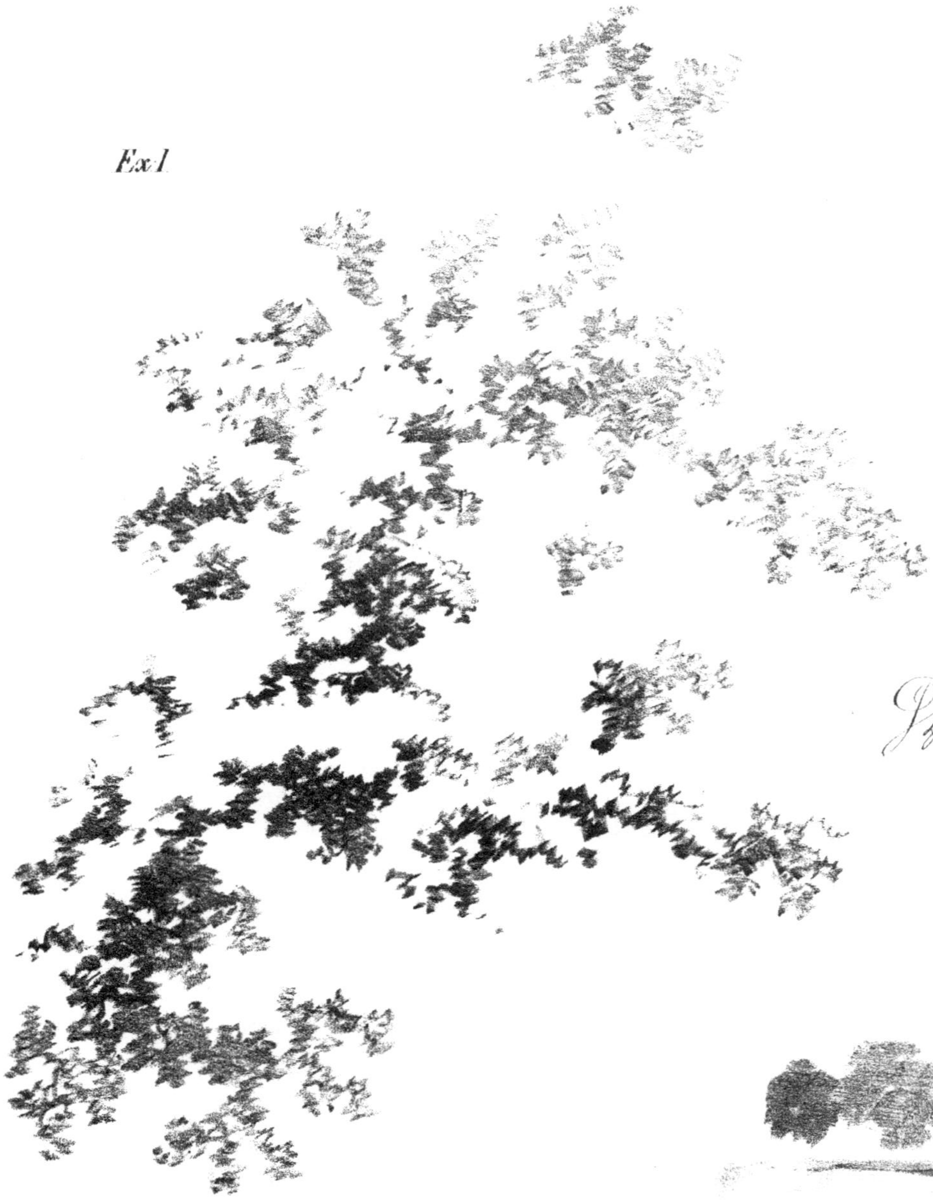

Ex. 2.
Ex. 3. 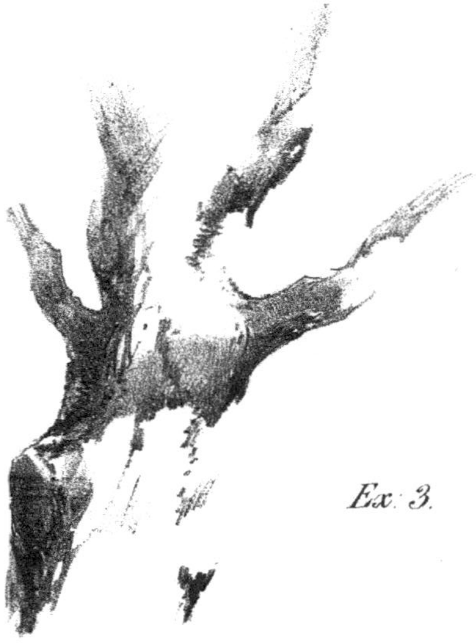
Plate 8
Ex. 4.
Ex. 1

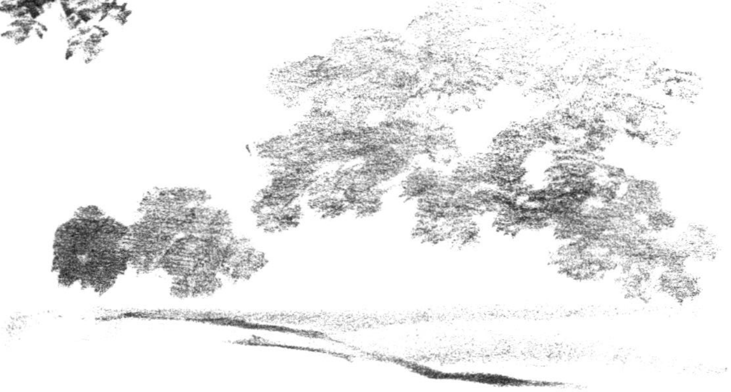

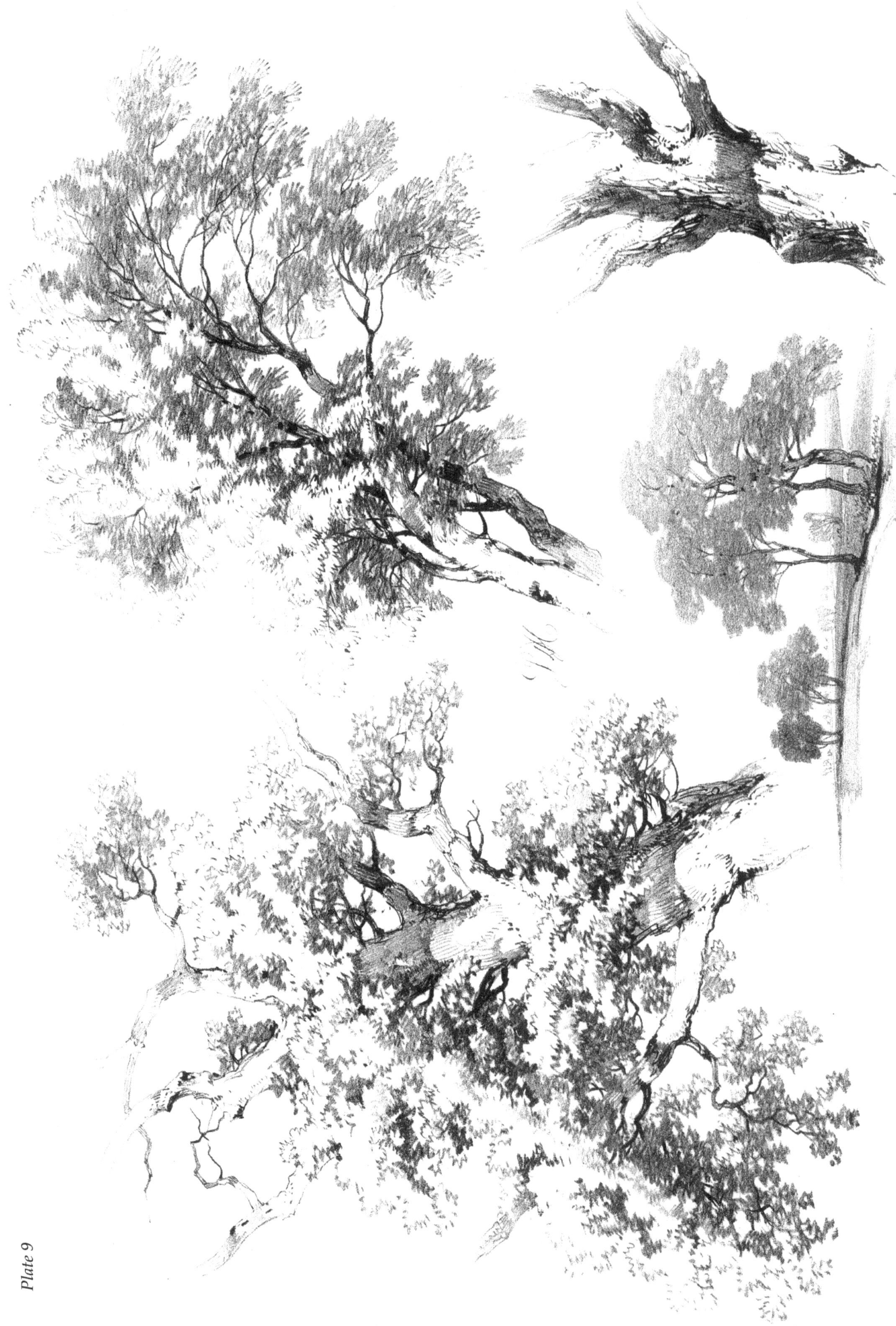

If, in placing on the paper the strokes for the Shade, the Student should find that they are too far asunder (which is a much less fault than being too close, whether in Skies or Distances), he has only to fill in the interstices to make a tone of colour as delicate as occasion may require, even to perfect flatness.

Besides the roundness of the folds of Trees, there is another marked feature to be observed,—*the general roundness.* The mode of expressing this is also determined by reference to Nature. As a Tree is a circular object, to a spectator standing in front of it, the middle portion of the circumference is nearer than the sides; and as it is a *tall* object, the lower part is nearer than the upper; and all the gradations are to be found between the two extremes in the intervals. To express then, in some degree, these properties, the leaves should be drawn gradually larger from the top towards the bottom, and from the extremities towards the centre. (See the various Examples of Trees.) To complete this effect of roundness in the general form, the Stems and Branches must be added; to the study of which the Student will now be led.

In concluding this part of the subject, it is necessary to observe, that the Leaves of Trees appear more abundant on the light side of a Tree than on the dark side; for the contrast between its local colour, and that of any bright object behind it, such as the sky, being less on the light than on the dark side, the interstices are not so evident in the one place as in the other.

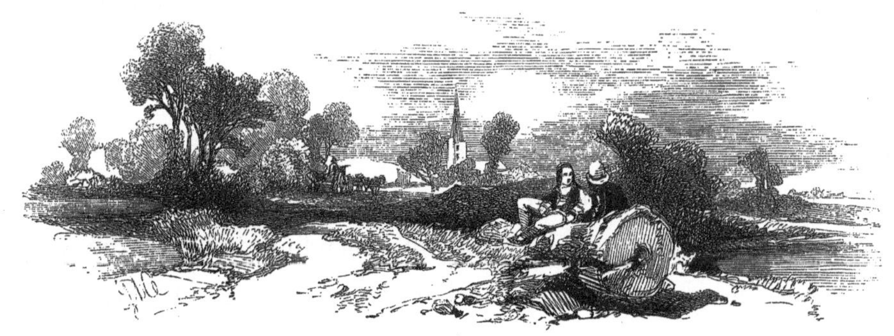

CHAPTER VI.

ON STEMS AND BRANCHES.

THE properties common to the Stems and Branches of most Trees are the following :—the Stems, from the root upwards,—and the Branches, from the point where they unite with the Stem, or with any Branch supporting them,— become gradually smaller; the Branches proceeding from the Stem, or from each other, are never so large as that part of the Stem or Branch whence they proceed; the uppermost Branches approximate to the direction of the parent Stem; and the others gradually form greater angles with it, as they grow lower down on it, till they eventually turn towards the ground: the same will be observed of the ramifications of the leading Branches.

These observations are exemplified by an Avenue: the Branches on the side of the Tree which is turned inwards to the Avenue, being obstructed by those from the Tree opposite, shoot upwards (the lower ones more remarkably so) for the light indispensable to their growth, and thus form what is said to have given to the Architect the first idea of an Aisle (see Plate 10); whereas on the outside they are found to grow as above stated,—the lower Branches extending laterally, and the upper becoming more vertical, according to the height of their shoot from the parent Stem. These observations apply to the Oak, Elm, Ash, Birch, Beech, &c.

The various Firs present, directly or indirectly, exceptions to this rule. The Scotch Fir has the Branches at top thrown out in a more horizontal direction; thence, as they grow lower down, gradually bending towards the ground, to a degree commonly greater than in other Trees; though by obstruction the Branches of the Fir are altered in their growth, as well as others. The Larch, and its kind, have all their Branches at right angles with the Stem, or nearly so.

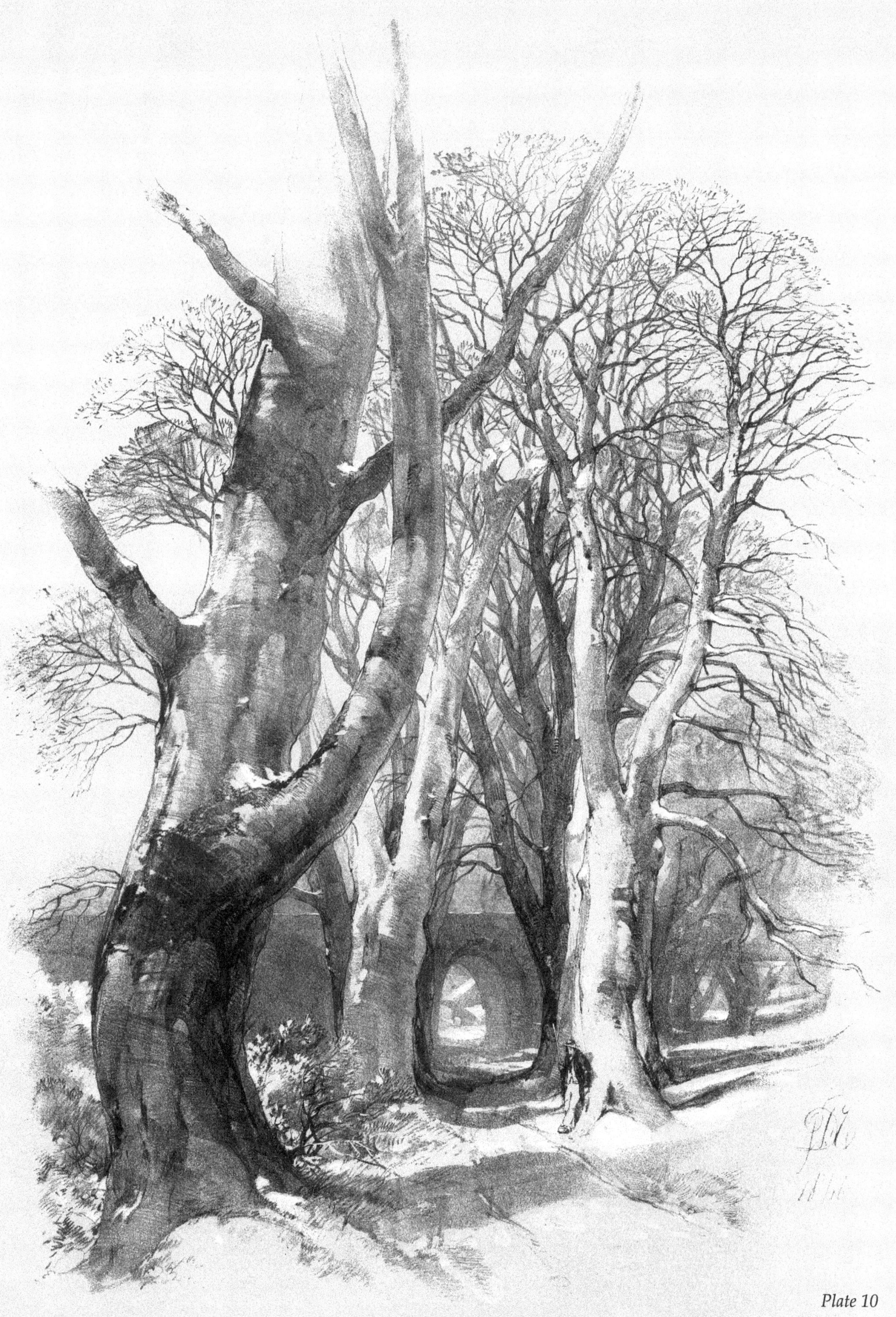

Plate 10

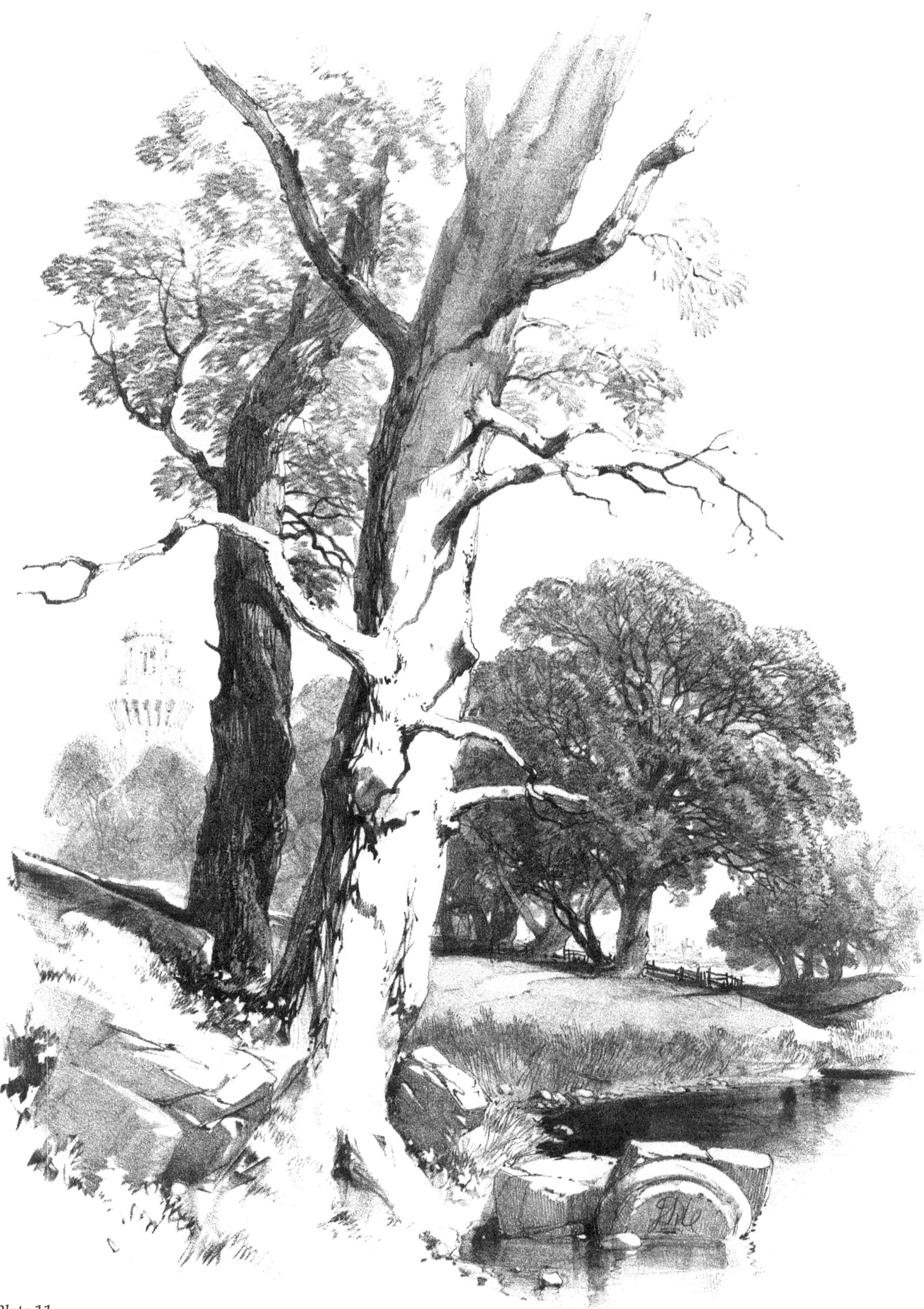

Plate 11

The Branches shoot out all round the Stem, and the smaller Branches shoot from the greater in the same manner. By examining the Example here given,

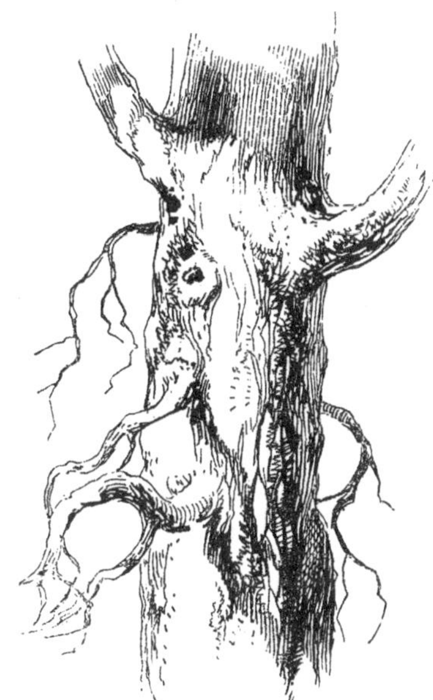

and Plate 10, it will be seen how this principle is carried into practice: those Branches, which grow on that part of the Stem turned towards the spectator, cross its outline, and are united to the surface; those on the sides are inserted on the outline of the Stem or Branch to which they are attached; while those growing on the unseen part of the Trunks appear to be cut off by its outline, and their insertion is therefore unseen. In drawing Stems and Branches, such lines must be adopted, whether straight or crooked, broad or thin, as will best express the character of the Bark.

Much care is required to *attach* properly the Branches to the Trunk, and to each other. Not unfrequently this is done in the clumsy manner shown at *c c,* in Example 1, where the Branches at their shoot from the Stem appear swelled, and then suddenly and unnaturally become taper. The best and simplest way to affix the Branches to the Stem is by first drawing the lines for the Branches, so as to make well-defined angles with the Stem, and the same with the Branches, where they unite with each other,—as *a a,* in Example 2; then by merely cutting off the extreme sharpness of the angles with curved lines, they become properly, because naturally, united.

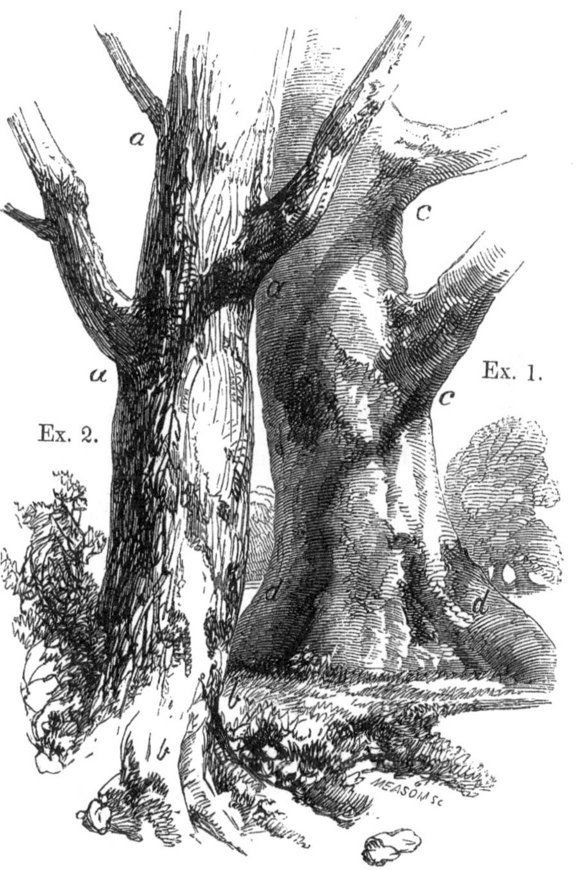

To attach the Stem properly to the ground, the outline on both sides of it must be brought down to, and united with, the ground, as at *b,* in Example 2, in the same way that the Branches have been united with the Stem, and with each other; and the surface included within the outline should imperceptibly unite with the ground, as in Example 2, so as to leave no distinct termination. It is very important that this should be attended to, as the appearance of rotundity is greatly assisted by doing it properly. On referring to Example 1, it will be instantly seen that, however round the Stem might have been made to appear on its surface, the way in which it is cut by the straight line of the ground, would be in opposition to the idea of its rotundity. This mode, however, of attaching a Tree to the ground is by no means uncommon.

Both Branches and Stems now require covering with the Bark; and here it will be observed that, on the Stems at the Root, and on the leading Branches towards the Stem, the character of the Bark is more strongly marked than in the more remote ramifications. The Bark is more or less rough and cracked, according to the kind of Tree, or its age; and in proportion as Trees grow older, the Bark is more deeply furrowed. Some have a very thin, smooth, and light Bark: of this kind is the Bark of the Beech and the Birch, which contrasts so beautifully with their Foliage.

Before attempting to pourtray these appearances, the Student should observe that the Trunk and Branches of a Tree, being cylindrical, receive the light and shade as cylinders do; that is, the brightest part is some little distance from the outline, on the *light* side, and the shade is darkest, at some distance from the outline on the *shaded* side, according to the direction of the light. See in illustration, the Beech Stems, Plate 10, and the cut at page 59. The peculiarities of all Trunks and Branches must be subject to these general considerations; although from the roughness of the Bark they are apt to escape notice. The lines chosen for representing the Bark must be made dark or light, broad or thin, according to its nature. See the Stems, Plate 11, the *first* stage of the Drawing, where, in addition to the considerations above-mentioned, it will be found that, on the shaded side, the lines are placed so near to each other as hardly to convey any idea of the character of the Bark, because the shade obscures the furrows. As no attempt is made to depict leaves in shade, so none need be made to depict the Bark in shade: indeed, as a general rule, it is better to give too little of the character of any object in shade, than too much.

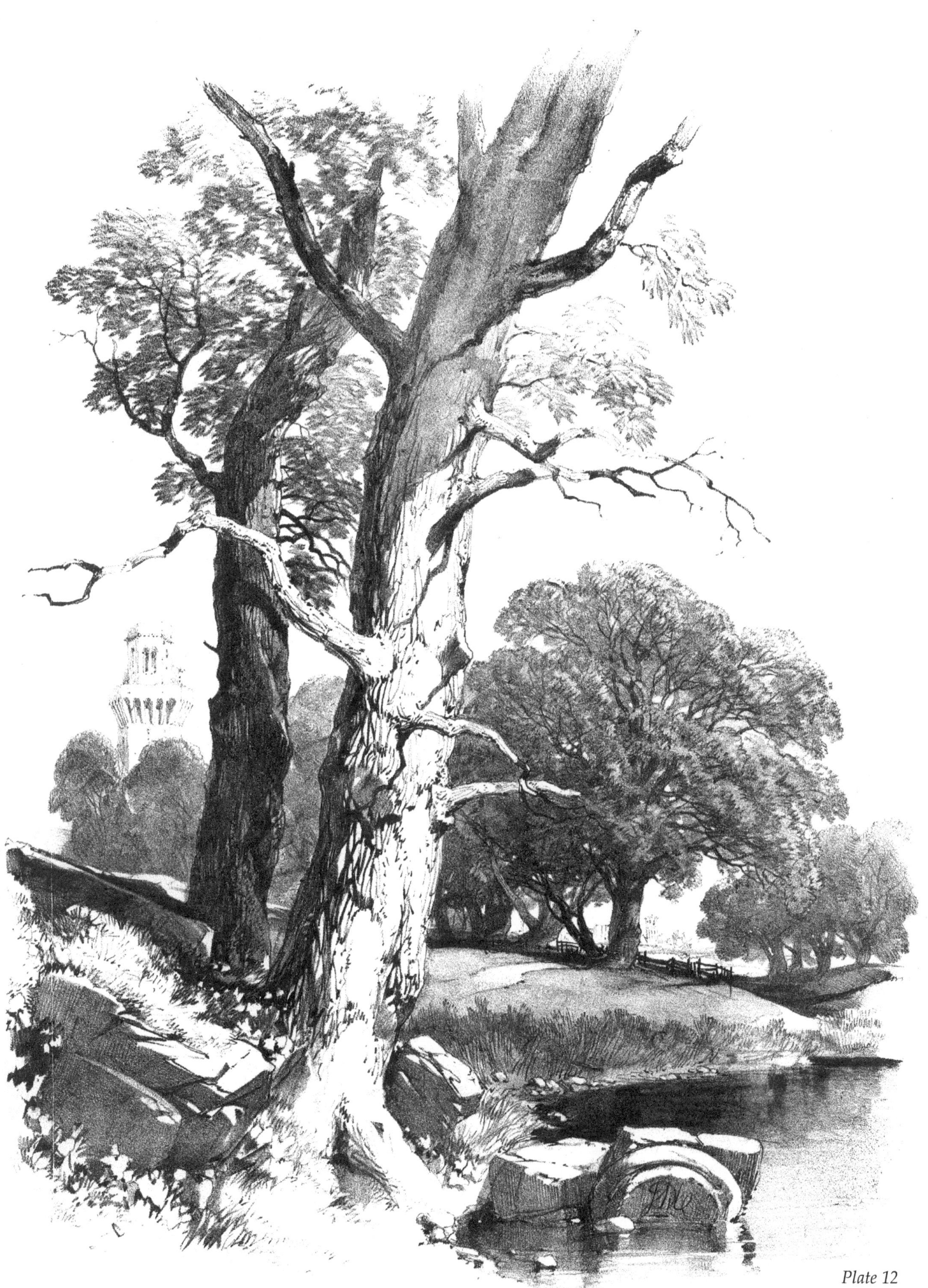

Plate 12

It has already been observed that the leaves of Trees are most plainly seen where the light separates from the shade. If the Student turn to Plate 5, he will there see that the character of the materials composing the building is most forcibly marked on the edges of the lights and shades, just where they separate from each other. The same observations equally apply to all cylindrical and rotund objects. For instance, in the Basket here given, the line of wickerwork, which lies on the limits of the light and shade, is most plainly seen; and the others, as they gradually approach the light, or are obscured by shade, become less and less distinct, till in the lightest or the darkest part they are scarcely

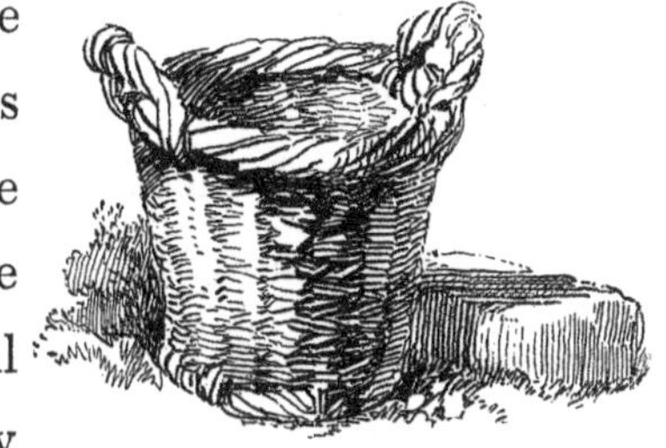

perceptible. As the Bark on the Stems of Trees is, in the same manner, most plainly seen where the light becomes blended with the shade, its character should be there marked most plainly, the lines being there made darkest, and gradually becoming lighter towards the light. By these means, both the character of the Bark, and the roundness of the Stem, are at the same time most significantly expressed.

For proof of this, and of the attractiveness of all light parts, compare Plate 11 with its finished state in Plate 12. It will be seen that the characteristic lines are of the highest service on the light parts, and that it is only there they are required, since the shades have not again been touched. In Plate 11 the light sides are bald and thin, unmeaning and unsatisfactory; but by the addition of such character as is given to them in Plate 12, they are made to look emphatic and dense, round and complete.

An Example of the effect of this principle is to be found in the upper Hand, Plate 1. The Student will perceive, if he examine attentively, that just where the light falls into the shade, the lines employed to express the rotundity of the Fingers are there more distinctly marked and separated. So in Plate 4, immediately along the outline of the Deer, and along the line of the Back, and down the side of the Face,—on the confines of the light where it is merging into shade, —its hairy covering is the most evident: but in the shades, in both Plates, the lines indicative of the texture are hardly distinguishable.

Were I, in this instance, calling attention to an Example of my own Drawing, the Student might perhaps suppose, that what has been pointed out was referable to some peculiarity in my style of Drawing; but when these things are found to exist in the works of others, and those the most distinguished, whose objects of study are so widely different from my own, they cannot fail to strike him, and make him see and feel that there are laws which govern Art, and that their application is not confined to one class of subjects. This should encourage him to unremitting diligence, and should kindle in him a determination to acquire the power to apply these laws successfully in the department of Art to which he intends more especially to devote himself, seeing that in so doing, he has made sure advances towards their universal application.

We come now to the Branches of Trees, which, in consequence of their twisting very much more than the Stems, require, not only the application of all the instruction which has been given concerning the latter, but something in addition,—depending on the Laws of Light.

All objects, and parts of objects, receive the greatest quantity of light when the rays are at right angles with their surfaces, and less as the rays fall on them obliquely. Let *a a*, in the annexed Example, be rays of light; and A B C, the

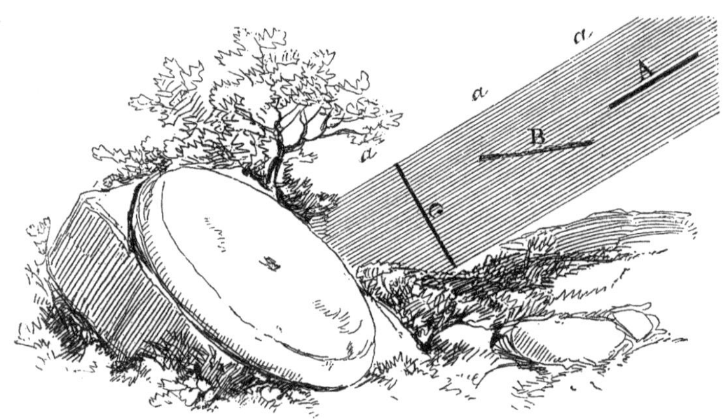

surfaces of three objects of equal size, placed at different angles with them: it will be seen that the surface A does not receive any rays to illumine it, on account of its being precisely in their direction; but B, being somewhat inclined towards them, receives the light partially; whilst C receives it in the greatest degree, in consequence of being at right angles with the rays. From an observation of these facts, as here shown, the light and shade of the Base of the Column will be easily understood and accounted for. The application of this principle to the Branches of Trees is shown in the first Example on the opposite page: the light being supposed to fall obliquely from the left, those parts, such as D D, which have the same inclination as the rays, are, of course, in shade; in other parts the shade is regulated accordingly as they recede from the light; and, *vice versâ*, those parts are left most bright, as L L, which are the most directly opposed to the rays. Now let all the circumstances belonging to the Stem be added, as before explained, and the result will be like this Example, or as Plate 12, the finished state of Plate 11. The effect, both of the Stems and Branches, will also be more vigorous, by the indication of the moss which is found on them; this being often of a dark colour, affords considerable contrast and animation, as well as additional likeness.

Branches do not grow on a level with each other, from opposite sides of the Stem, or of other Branches, but alternately, all round, at different heights, as in each of the Examples given in this page. The angle of their separation must not be overlooked, as this not only shows from what part of the Stem they grow,—whether the upper or lower part, or from each other, whether near the extremity, or near the Trunk,—but also indicates, in some degree, the kind of Tree to which they belong. In the more sturdy and spreading Trees, such as the Oak and the Elm, the Branches—more especially the lower ones—diverge abruptly from the Stem, appearing to interrupt the continuity of its direction, as is shown in Example 1 below; while in the more delicate and slender, such as the Birch and the Willow, the Branches shoot at a more acute angle from the Stem, forming with it, and with each other, as they grow up in a similar direction, an assemblage of graceful lines of a like character. See Example 2.

The Student should now compare Plates 14 and 15, with Plates 16, 17, 18, 19, 20, 21, and

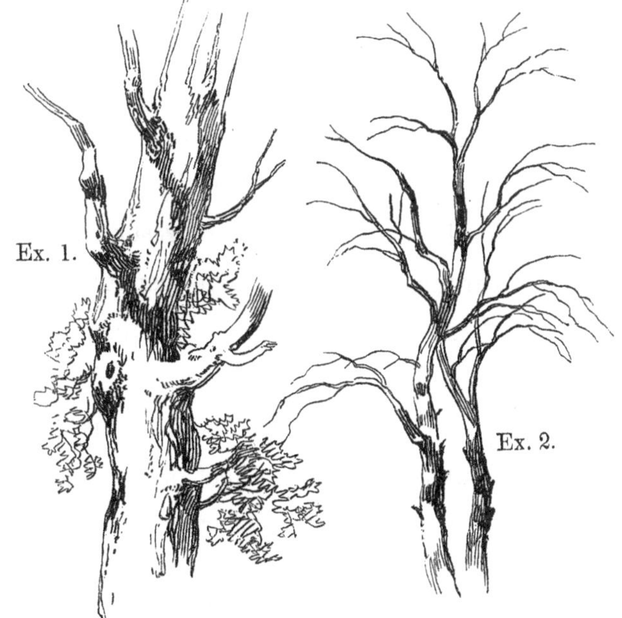

22: if he has profited by the instructions which so far have been given, he will not only perceive their respective merits or defects, but will be able to account for them.

By thus exercising his judgment, he will become more thoroughly sensible of the advantages of following the Laws of Nature closely; and from what he already knows of these laws, he may estimate their additional importance in a more advanced stage of pictorial art. He will now be able to understand why a slight sketch, from the hand of a skilful Artist, is often preferred to a more laboured production, which may yet be very imperfect, notwithstanding its greater pretensions to completeness. Such a sketch will be preferred, because it displays the effects of a concentrated knowledge, expressed with simplicity and power, and apparently without an effort. Its merit, however, does not consist in its slightness,—in its being devoid of the evidences of labour,—but in its truthfulness, with regard to the objects represented and the means employed. No gratification is afforded by a sketch, however free, where truth has been sacrificed or neglected, as in Plate 14; and as little is derived from such laboured productions as are exemplified by Plate 15, where a pains-taking workman has toiled, without knowledge, to make the means attractive.

Up to this point, it is to be presumed that the Student has been able to follow out his instructions, and to carry them into operation successfully and with certainty. He can now imitate the leading characteristics of Foliage, and of the Stems and Branches apart from each other. It must now be his business to unite them, and produce, by their union, effects not otherwise to be obtained. Before he attempts this, however, he should attend to the following observations.

The Branches are so *lost* among the Foliage that no one can be distinctly traced to its *extremity*. It is by the Branches that we are able to distinguish more clearly such lights as represent the illumined folds of the Tree, or those spaces through which the eye penetrates to the sky beyond; and it is here, across these spaces, large and small, that we most plainly distinguish the Branches, and are able, by these occasional glimpses of both Stems and Branches, to obtain an idea of their continuous form. The Stems and Branches also greatly contribute to the effect of the general roundness; and additional force is given to the expression of roundness, by the shades cast on the Stems and Branches by the Foliage, such as *a*, in the Example on the opposite page. These shades should always be darkest at the lower part, and lighter towards the Foliage, which will thus immediately appear to advance, while the Stem or Branch will appear to retire.

Among the impressions we derive from Trees, are those of semi-transparency in the Foliage, and of opacity in the Stems and Branches. Before our portraiture can be complete, ideas of those qualities must be excited in the mind. The Branches and Stems in shade being made darker than the Foliage in the drawing, cause the Foliage to appear semi-transparent; whilst the lightness of the Foliage acts, in its turn, on the Stems and Branches so as to make them appear opaque: and when these impressions, of transparency in the one and of opacity in the other, are produced, their relative depth of colour is right. Those parts of

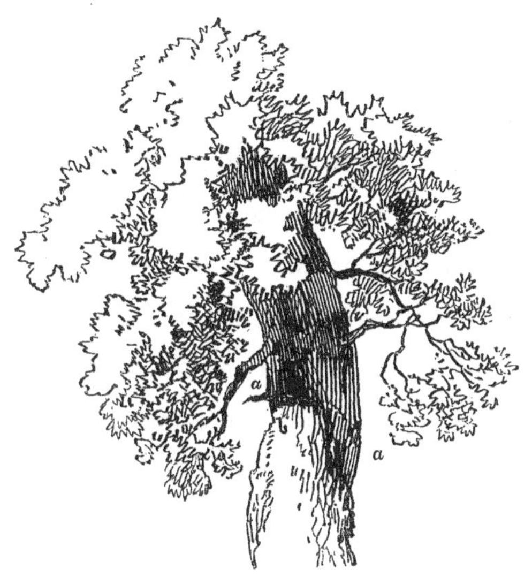

the Foliage also which are in shade are made to appear *distant*, when the Branches are seen continuous across it; or *nearer*, when it spreads before them, and their continuity is hid from our observation. The Student should now turn to Plate 9; he will there find parts of an Oak and an Ash complete, which will assist him to comprehend and to feel the above observations. Intricacy is another attribute of Trees; it is to the shaded parts that this observation more especially applies; and this effect of intricacy is given entirely by the number of the Branches, which are traced across the spaces seen in the shades, where the masses of Foliage separate.

If what has been pointed out be thought minute and dry, my reply is, I write for the uninstructed, for the inexperienced, and the young,—not for those who are wise in these matters. Though the explanations may have appeared long to the Student, he must remember that he has now learned the *leading features* of *all* Trees, and therefore is so far prepared to draw *all*. He has now but to add to his previously-acquired knowledge of the general characteristics of Trees, the peculiarities of each, and very little practice, comparatively, in them, will render him master of Foliage.

"Nothing is denied to *well-directed* labour—nothing is to be obtained *without it*." The Student must not expect the hand immediately to execute what he perfectly understands; it requires diligent practice to obtain perfect command over it.   He must be content to go on surmounting his difficulties and weeding out his errors, one by one, as his judgment improves; and if he see them disappear, though ever so slowly, he is certainly cultivating the ground to advantage.   It is indolence which leads us to complain of the difficulties. Certainly, to imitate Nature well is not the easiest thing in the world; but if the Student be willing to labour, he will have his reward.   None can find their way by a readier road than a right one; and it is mere delusion to talk of this or that style being easier than that which has truth for its object, and sound principles for its basis.   Many who are anxious to avoid the difficulties which diligence is content to struggle with, run off from one " *style*," as they call it, to another,—or, more properly speaking, from one *manner* to another, —always fancying that to be the most worth having which they have not yet tried; till at length, when more time and labour, in a thousand mistaken ways, have been wasted, than, if well spent in a right one, would have insured to them the largest share of gratification in the exercise of Art, or in the contemplation of Nature; they find that they have been only running round in a circle of errors, without making any advance towards excellence in the practice of Art.   They have merely acquired a smattering and confused know-ledge of a language which they can neither speak nor understand; and mortified, at last, to discover the truth they at first refused to be persuaded of,—that it is on knowledge, and not on nostrums, they must depend,—and blushing for their elaborate mistakes, they excuse themselves in the affected candour of their self-accusation,—" I find I have no genius for Drawing."

To those who are seeking a short road to Art, it may be unpalatable to be told that none can be shorter than that which knowledge makes short; and that there are no by-paths by which idleness and indifference may find their way to a goal, which is only to be reached by industry and intelligence.   The really short road is that which is made so by entering on a right course from the outset, taking advantage of the instruction to be derived from the experience of others, and persevering until what is seen to be right be accomplished.

The Student should now know that what has hitherto been done is yet capable of inprovement, and by what means this is to be effected.   Looking again to Example 8, Plate 7, he will there see that all that is done in giving roundness, is done by the Outline alone, but that one circumstance, common to the light and shade of round objects is omitted, viz., the half-tone

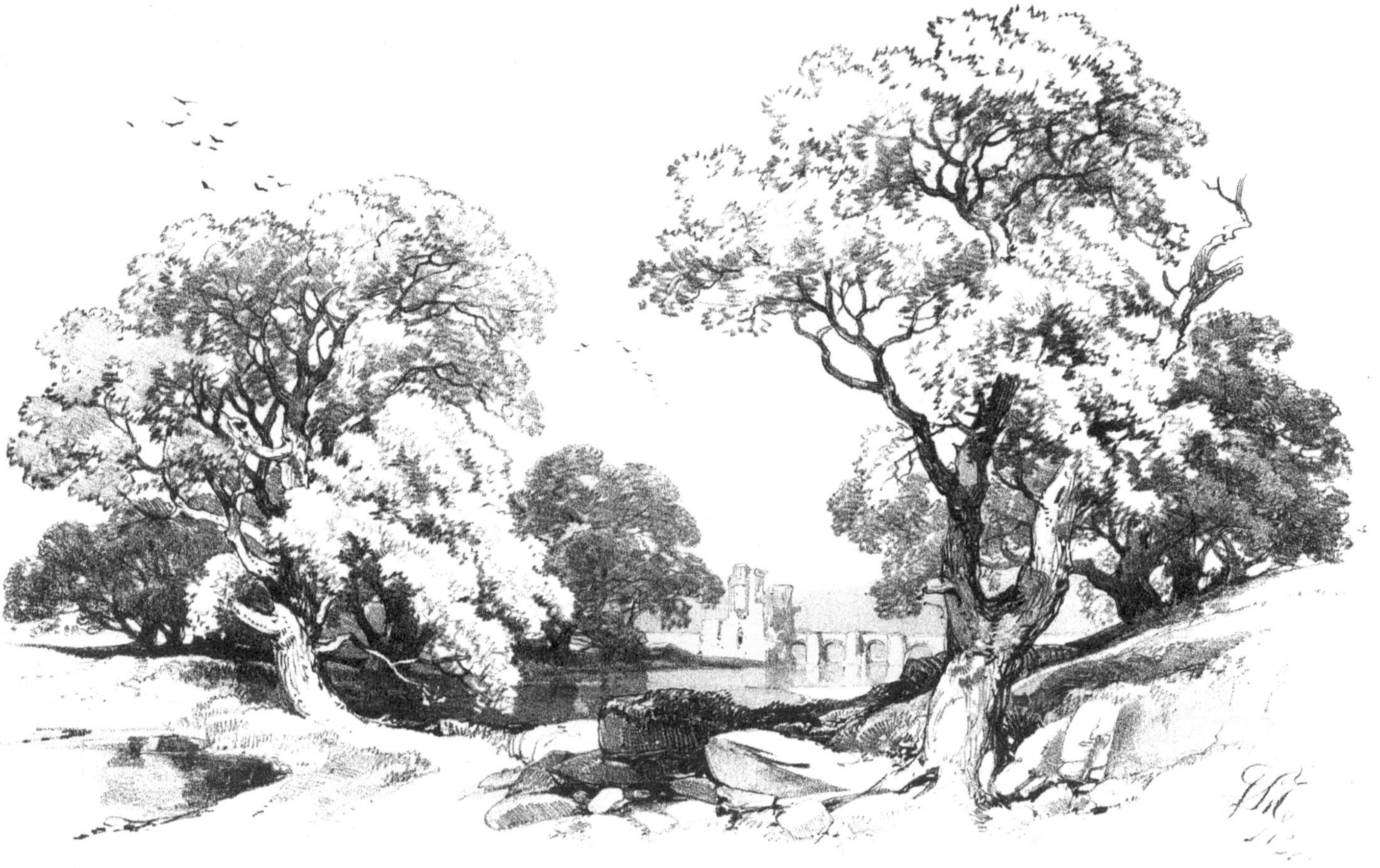

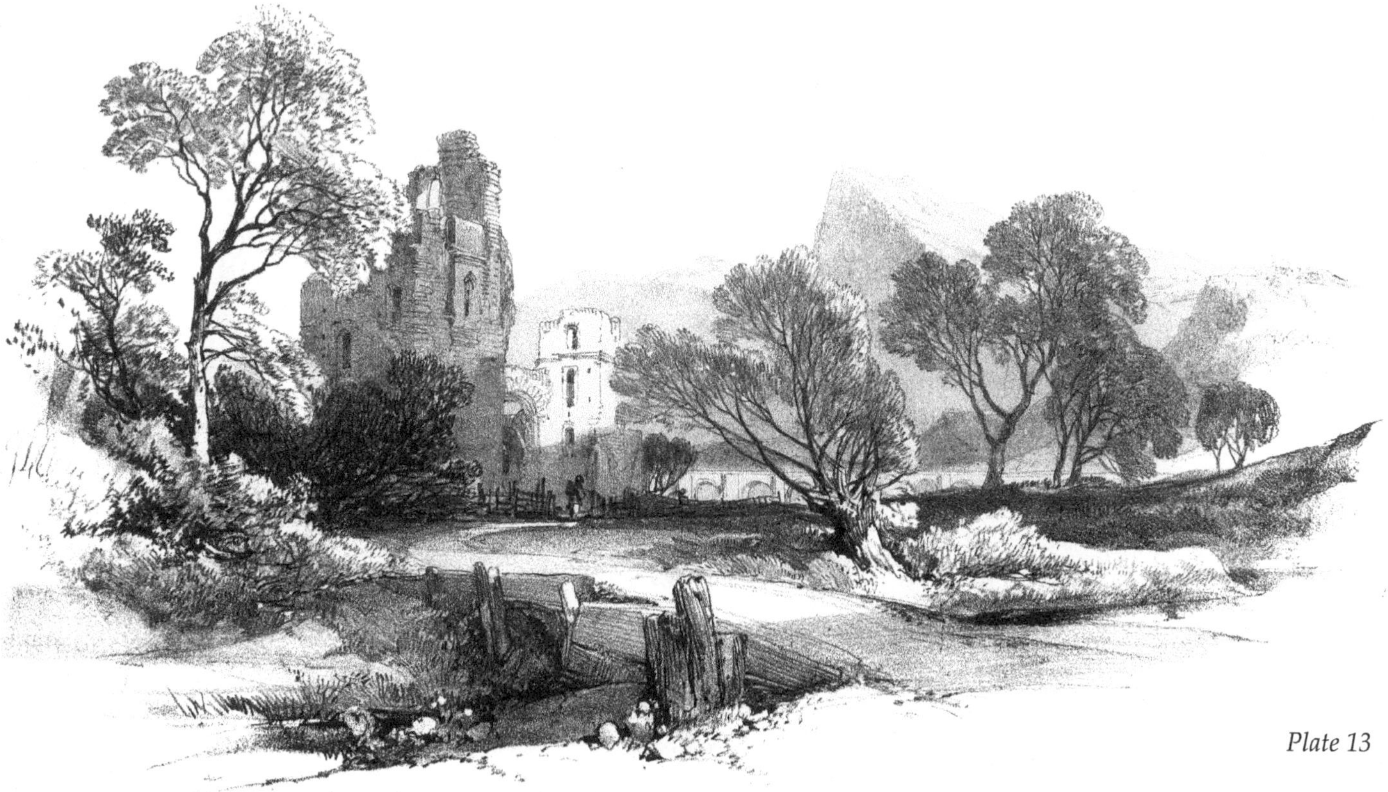

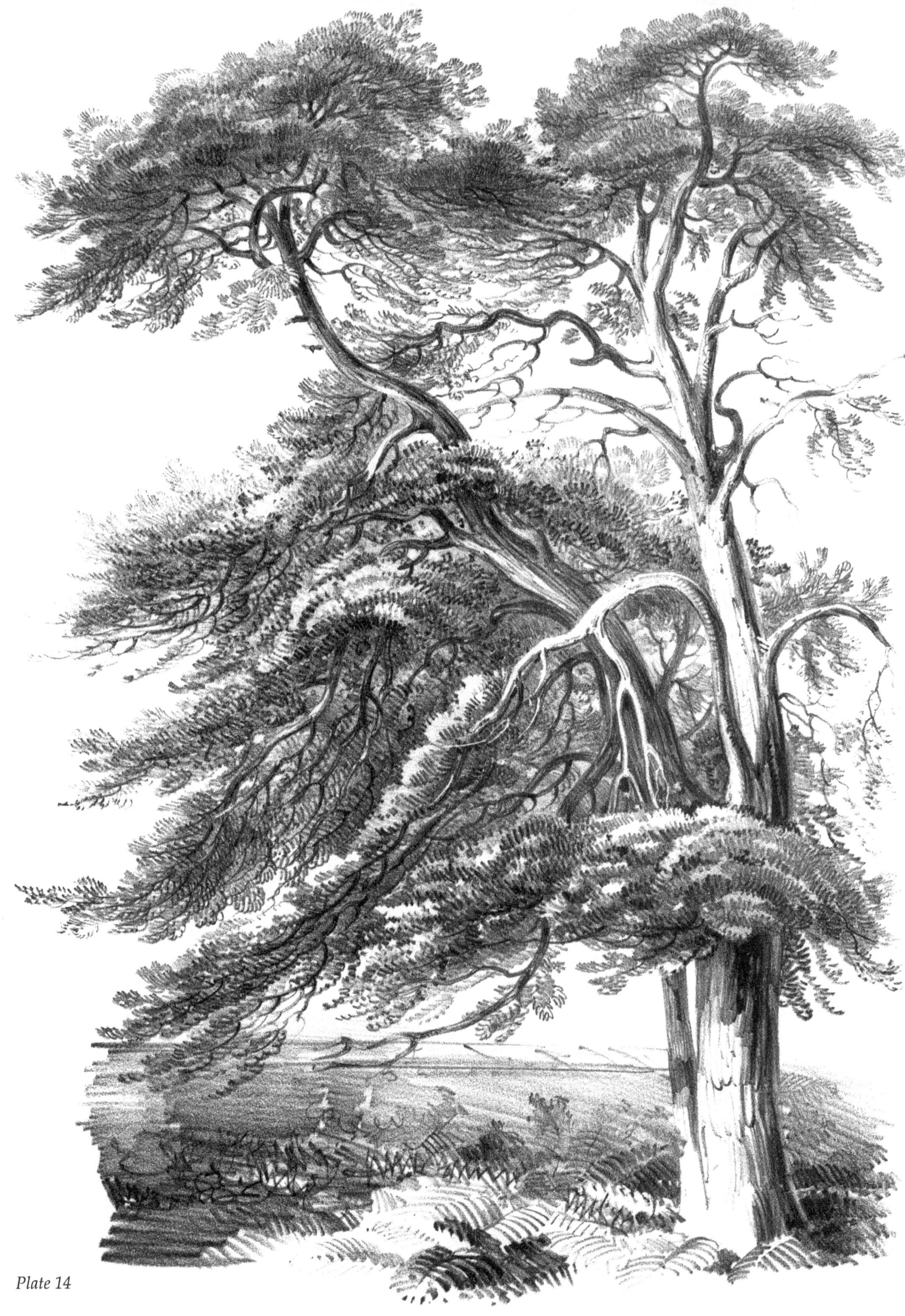

Plate 14

of colour existing between the brightest light and the deepest shade. The addition of this middle tone causes the light parts to appear more round. This should be done by lines, indicative of the *kind* of Foliage, placed near the Outline, and next to, and lighter than, the Shades, but by no means allowed to interfere with either. Examine the Examples in Plate 9.

As the forms of Trees are, apparently, changed much more by a different arrangement of the Stem and Branches, and an altered position of the light, than by alterations in the forms of the Foliage, the eye consequently does not so easily detect any change in the lattter as in the former. For proof of this, examine Plate 13, where, in each of the Examples, a separate form of Tree has been adopted, and in each this form has been preserved throughout; consequently, in the forms of the Foliage, all the Trees are so far exactly alike; yet, from their having Stems and Branches differing in shape, size, and quantity, they appear, as a whole or in groups, strikingly dissimilar. It is for this reason that, when drawing Trees, the Student should be especially careful, in the first place, to obtain a correct representation of the forms of the Stem and leading Branches, and then to add the masses of Foliage; drawing these last by light lines, and marking the *kind* of Tree, as distinguished by the shape and arrangement of the leaves. This may be well done in such Trees as the Oak, Ash, Elm, or Willow, because the forms of the folds partake so much of the form of the leaf,—being in the Oak irregular; in the Elm, of a broad oval; in the Ash, of a longer and narrower oval; and in the Willow still longer: sometimes for the forms of the folds it is only necessary to adopt the general form of the leaf, and thus to indicate, by the slightest means, the kind of Tree intended.

In attempting to draw Foliage for the first time, the adaptation of the shade and character to positive forms usually increases the difficulties so much felt by beginners, as seriously to impede their progress. The Student, moreover, is often induced to believe, that unless the precise form of the original be secured, he has no hope of ultimate success; and this leads to the same impression in regard to details, which he labours to copy minutely, a thing, of all others, I am most solicitous, for his own sake, he should cautiously avoid, if it be his wish to draw *Foliage* well. Such minuteness is not only unnecessary, but is positively detrimental. Should he be ambitious of attaining the excellence which he admires in the works of others, he must look beyond the acquisition of mere

dexterity in the mechanism of Art. He should devote his attention to matters
of a higher kind,—to the causes of the pleasurable feelings he has experienced;
and under the guidance of his model, endeavour to produce the like impressions for himself, and with the like force. Although, in the beginning, it may
be desirable to adopt the methods we have seen successfully employed by
others, yet, eventually, in a mind acting for itself, they become greatly modified, or entirely changed, and better adapted to the expression of its own views
and feelings.

The impracticability, as well as the uselessness, of copying the forms of
Foliage minutely, have been shown in page 41; but the same reasons do not
apply to the Stem and leading Branches,—features of so much importance.
Though their various shapes may be more accurately ascertained than the forms
of the Foliage, and drawn with more ease and precision, it is yet necessary to
attend carefully to their general properties. The Student will experience greater
difficulty than he at first might imagine, in depicting the intricate sinuosities of
the Branches; and will often find that, with all his labour, his Drawing is not
exactly true. If the first line he draws—which should in every object be that
to the left hand, or the upper one—vary from Nature or his model, the next—
the right hand, or lower one—must vary in the same degree, as the second
must be entirely dependant on the first; nor is this more the case with the
Stems and Branches of Trees than with *all other* forms. In the perfect correspondence of the second line with the first consists the truth of the drawing in
both; and to make either the Stems or the Branches true, the lines must be
fitted to each other, so as to preserve their gradual diminution; and this property, before spoken of, must be as strictly observed in the smallest as in the
largest (see Examples in Plates 10 and 12). A very usual method of drawing
Branches, but which is grossly incorrect, may be seen in Plate 14. Though in
speaking of this, or any other error into which the Student may fall, it may
seem hypercritical to complain of errors in individual features and lines, instead of
general defects, it must yet be remembered that his Drawing is composed of a
number of parts of various forms, and lines of various directions; and that though
the error of a single line may be minute, yet if that minute error be found in
every line of the same kind, its repetition becomes a general and an obvious
defect. It is certain, therefore, that to remedy the general fault, he must refer

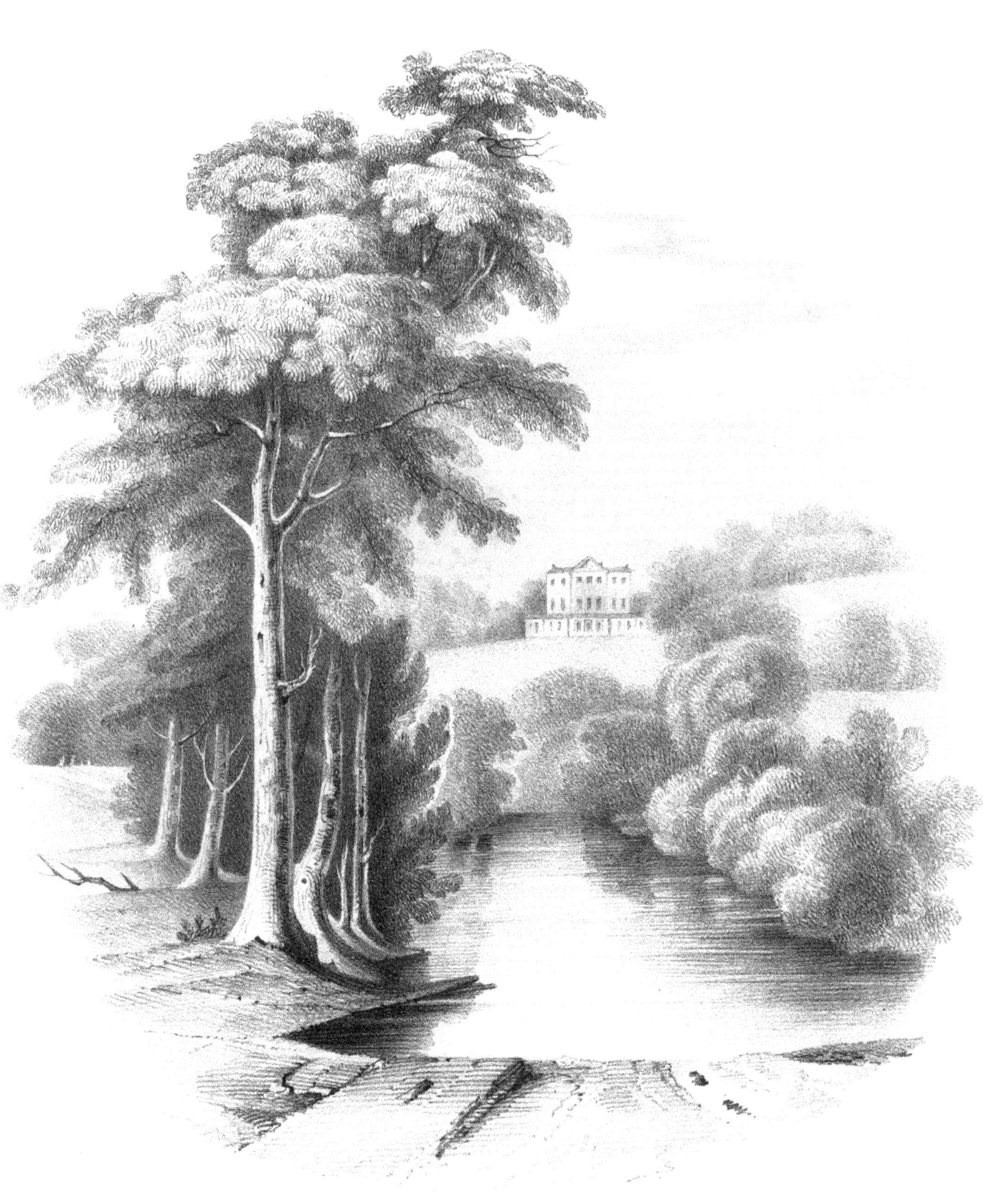

Plate 15

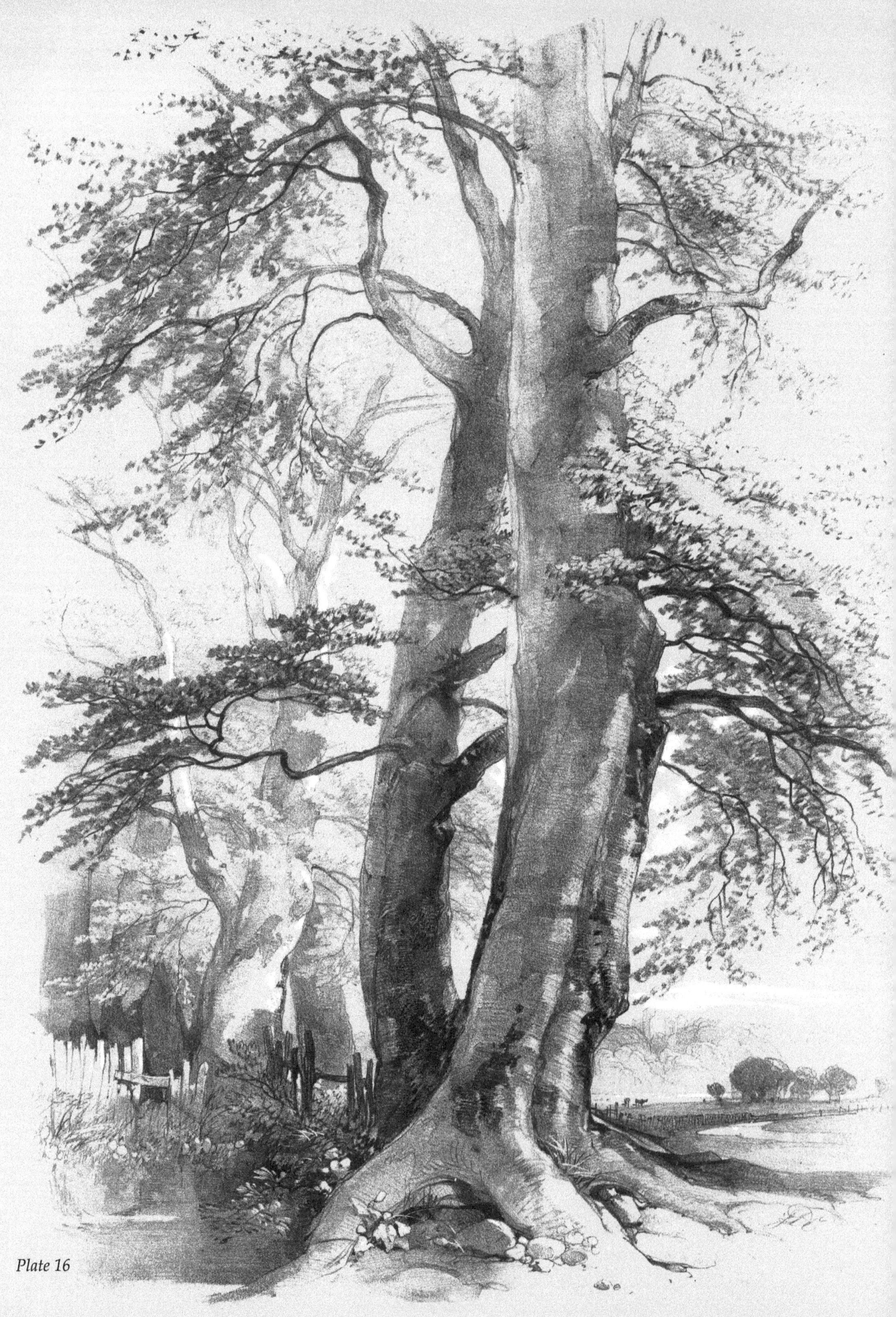

Plate 16

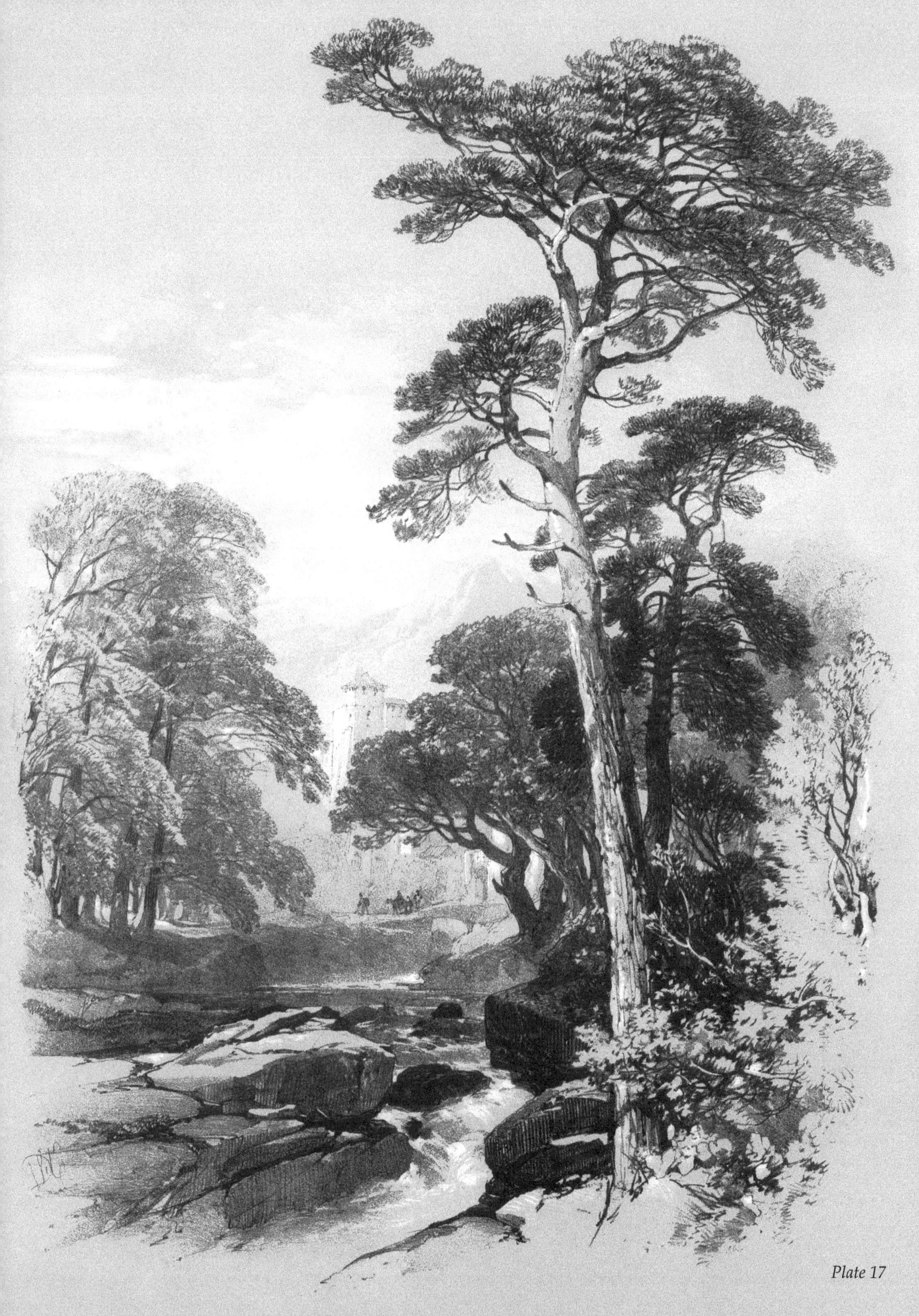

Plate 17

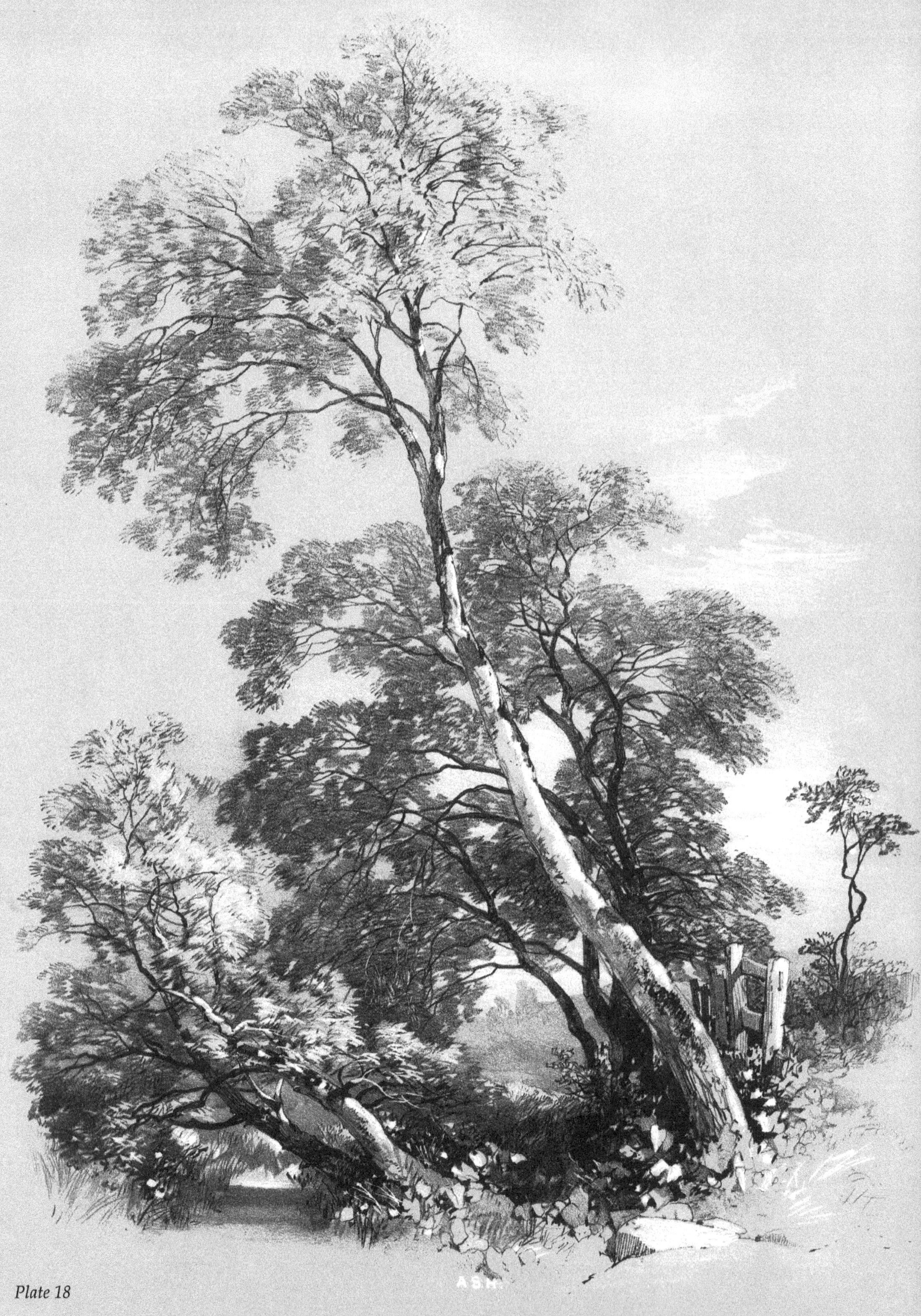

Plate 18

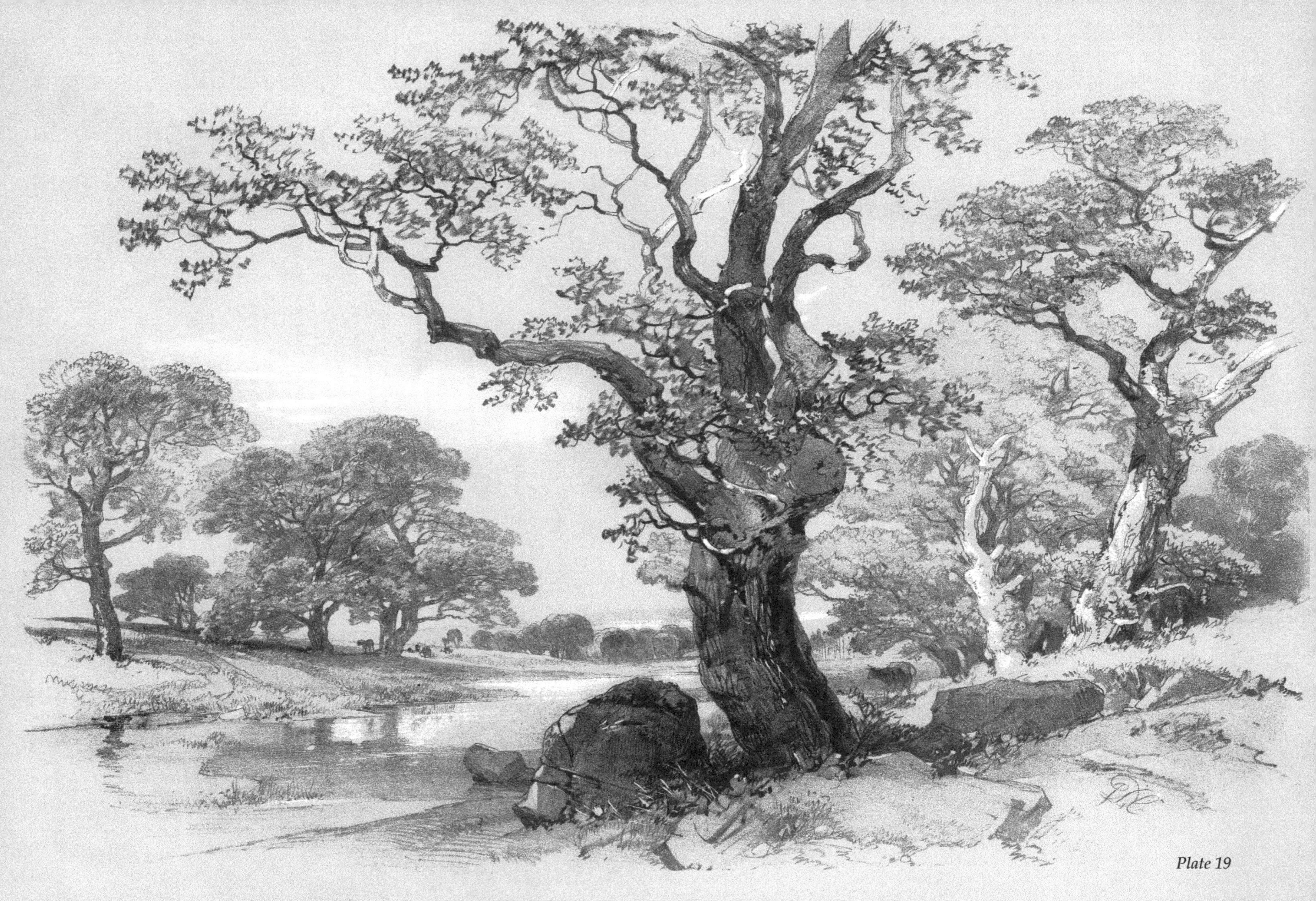

Plate 19

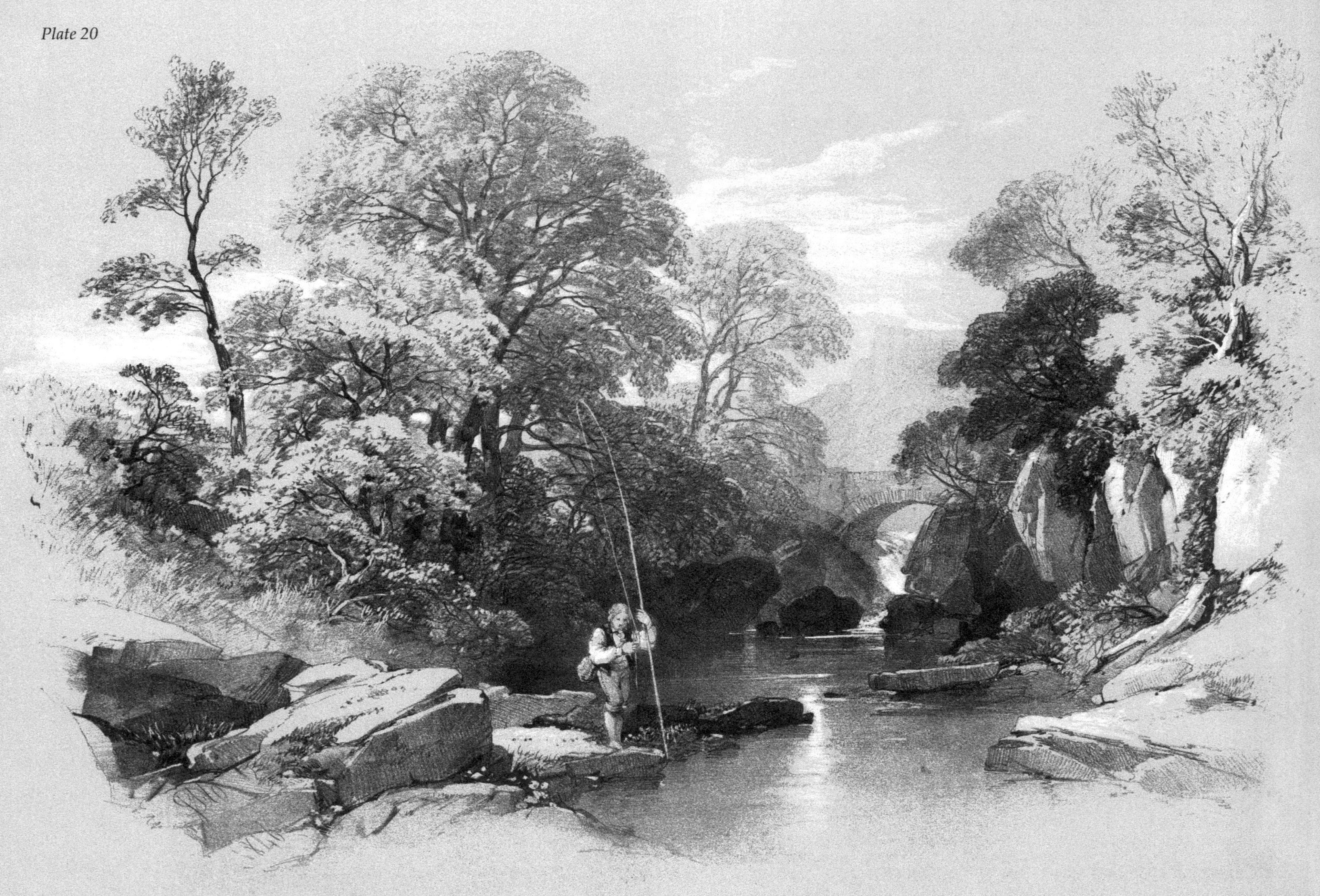

Plate 20

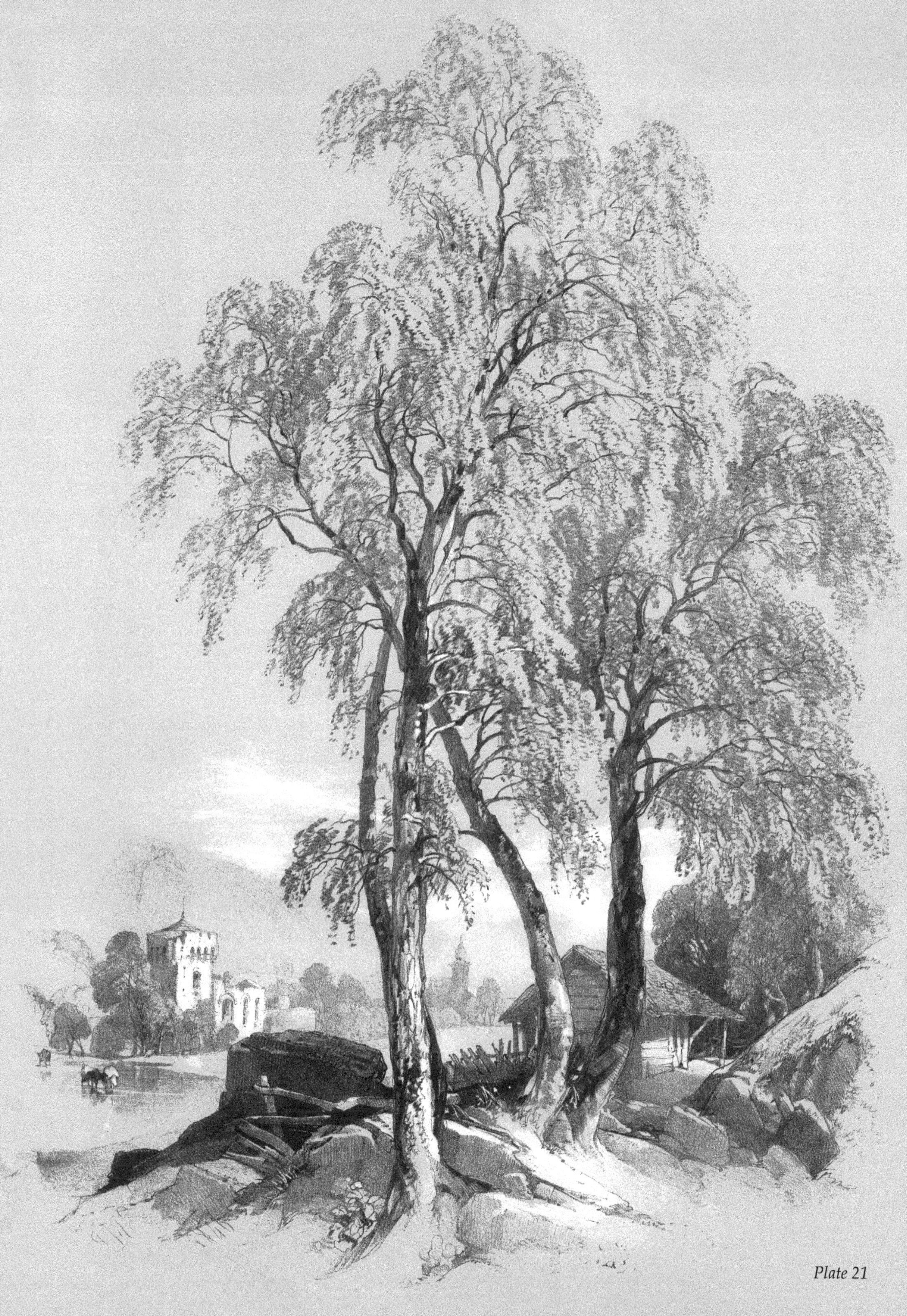

Plate 21

to the original minute cause of it, and correct the particular error in every line in which it occurs. On a further examination of Plate 14, the Student will discover a combination of errors and defects. Here thick Branches are attached to slender, and are less thick at their origin than elsewhere; instead of diminishing gradually in size, they are now slender, now thick; thicker Branches are seen growing at the top than towards the root of the Tree; Branches placed near the root, are represented as growing upward; the lower Branches, and most of the upper, by reason of the regularity of their bifurcation, and the sameness of their curves, look like pitchforks; their extremities, instead of being lost among the Foliage, are constantly to be seen; and so far from appearing to support the Foliage, they are but a collection of coarse, dark, or black lines, lying upon it. Were it possible to separate any one from the Foliage, and to view it by itself, it would be difficult to imagine it to be the Branch of a Tree. Compare the difference between the Examples in this Plate and Plates 10 and 12. Even the least instructed would not prefer the former to the latter.

In concluding this portion of the subject, it will be as well to point out to the Student the mode of study on which his improvement must, from the first to the last stage, in a great measure depend.

We will suppose him to have completed a Tree, or a part of one, and to be dissatisfied with its execution. Instead of condemning his Drawing, because, on the whole, he sees a manifest difference between it and that which he has tried to imitate, and preparing instantly to attempt a second, let him first patiently criticise what he has done. Let him begin his examination at his first step, the Shade, and ascertain if he have observed its qualities: if he have not, he must try to discover to what cause or causes its defects are to be attributed. Having discovered these, and corrected them, let him then examine the Outline, and proceed with every other part in succession, step by step. Such investigation will not only enable him to detect his failings from the beginning to the end, but will also excite his ingenuity to provide means for their correction, so as to make his Drawing more like the original, by exhibiting the same truths with corresponding power; and even though his efforts to remedy the errors of his copy be in-effectual, he will, from thus having ascertained his mistakes, be less likely to repeat them in a second effort. His feelings, aroused by investigation, will prompt him to renew his exertions; and from having discovered his failures and their causes, he will apply himself more confidently to the same task, not as a toil, but as a trial of skill.   He thus learns to think and to act for himself; his inquiry is no longer,—" How like is my copy to the original ?"   He now asks,—" Is it equally true to Nature ?"   He no longer servilely follows the steps of another —taking for granted that they are right—but, guided by his acquired knowledge, he finds his way to Nature by himself, and expresses his sense and estimation of her beauties without requiring to be prompted.

It is a good plan for the Student to preserve and date his various essays; as by referring to them he can ascertain the degree of his improvement.   Many, from neglecting this useful test, are discouraged more than they otherwise would or ought to be; for as their judgment has become matured, they are more alive to the faults which they still commit, while they forget the progress they have made, and the faults which they have learned to avoid.   Defects are more clearly seen, too, in proportion as the Student is more sensitive; and he is often so engrossed by them as not always to be aware when he is right.   His feelings thus become constantly excited; and, from his supposing that he is always in nearly the same track, and from his success not keeping pace with his desire to improve, he is apt to conclude that the progress he makes is but trifling.

When it is his object to make trial of his skill in drawing any particular Tree, he must first look for, and study, its leading peculiarities,—as displayed in its manner of growth, in the form of the Leaf, in the character of the Branches, and in the angle of their separation from the Stem and from each other, as well as in the colour and texture of the Bark.

Before the Student ventures on the study of a Tree of another kind, he should first be able to draw well that which he commenced with,—I have usually found it best to begin with the Ash,—that by comparing what he has been able to do with what he wishes to attempt, he may the more readily discover the most appropriate means.   We will suppose it to be his desire to draw the Beech, in Plate 16, a study from Buckhurst Park : he must first observe the form of the Leaf, as from this he must decide on the shape of the Outline; and then the form and arrangement of the Lines in the Shade.   In the Beech, the Leaf is rounder than in the Ash, consequently the form of the Outline must be rounder, something more like that employed for the Elm, in Plate 20; but the Lines, instead of exhibiting round general forms, like those of the Elm, must express long and undulating general forms, and must be much detached, to give freedom, and to represent the way in which the Leaves grow on the Branches. The Foliage of the Beech being more loose and flowing than that of the Elm, it requires that the Outline should be very sparingly introduced, and should by no means be rigid and connected. Much more, however, depends on the distribution of the Shade. The Shade should be done by Broad and Short Lines—though they can hardly be called lines; and the Sets of Lines, instead of being short, like those seen in Example 6, Plate 6, or Example 1, Plate 8, should be long, undulating, and continuous. These undulating forms may be easily detected in Plate 16, as I have there left them tolerably obvious, in order that the Student might be the better enabled to follow them, and to comprehend what I mean. These sets of lines should be made to correspond with the direction of the Branch, and to follow its various windings. Though for the most part they are horizontal, or nearly so, singly, it will be generally found that, collectively, they are passed in long flowing lines, sloping on each side of the Tree, so that the *lower ends* may be *farther* from the trunk than the *upper*, as has been explained in page 45; and this position will be found constant, especially towards the lower part of the Tree, and towards the extremities of the lower Branches.

As the Branches are separated from each other at longer intervals in the Beech than in most other Trees, and as the diminution in their thickness is still more gradual, and less perceptible, they produce those long sweeping lines so characteristic of this Tree; those which shoot nearest to the Root, like the Branches of most deciduous Trees in the like position on the Stem, incline towards the ground as they leave the Stem, though at their extremities they generally turn upwards. Both Branches and Stem are covered with a smooth, silvery Bark, which naturally suggests that the Lines on it should neither be too evident nor have the same inclination, as in the Stems of other Trees, but should be placed transversely, as seen in the Example on page 59, and as applied in the drawing of the human figure; and just sufficiently shown as to exhibit well the roundness. See Plates 10 and 16, where, in the darkest parts, the lines are placed so close together as to be undistinguishable: where they are required to be seen, the Student has already been instructed by what has been said in pages 60 and 61. He will also find that these lines are more and more curved as they are placed higher up on the Stem (according to the laws of

Perspective); this helps to give height, and likewise aids the expression of roundness.

Moss, of a dark and rich colour, is mostly found on the Branches, and, I believe, always at the Root of the Beech. This gives occasion for the dark patches of colour to be seen on them in the Example. These patches contribute to give vigour and richness: they must not, however, be left, as they often are, like so many ink stains.

I have now placed before the Student the peculiar features which this Tree possesses *in addition* to the leading properties common to all Trees. But before he attempts this, or any other subject new to him, his best plan is to do with it as he would do with a machine, the construction of which he might wish thoroughly to understand ;—that is, to take it to pieces, and learn how each part is made, that he may know how to put the whole together. Let him first try the Shade and the Outline separately, then the Stem and the Branches, each in their turn. In putting these together, one Branch, with its Foliage, is enough to begin with ; and when he can do this successfully, he can surely do all,—to depict the whole tree he has but to repeat, again and again, what he has once perfectly done in a single branch.

As the Student, when drawing all the various Trees in succession, will find that he has, of necessity, to repeat in every succeeding one much of what he has done in the one preceding, he should sedulously endeavour to first acquire the ability to draw *some one* really well. In consequence of this repetition, under certain modifications, he will find that, supposing it to have cost him fifty trials to do the first, as required, *really well*, he will be able to do the second equally well after thirty, the third after fifteen, the fourth after five, and so on until, at length, he is able to effect his purpose at the first attempt. I have made use of these comparative numbers for the sake of explaining more simply, by their proportion, the extraordinary acquisition of power which the Student may derive from his future tasks, in having executed one well.

The only new difficulty the Student has to contend with in delineating a number of Trees in the same Drawing, is so to proportion the separation of the Lines, or so to unite them, that each may accord with the relative size and distance of the others. This is chiefly done by making the Lines tolerably distinct, and plainly marking the character of the nearest Trees ; and, towards the distance, placing the lines gradually so near each other as entirely to lose them in a perfectly flat tone of colour, whatever may be its depth.—Examine particularly those Drawings where the foreground objects are immediately contrasted with those most distant.

In the observations which I have made on the Examples of the Beech Tree, I have avoided all mention of what has, in the former pages, been placed before the Student; because he will find, if he examine, that most Trees possess the same general features, with which, by this time, he ought to be thoroughly and intimately acquainted. I have only thought it worth while to mention that there are incidental varieties and individual peculiarities;—and these he will surely be able to detect by studying the Plates. Nor ought he to be disappointed that more than this is not done for him, however he might desire it, or believe it to be necessary, to save him trouble; for after all that has been presented to him, either here or elsewhere, he must expect to have much to do for himself; and he who waits to learn till all he requires to know be presented to his notice, will never learn at all. Something must ever be left to his own diligence and penetration, which the instructions contained in this Volume are meant to awaken and strengthen rather than to supersede. Indeed, the constant reference to the various Examples is intended to promote, as much as possible, a disposition in him to observe for himself, and to draw his own conclusions, so that he may fairly become his own master, and, by applying what he has learned from the guidance of others in the beginning, be enabled to guide himself to the end.

I have not here entered on what constitutes Beauty in Foliage, either as regards the form of the individual Tree, or the beauty arising from the arrangement and combination of Trees; on these subjects the Student will find ample information in pages 48, 49, and 80, of " The Principles and Practice of Art."

CHAPTER VII.

ON FOREGROUNDS.

IT is not my intention, in this part of my subject, to speak of the various objects which may be brought in to aid this very important portion of a Landscape. At present, I would only enter with the Student on the consideration of Grass and Herbage, the study of which seems properly to follow that of Foliage, as they partake so much of its nature, and are inseparable from the Foreground of Landscape.

In these, again, the Student must be reminded to imitate the general character, not the individual details; he must not, therefore, pretend accurately to depict the various Grasses which he finds, but must rather endeavour to convey an impression of the length or shortness of Grass generally, its scarcity or abundance. With these differences it is found everywhere; and its different effect, whether appearing on an even lawn, or on a rugged bank, arises from the difference of the ground on which it grows. For this reason, whilst drawing the Blades of Grass,—which must be represented by a number of strokes of every varied position,—he must so arrange them as to distinctly convey an idea of

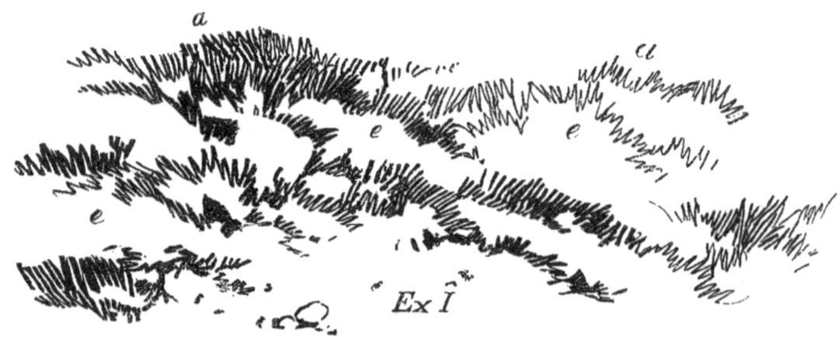

the degree of evenness or unevenness of the ground underneath, as in Example 1 here given. In this *preparation* it will be seen that most of the lines for the Grass are bluntly terminated at top and bottom, and almost unavoidably so, especially if they be dark; as it is barely possible to produce dark lines except thus contrary to Nature, where we see every blade of a taper form, as every line should be, as at *a* and *e*. Turning to Example 2, it will be found that each blunt line has been afterwards made taper; and that the results at each part, *a* and

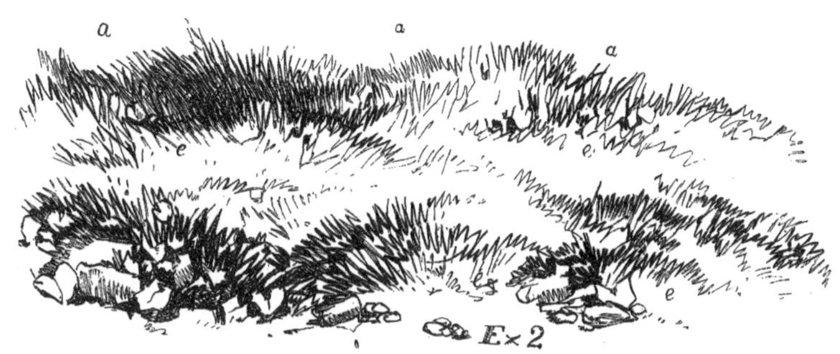

e, are different. At *a*, the lines give distance to the light beyond, the lines *themselves* having the form of the blades of Grass, and standing as their representatives; but

at *e*, where also they are terminated in a point, the blades of Grass are not there, represented by the *lines* themselves, but, on the contrary, by the *white paper* enclosed between the lines: the character of the Grass being thus given to the white paper below, the strokes then stand for the *Shade* between them; and now the white paper, in its turn, gives distance to these masses of Shade.

The Student will observe, that here the like effects take place as in Foliage; the character is seen and most distinctly marked in the same places, namely, on the extremities of the Shades, where they separate from the Light, and on the extremities of the Lights, where they separate from the Shades. The groups of lines require to be modified and blended with the paper at each end by lighter lines, made smaller, and more apart, as they recede from each group. The other separations between the masses of Shade should be of various sizes: the largest must have light lines, inclining in various directions, to break the monotony of the broad masses of Light, and also to make it the more completely understood that these masses are meant to give the idea of Grass, as much or even more than the lines themselves. The smaller portions of paper intervening between the groups of lines, may be employed for leaves of the Acanthus, or the Mallow, or of other kinds, of various sizes; this may be done by uniting the lines above and below these portions of paper, as may be seen in different parts of Example 2. Leaves, of all sizes, are also formed by taking away the serrated terminations of the masses of lines, so as to form a clear edge to each; and in the largest, the central fibre, which, in Nature, separates the leaf into equal portions, should be marked by a line more or less distinct. All this increases the attraction of the Lights, and contributes to the grand object of making the likeness most remarkable where the lines are fewest. Compare the preparation of every part of the Foreground in Plate 11, with the Foreground completed in Plate 12, to see how these things have been prepared, and afterwards completed. What is found here, however, is not enough; the Student ought to look attentively at every Drawing in which there is a Foreground represented and described, especially at Plate 21, that, by viewing the varieties each presents, he may be fully convinced that these principles are constantly followed out. From being previously acquainted with them, he will know how to trace their operation, and will be able readily to discover such a manner of employing the means or materials he uses, as will best insure success to his efforts.

The varieties of Herbage present a wide field for the Student's observation. The Burdock, the Acanthus, the Thistle, with many others, possess the most beautiful and varied forms, and serve, by their judicious association with other objects, to enhance the characteristics of the Landscape, and by their portraiture, to augment the general truth of the whole Picture. The effects produced by their introduction may be seen in several of the Examples given, particularly in Plate 21.

For an instance in proof of the trifling difference which may exist, and often unavoidably, in the manipulation of the materials of Art on totally dissimilar objects, the Student—bearing in mind what has been said to him on the subject of Grass—where its character is marked—the form of the ground underneath, &c.,— has only to turn to Plate 4, where he will see that there is a great similarity in the individual form of the lines themselves, whether for Grass or for the hairy covering of animals: perceiving this, he cannot fail to be convinced of the impossibility of rightly applying them in such instances to the surfaces of bodies, except with reference to, and with a perfect knowledge of, the forms underneath; and that but for this knowledge, the small individual variety of the lines could never be made to convey such varied and distinct ideas.

The delineation of every blade of Grass by an equal number of strokes is no more required than to represent in Foliage each individual leaf; for who could ascertain the number there may be in either case? All, however, can judge of the abundance or scarcity of Grass, whether it looks flexible, and as if it would give way to the pressure of the foot or not. See Plate 14; in the Foreground of which are exhibited some such mistakes as must inevitably be made by those who attempt to be *bold* and *dashing* at the expense of truth—who display their *swiftness* by their rapidity in doing wrong, and their *freedom* by the liberties which they take with Nature. In this Drawing, much of what is meant for Grass looks like the teeth of a saw, or anything which the spectator's imagination can suggest, equally remote from the real object; and it is difficult to say what the other random lines intended for Fern look like,—certainly not like Nature. It is surely sufficient encouragement to study Nature, if only to avoid the certainty of committing such gross mistakes. Can it be matter of congratulation to deal thus roughly with her, and thus to confound all her beauties in one unintelligible mass of lines, which the hand, without guidance from the mind, has liberally distributed in every direction but the right, when the truest imitations of her may be effected, even more speedily and more freely?* I cannot possibly comment on all errors; but for the sake of those who would study Art, I point to such as are most common, and even popular; so that by contrasting the different results of truth and error, I may be able to make the greater impression.

While some are waiting the inspirations of genius, and others are giving the reins to impulse, erroneously believing that their dashing, or their laboured counterfeits, look like the productions of real talent, the more rational Student, whether Artist or Amateur, will be continually gathering his materials from all the sources presented to him; and, by diligent mental labour, correcting and refining his practice, knowing that the productions of a cultivated imagination will be so imbued with the true spirit of Nature as sensibly and effectually to address themselves to the taste and feelings of all.

Having so minutely detailed the operations of the Pencil, and having led the Student to such a careful investigation of Nature, I may have risked objections from those who argue for general breadth, and the effect of a whole, rather than such particular attention to individual objects. I acknowledge the attention of the spectator may be best arrested by a union of the parts into one general and effective combination, rather than by the individual portions of a Picture. Yet how is that powerful whole to be produced, when ignorance is displayed in

---

* In Plate 15, Nature is equally disregarded, even by the more pains-taking; though of the two, these errors, if not less objectionable, are perhaps less mischievous, in their results.

each of the parts composing it, be it what it may,—a Picture, a Building, or a Machine ?   Now, as nothing can come of nothing, and as a knowledge of the whole must be made up of a knowledge of the parts, the whole, to be good, necessarily involves the goodness of the parts.   He who best knows all the properties belonging to each part is most likely to know what are essential to his purpose, and can either bring all to his aid, or reject such as he does not require.

Surely it is too soon to urge the Student, young in Art, to aim at *general* effect,—to grapple at once with the combined difficulties of a more advanced stage of Art,—Composition, Light and Shade, and Colour, with all their properties.   To expect all this from one who, as yet, does not clearly understand the properties of a single object, is to look for fruit ere the blossom be expanded. Does the Musician press his Pupil, who scarcely knows the names of the notes, to consider and attempt the general effect of concerted pieces ?   The art of Painting cannot be seized by a *coup de main* any more than that of Music. The knowledge of either is no inherent gift.   To advance with certainty in any study we must proceed with caution, and step by step.

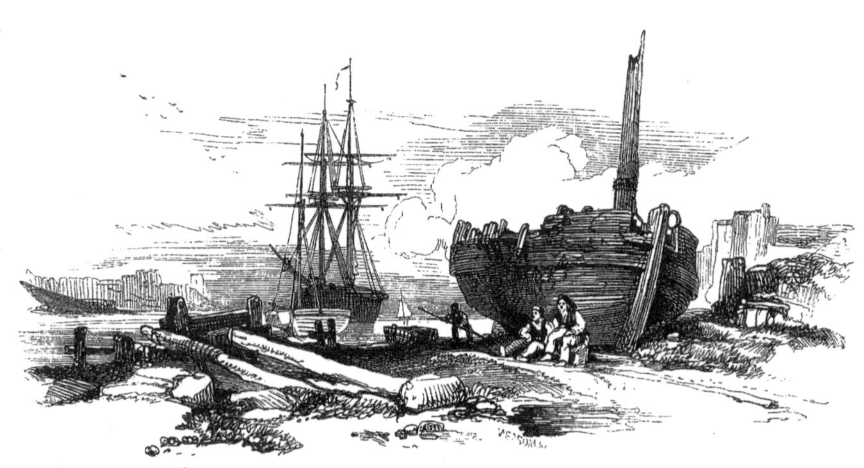

CHAPTER VIII.

BEFORE entering on this department of Pictorial study, I take it for granted that the Student can produce a correct Outline, be the object of his pursuit what it may. If unable to do this, Light and Shade will not assist him in rectifying any of his errors, but will rather tend to expose them. Nor can he properly understand or apply Light and Shade without a knowledge of Form. He has already been told that Light and Shade do not effect any change in the Form of an object, and that they constitute a distinct and separate study. Light and Shade, as here treated of, will be confined to the individual objects. For their application to an entire Picture, whether embracing few or many objects, the Student should consult Chapter VI. of " The Principles and Practice of Art," where it is explained at large.

Light and Shade, in the practice of Art, should be considered as the means of representing a surface in such a manner as to convey to the mind a correct idea of the character of a solid body—whether convex or concave, prominent or indented. In a Drawing, the Outline is to the *contour* of a real figure, or body, just what the Light and Shade are to its *surface:* the one leaves an object superficial, the other makes it appear solid. It is, therefore, necessary to be acquainted with Form, before attempting Light and Shade; for though the latter produce the greatest illusion, by imparting to all objects their peculiar character as solids, thus powerfully counteracting the influence of the flat surface on which they are drawn; yet all this power would be rendered nugatory by an incorrect Outline, whilst that incorrectness would become more strikingly obvious by the application of Light and Shade.

In the use of the Chalk or Pencil, it is to be observed, that no absolute and positive likeness to Nature is produced by the lines themselves, abstractly considered. It is, therefore, a matter of the first importance, in any attempt at Shade with these instruments, to study the proper application of lines, when their repetition, in order to obtain Shade, thus becomes unavoidably necessary. To obviate the anomalies consequent on the employment of the Chalk, or Pencil, for this purpose, these observations are called for; the more so, as the *number* of the lines, as well as their intensity, is increased in order to obtain the Shades, and on these all the labour is bestowed; whilst on the Lights *few* lines are either used or required. Now, by separating in the mind the consideration of a Shade partially, or entirely obscuring an object, from the character of the object as seen through the Shade, according to its intensity, we shall have the idea of a perfectly *equal* and *unbroken* tone of colour,—such as may be seen in open doorways, or on perfectly flat walls. From this it might be concluded, that in the Shades there should be no positive evidence of the direction of the lines, in order that the perfect evenness of the Shades, which is their distinguishing quality, should be preserved. As the character of a surface in Shade, however, is generally more or less seen through it, the lines employed to express Shade should, where the character of the surface is perceptible, be so adapted as at the same time to indicate that character; when portions of the surface have any particular direction, the lines should have the same, and yet should be so close together, and so equal in depth of colour, as to convey distinctly the idea of Shade. These observations may be seen carried into practice, in the Trunks of the Trees of Plate 12; they may also be understood as applicable to the tiled Roofs of Buildings, where the tiles, not being entirely obscured by the Shade, require the strokes on the Shade to follow in their direction, so that the Shade and the character of the surface, partially obscured, may at the same time be represented. This application of the suggestions of Nature prevents the Shades from being poor and unmeaning, as they would be if they were made perfectly smooth, and forms a corrective of the opposite extreme also, of making lines in the Shades too obvious, by which all appearance of their retiring is destroyed. See again, Examples 1 and 2, Plate 8, and Plate 11, where the Shades only are done, so that the influence of the character given in the light parts of these subjects, as completed in Plates 9 and 12, may be the more apparent, and thus more forcibly prove how much is obtained by giving the interest to the illuminated parts of objects, and there with all possible power.

When looking at objects in Nature with which we are well acquainted, we are so perfectly conscious of their forms, and of their surfaces, that the eye no longer voluntarily follows the contour; indeed, it is impossible to see the precise limits of any object, unless it be superficial, and very violently contrasted. The most familiar objects will prove the truth of these remarks. Let the Student regard any object or objects around him, at the moment he is reading this, and he will find that their forms are so variously contrasted,—sometimes having their Outline strongly relieved by the darker or lighter colour of others behind, sometimes mingling with another of like intensity of colour, or so involved in Shade of unequal intensity, or so extremely unequal in their own local colour,— as to render it absolutely impossible to follow the precise form of any one. The Student on examining each of the Shaded Examples given in this Work, will find that this important fact has been constantly observed in all.

In Plate 10, the light Beech Stems are, in one place, separated by some very dark ones beyond them; in another, they relieve, by opposing their own dark colour to what is light and distant. Through the whole course of their Outline, either on the illumined or shaded side, they are alternately contrasted by light or dark, plainly or indistinctly seen, so that we are affected less by the impression of their different shapes, than we are by their apparent roundness and solidity, and with the space which intervenes between them in every part, from the nearest to the most distant object. These oppositions, and consequent separations of one object from another, take place in every varied degree, whether with the stubborn and opake Stems and Branches, or with the flexible and transparent Foliage,— with large or with small objects, with the whole as with the parts. It should never be possible, in Art, to trace the Outline of objects equally in every part whenever Light and Shade is added, otherwise they will not appear to be solid and round, nor will the attention be arrested, as in Nature, by their surfaces.

The Student will find the same peculiarities, if he examine the Outline of the various Trees in Plate 20, where they separate from the Sky behind them, or from each other, and where the confines of the Stream are lost among the Rocks; indeed, if he direct his attention to the Stream, the Rocks, the Trees, or the Figure, or to any part of this or the other completed Drawings, he will find it difficult, if not impossible, to precisely follow the course of the Outline of any object, whenever Shade or Shadow has been added to explain the surface.

Sometimes it is necessary to produce, in the first instance, a perfectly flat tone of colour, where the Shade passes over a smooth object, or one comparatively so,—as across the Water, in Plate 21 ; and this is absolutely demanded, when it is required to detach from Shade any object of a darker colour, such as the dark Cow, and at the same time to give character to it. For if the Shade across the Water were composed of lines distinctly separated from each other, no matter what their direction, those intended to characterise the Animal would scarcely be distinguished,—all would be one mass of confusion.

Roundness and solidity are, or ought to be, the consequence of Light and Shade, as certainly as Form is the result of the Outline ; but as Light and Shade are more powerful in their influence on the mind in creating illusion,—withdrawing the attention from the flat surface on which the Picture is painted,—the moment Light and Shade are introduced, the Outline should cease to exist as an Outline ; it is no longer required. That which Nature takes so much pains to conceal, namely, a distinct Outline, the young Student is mostly to be found exerting himself to display ; but now that he knows this truth among others, he will see that it is much more profitable to spend his time in following up, with sedulous attention, the study of those principles, the importance of which I have endeavoured to impress on him.

In Light and Shade, distinction must be made between *natural* Shade, and *accidental* Shadow. Natural Shade is that which is inseparably connected with every object receiving the light. Accidental Shadow is that which one object casts on another, by interposing between it and the light ; and this accidental Shadow may be removed by removing the object which produces it.*

An accidental Shadow is darker or lighter than the shaded side of the object casting the Shadow, accordingly as the object on which it falls, is, in its local colour, darker or lighter than the object casting the Shadow. For instance, if the Shadow of a white building be thrown on another white building, the Shadow thrown will be darker than the shaded side of the building throwing it ; but if the building which throws the Shadow be of brick, or any material darker in colour, then its shaded side will be darker than its Shadow, on the white building which receives it. In these cast Shadows there are two other circumstances very important to notice,—first, the form and intensity of the Shadow thrown ; and

* See " Principles and Practice of Art," pages 95, 96, and 97.

secondly, the form of the object or surface over which it passes; becàuse on the edge of this accidental, or cast Shadow, the Student must mainly depend for the indication of the nature of the surface which receives it.

For a further illustration of this, see the Example below: where the Shadow of the Stick, across the moulding of the base of a Column, shows distinctly which parts of it are concave, which convex, and which upright, and to a

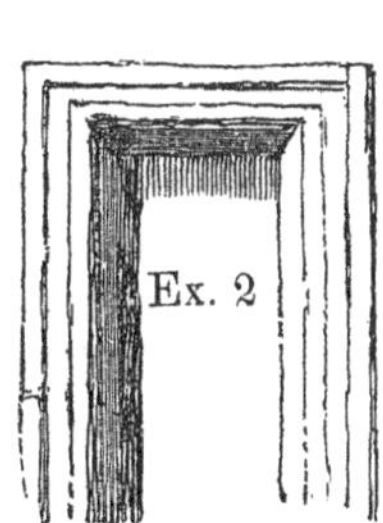
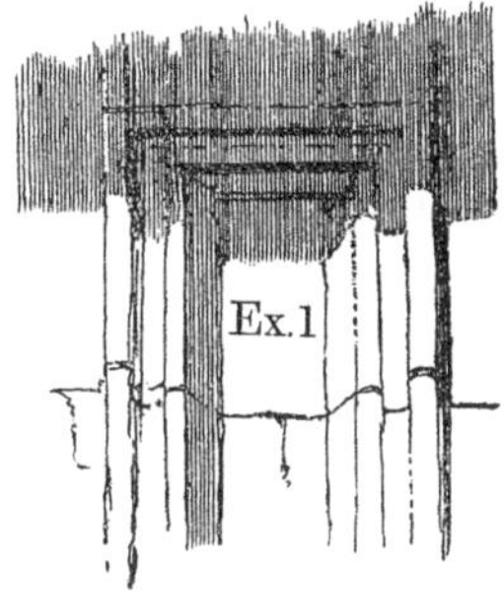

degree which we look for in vain from its natural Light and Shadow. So with Example 1, in the annexed cut; where, from the edge of the cast Shadow, it is evident how far the Wall, in the blank Window, recedes from the general surface, and how much above this the Architrave around it projects: whereas, in Example 2, it is difficult to believe that any part of the Architrave comes forward; although the recess may be as well understood in this as in the other example. The Student must attend to *this* as a point of the greatest consequence; as the forms given to the Outline of these accidental Shadows, help him more than the Light and Shade necessarily belonging to an object,

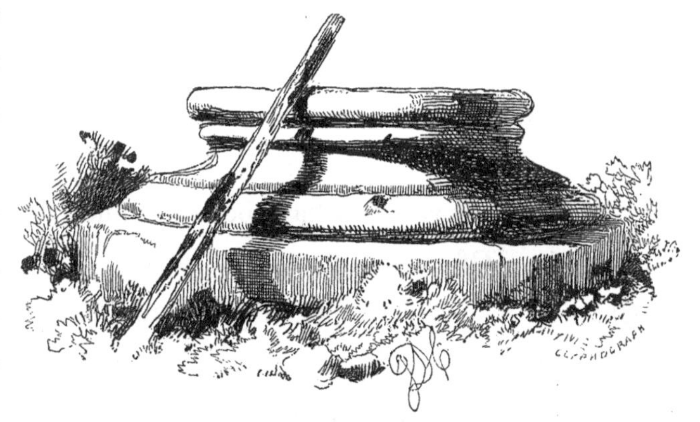

to explain clearly the precise undulations of all surfaces, and to give them the appearance of solidity. More instances, occurring in other Examples, might be enumerated; but these I leave the Student to discover for himself.

Though the shaded parts of objects, in any degree round, do not separate from their light parts abruptly, but gradually, and the rays of light glide over the surface, yet the Shadows which such objects cast,—whatever be the surface on which they fall,—are just as well defined on the edge, as those from any angular object, the light and dark parts of which separate abruptly. See the Shadows of the Trunks of the Trees on the ground in Plate 21, and in Plate 10; and the Shadow of the Pollard Willow across the white Cow; the Shadow of the ear across her face, and of her leg across the dewlap; which are just as sharp and well defined as are the Shadows of the Leaves in the foreground on each other. Shadows, whether they be cast by round or cylindrical objects, such as a globe, or the stem of a tree, have their edges just as well defined and clear as the Shadow which falls from the blade of a knife.*

All lines for the Shades and Shadows should be firmly drawn, as shown in all the Examples, and of equal colour, whatever be their direction, so that the colour of the Shade or Shadow may be even; but on Flesh, they require to be lighter, either at one end or at both ends, and curved, whether the surface be concave or convex, as in the upper Hand in Plate 1.

Lines put on for Shade, or Shadow, if too light, must not be gone over in the same direction, to increase the colour. It is difficult and tedious to follow exactly those first made; and in making one set of lines over the other, with the speed of the first, some of the first lines are increased in their intensity, two-fold, by the second, or the spaces between them are filled up, and thus the *evenness* of the Shade is destroyed. Should the lines for the Shadows be too evident, or come forward instead of retiring, or mark the character too much, the Pupil has been already instructed how to remedy this, in page 46.

Hitherto my remarks have been confined to the Light and Shade of objects individually. Of their influence on objects collectively, I have treated at length, in Chapter VI. of the " Principles and Practice of Art," as a separate study; for, though Effect be produced by Light and Shade, there may, nevertheless, be Light and Shade, without producing Effect. The latter is not the invariable consequence of the former.

Most Amateurs, in their too great eagerness to use the Brush, are apt to overlook the importance of first acquiring a knowledge of the elementary principles of Art: allured by the fascinations of colour, they fail to perceive the utility of the Chalk or Pencil. In their inconsiderate desire to attain the end, they neglect the means; and abandon as an impediment that which in reality would facilitate their progress, and is indispensable to their final success. Taking up the Brush before they are prepared to use it, they meet with obstacles which they cannot surmount, and being dissatisfied with their abortive attempts at

---

* See " Principles and Practice of Art," from pages 97 to 100.

colour, and disinclined to resume a course of elementary study, they relinquish the pursuit of Art, and moralise on their former infatuation.

Most beginners in Art look on the Study of Form as dry and unprofitable, and pursue it with more haste than good speed. Buoyed up by false hopes, flying from the troubles "they know, to others they know not of," they hurry to the study of Light and Shade, to gain what is termed a "bold Effect,"—in other words, a violent contrast of black and white, to hide or excuse their bad drawing. This specious "Effect" may, indeed, impose on the entirely unlearned in matters of Art; but those whose minds are enlightened, in however small a degree, see through the specious veil, and find every original defect of drawing rendered more intolerable by the very means employed to conceal it. Here again, as with Form, there are difficulties equally tedious and difficult to overcome, augmenting those which they thought to evade; and, in the same ratio as these increase, the courage to face them diminishes. But one more step remains,—Colour. They heedlessly rush to this as their last resource, with the same vain expectations that led them from Form to Light and Shade;—new difficulties present themselves in addition to the former, and no new power, and still less inclination, has been acquired to contend with them. What wonder, then, that total failure should be the result of this

" Chase of idle hopes and fears ! "—Byron.

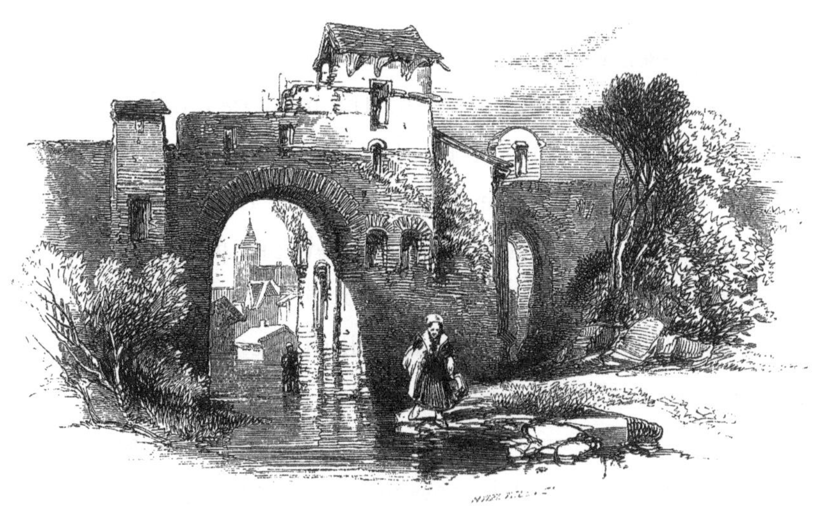

CHAPTER IX.

ON THE USE OF THE BRUSH.

IN entering on this subject, I shall first point out, as I promised, the relation between the use of the Brush and the Chalk or Pencil, and show in what manner the practice of the latter leads to the efficient use of the former. To do this properly and distinctly, it will be best to explain in what they differ, and in what respects the one has an advantage over the other.

As the use of the Chalk or Pencil involves the Artist inevitably in the production of lines which, as such, are more or less at variance with Nature, he is compelled to exert his ingenuity to conceal their defects as much as possible. The Brush does *not* naturally produce lines, and, consequently, its effects are, in that particular, so much more like Nature; the advantages derivable from its use are, perfectly flat tones of colour, and the imitation of local colour of every degree of depth. The sense in which I here use the term " local colour," is not to be understood as expressive of the difference of the colours of objects, but of the comparative depth of each. In this sense local colour may be represented by a single colour, sepia, for instance, which is one of the best pigments for this purpose, and the most generally used.

From the Chalk or Pencil is to be obtained every degree of depth of colour the instant it is wanted, from the lightest to the darkest, by the difference of pressure; and its operations may be suspended for any length of time that the Student may require either to collect his thoughts for what he is about to do, or to examine what he has already done; and all can be readily removed if wrong,— its chief advantage to beginners.

On the contrary, the operations of the Brush, in Water-Colours, require speed, especially in Foliage, and in passing over large spaces, inasmuch as the colour dries rapidly. Here, then, if the Student have not all his thoughts at command, and be not prompt in execution, from previous practice with the Chalk or Pencil, he can do nothing,—*absolutely nothing*. The tremor occasioned by knowing that what he is doing must be done quickly, and, if wrong, cannot be very easily erased, is of itself a great impediment to free execution; and, if to this be added ignorance of what is to be done, failure is certain. He is often obliged to apply to his Pallet, either to increase the strength of colour, or, by adding more water, to diminish it; and to heighten his embarrassment, his colour is drying because he is not sufficiently dextrous,—for if he have not the necessary knowledge, dextrous he cannot be. When previously accomplished, however, in the use of the Chalk or Pencil, he has but little to learn in the use of the Brush, as he will find. Let him review what he has already learned, and he will see that the principles of Art and Nature have not changed because he has changed his instrument or materials. Foliage still grows the same, whether imitated with the Brush or the Pencil. Objects retain their Forms, and are subject to the same laws of Light and Shade, and have the same character; but as he has already learned how to depict their visible qualities with the Chalk or Pencil, his only additional study is local colour. The mechanical difficulties of the Brush are speedily overcome; so very speedily, that I have invariably found persons who were capable of using the Chalk or Pencil well, use the Brush with equal facility and power, after a very few trials. From the consequent decision of the operations, that which has been thus done wears so much the stamp of truth, vigour, and courage, imparted by acquired knowledge, as to have the appearance of being done by an Artist rather than by an Amateur.

The Chalk or Pencil does not imitate local colour well without much labour; and such imitation, unless it can be done with judgment, should never be attempted. This defect of the Chalk or Pencil is, in a great degree, overcome by the employment of a tinted paper, as in the Plates 2, 3, 10, 16, 17, 18, 19, 20, 21, and 22. In these, dark objects, such as the Trees which cross the Sky, have their local colour suggested by the colour of the paper; and light in the Sky, or any brilliant lights, such as those in the Water of Plate 17, 18, and 21, or any white objects, such as the Cow in Plate 22,[*] have their brightness represented either by white opake colour, or by white Chalk. A more effective imitation of Nature is thus obtained; bright objects look more luminous, dark ones more rich, and solid objects appear firmer. An impression of permeable space is produced; the Trees

---

* See frontispiece

seem decidedly round, and the interstices of the Foliage pervious; the Sky appears distant; and an idea is excited of the whole subject being pervaded by atmosphere. All the Drawings on white paper, when compared with those on tinted paper, appear cold, harsh, meagre, and less satisfactory in many important respects. If the Student turn to Plate 13, he will see that, in the upper subject, the *light* parts of all objects are left *white ;* and if the Stems of the Trees appear darker than the Foliage, it is on account of the greater number and depth of the lines placed on them: but however the Rocks, Roads, Buildings, and Foliage may differ in their local colour, that difference here finds little or no expression— in all, the *bright lights are white.* The reason why this local colour cannot well be given with the Chalk or Pencil, and should therefore seldom be attempted, is, that it is necessary to cover the object in such a way, that such lines as come afterwards to mark the character may not be interfered with. The lower subject of Plate 13 will exemplify this. The largest portion of the Castle has a tone of colour over it, to indicate that the materials of which it is composed are of a darker colour than those composing the other portion of the Building; and this local colour is represented without any lines being apparent, so that such as are placed on it, to give the character of the materials of the Building, may be plain enough to be perfectly understood. There is also some attempt to imitate the darker local colour of the Trees, on the right of this picture; these attempts, however, are of necessity very limited, for here again the sun-lit parts of the Mountains, the Grass, the Road, and of some of the Trees, are all white. Local colour, however, is more beautifully and more effectively imitated with the Brush; and in this chiefly consists the difference between its use and that of the Chalk or Pencil. When using the latter, the Student has been directed to begin with the Shadows, because it is much more easy to adapt the Outline to the Shade than the Shade to the Outline, as no attempt is made to imitate local colour, and as the lines for the Shade can often be so arranged as to render an Outline unnecessary. In using the Brush, however, the operations may be re-versed; the general body of the colour, that is, the local colour, may be laid on first, and with this is given the same form and character of the Foliage that is given by the Outline from the Chalk or Pencil. See Example 1, Plate 23.

In Trees, there are of course a multitude of Forms to be expressed, and all must be accurate in character; but when a considerable surface is to be

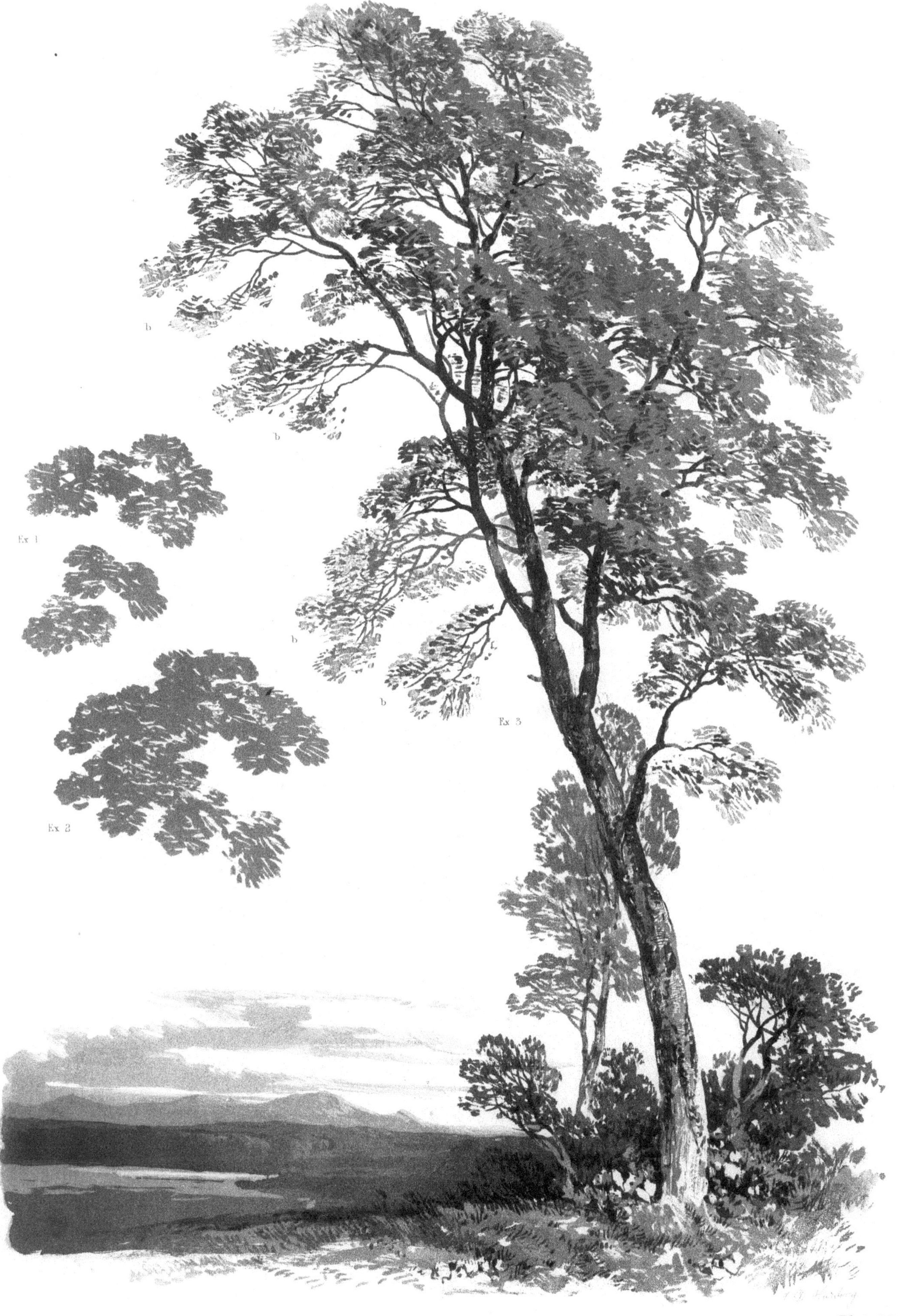

b
b
b
Ex 1
Ex 2
b
Ex 3
b

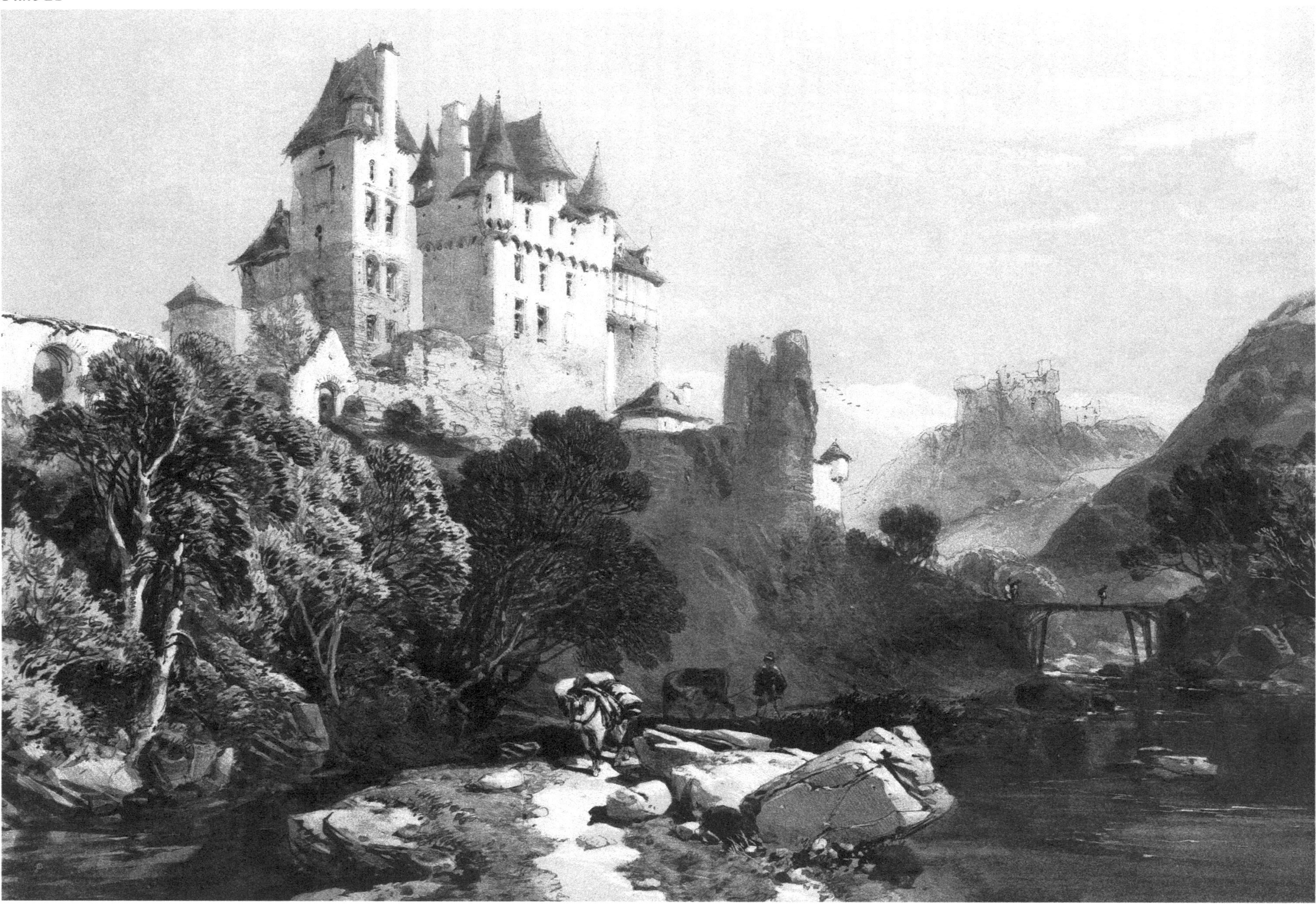

covered, the colour is drying during the operation, and is apt to dry too fast. To avoid, as much as possible, this inconvenience, and to accomplish all that is wanted, each Form (as Example 1, Plate 23) should be done separately; and the Brush should be kept moderately full, beginning at the top and towards the left-hand side of the Tree, and observing the same motion of the hand as when using the Lead Pencil. Whenever it may be desirable to attach to the first Form so made, a second of the like kind, it is easy to do this, because the colour will remain wet; to the second, a third may be added in like manner, and so on, till sufficient be done. See Example 2, which in its results, corresponds with Example 2, Plate 7; that is, the Form and Character thus given to the Tree by the Colour, are the same as are given by the Chalk or Pencil, in the Outline. By the former mode, however, instead of there being a quantity of white paper enclosed by the Outline, the whole, except the required interstices, is covered with colour, representing the local colour of the object; and herein lies the especial difference between the productions of the Brush, and those of the Chalk or Pencil.

When so much as is shown in Example 2 can be readily done with the Brush, no difficulty will be found in completing a whole Tree. In attaching the several masses to each other, the interstices, small and large, which, in all Trees, are seen between them, more or less numerous, are to be kept light, as may be required.

The form of the Tree and the Character of the Foliage being thus completed, it remains but to add the Shadow, the Stem, and the Branches,—following strictly the same order and the same principles that are to be observed in using the Chalk or Pencil. The Student has, therefore, no new difficulty of importance to contend with, except, perhaps, in preventing the second colour, for the Shade, assuming, on the Shaded side, distinct forms, which may be confounded with those produced by the first, which represents the local colour (see Example 3). This colour for the Shade should never come to the limits of the first, or local colour, on the Shaded side of the Tree, as at *b b*, Example 3; for if the form of the first colour were not exactly followed by the second, a new form would be created; and if it were exactly followed, the edge on the Shaded side would be too dark and hard. The colour of the Sepia, therefore, after having distinctly expressed the character of the Foliage towards the light side of the Tree, should be so mingled with the first, or local colour, on the Shaded side, as to leave no new Form; this is effected by using the Brush with but little colour in it.

The most effective mode, however, of using the Brush in Foliage, and of obtaining the nearest likeness to Nature, is to observe, from the beginning, the same order of operation as in using the Chalk or Pencil,—that is, to put in the Shades first, and the Light, or local colours, afterwards. By proceeding in this manner, we are, moreover, enabled to work more deliberately, as less inconvenience is to be apprehended from the colour drying. In applying the local colour to the Shade, we can not only adjust it so as to leave any number of interstices, but also in such a manner as to express most distinctly either the lightness or density of the Foliage. The same mode of procedure may indeed be employed with advantage in depicting all other objects.

In representing Grass and Herbage, Character on the Outline is not required in the first tone of colour, as in Foliage; the forms of the masses only are wanted, to show their Outline when a path or road divides them; Character must be gained by the second operation, and this again is *exactly* the same as that of the Chalk or Pencil, which has been previously explained; the end is always to be obtained in the same simple manner. It would be useless to multiply Examples; either the local colour should be first laid on, and the Shade and Character afterwards added; or these operations may be reversed, the Shade being put on first, as with the Chalk or Pencil, observing the same principles, and obtaining the same results.

As from the Brush even washes of colour are obtained, the Student should carefully observe to pass all light colours over intervening objects of a darker colour, or over the places where such objects are to come, so as to avoid leaving any unnecessary interstices of white paper; and when Trees, or any objects whose local colour is dark, cross the lighter colour of Skies and Distances, the Skies and Distances should be first put in, and their colour should be passed entirely over the places which Trees or other dark objects are to occupy. Such lighter tones of colour as those on the distant Hills and Cliffs, to the right, in Plate 24, should be passed without scruple over the places which are to be occupied by the darker Rocks, Trees, and Buildings immediately under them; and in a like manner the colour on the Tower, in the centre of this Picture, and the Rock on which it stands, should be passed over the place occupied by the dark Tree. As it would be extremely embarrassing to leave, in the midst of masses of Shade, minute and scattered lights,—such as the lights across the Water, and the light on the Figures in the foreground, and on the Stems of the Trees to the left,—the broad wash of light colour in the foreground must be taken over them all *fearlessly,* and when that is dry, these lights must be obtained by scratching them out of these broad washes with a *sharp* penknife, or by wetting the place with clean water, and when nearly dry, rubbing it smartly with a silk handkerchief over the finger, or with the Indian Rubber. The great object is, to do this in such a way as to avoid leaving the edges of the lights thus obtained, or the surface of the paper, *woolly.* The Student must here be reminded to observe most rigidly the form of every portion of colour he is putting on, so that he may make the Lights true and attractive. He must not have unmeaning blots of colour, but should recollect that every touch he gives to his Picture should have a form perfectly consistent with the object to which it is applied. The best practice I can recommend to the Student is, to copy with the Brush, attending to its peculiarities, the Examples which are here given to him for the Chalk or Pencil. I have found by experience the value of this method, as a sure means of acquiring facility and power of execution.

Should these Examples, with those I have already published, be insufficient to satisfy the Student—to explain every point of practice, to resolve every doubt, —he must apply to his Tutor, to do that for him which could not be done here, without extending this volume beyond all reasonable bounds. Here, he must not expect more than to learn sound principles,—to witness the proofs that they can be carried into practice,—and to have presented to him instances of their effects. All works of Art, to be good, must contain them; but the endless methods of combining them it would be quite impossible to show. When he has attained a thorough knowledge of those principles, he will select such Examples as are most accordant with his own taste and feelings. Thus prepared, he will be in little danger of being either awed by the grave dogmas of antiquated authority, or captivated by the *éclat* of fashion; for it is unlikely that he should select Examples for imitation which his judgment, founded on attentive observation of Nature, does not sanction. Even supposing that sufficient time cannot be commanded for the continued practice of Art, he will still be able, by being correctly informed, to speak well on a subject which all make a part of their almost daily conversation: he will neither unthinkingly applaud what is worthless, nor condemn what is truly excellent.

I here take leave of my Reader, having placed before him, to the best of my ability, some of the simple principles of Nature and of Art,—principles which are essential to Art in its perfection, as well as in its rudiments,—which are not a Lesson for the day only, but such as he must observe from the beginning to the end, so often and so long as he continues to practise Art. Their constant applicability, in every stage and in every department of Pictorial Art, is indeed their best recommendation to the Student's attention; and instead of considering their repetition irksome, he should be delighted that they are so *few*, so *simple*, and so *universal* in their operation. To teach him these has been my chief purpose; all that he has learned is applicable to all objects on which he may employ his Pencil, of whatever kind; and I strenuously urge him to test their truth again and again by a reference to Nature, and to look for their practical exemplification, not only in the Examples here given, but in every work of Art, having merit, ancient or modern, by whomsoever painted. According to the relative excellence of such works, he will assuredly discover those principles in a greater or less degree; and this of itself should induce him to persevere in following that which he finds to be true, as the only secret of Art which is worth knowing.

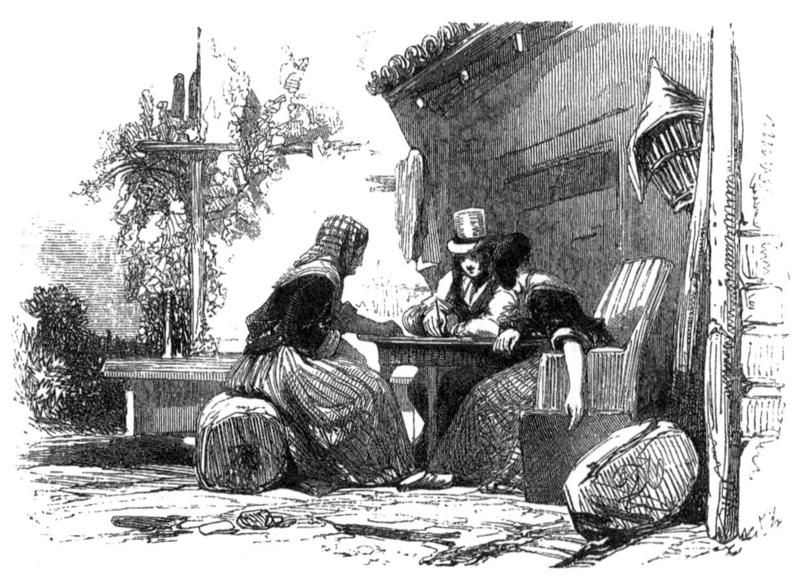

APPENDIX.

ON THE MATERIALS.

THOUGH it be true, in a great measure, that materials are good or bad in proportion as they are skillfully used or not; it is equally true, that from some are to be obtained effects, and expressions of qualities, which no skill can obtain from others: for this reason, I think it advisable to say what I consider the best, and why.

That Paper is the best on which can be readily obtained not only the delicate tones required for skies and distant objects, but also the vigour required for strongly marked objects in the foreground. These qualities of delicacy and vigour are best obtained on a Paper, the surface of which is moderately smooth, such as imperial hot-pressed, or finely-woven, which is better. Bristol-board is frequently used; but in consequence of its glassy smoothness, the pencil slides over it, so that no depth of colour can be obtained, except by such pressure as deprives the hand of freedom: for the purpose of Chalk-drawing it is nearly as objectionable; it is impossible, without great labour, to obtain any power; and if it be chosen to make what is called, or rather mis-called, a highly-finished Drawing, it would be better at once to take the Brush, which does ten times as much in one tenth of the time. Rough paper is as bad, in an opposite extreme: this resists the Chalk or Pencil so much, that everything looks coarse and powdery; and it is vain to try to gain delicate tones, such as are required for Distances, and in Figures; and as it also offers to the Chalk or Pencil a greater resistance in some places than in others, the evenness of colour, indispensable to Shade, cannot be obtained. Instead of a Drawing *Board,* a substitute formed in the following manner, is commonly employed: a number of sheets of equal size are pressed together and glued at the edges only, and all round; these are fixed to a tolerably strong mill-board, and the whole forms a most advantageous flat surface, as solid as a board. The sheet on which the Drawing is made can be removed instantly. For sketching from Nature it is quite a luxury. Such substitutes for Boards are called French Blocks, and are to be had of all the Artists' colourmen.

The Chalk I prefer is that called *Conté*. It is to be had of different degrees of hardness; but for general purposes that which is cylindrical and glazed, is the best.

Recently the quality of Lead Pencils, both for the purposes of Art and for general use, has been greatly improved, in consequence of the discovery, made by my friend Mr. W. Brockedon, of the mode of preparing pure Plumbago. For years, no fresh lead has been obtained from the Cumberland mines, and the best having been exhausted long ago, Lead Pencils were getting every day worse, and insufferable from grit. To remedy this, composition pencils have been manufactured; but these possess no lustre nor depth of colour, and it is difficult—sometimes impossible—to efface their markings. By Mr. Brockedon's invention, we obtain the pure Black Lead, in all its lustre and depth of colour, without a particle of grit, and of every degree of hardness or softness; and the markings from all are easily effaced. So great is the improvement in all respects, even over the Plumbago in its native state, that it may truly be said, that until now a perfect Lead Pencil has been unknown. Lead Pencils from Mr. Brockedon's pure Plumbago, are now manufactured by Messrs. Mordan and Co., and by Messrs. Winsor and Newton.

To get over the difficulty of obtaining local colour with the Chalk or Pencil, coloured paper is used. On this the high lights are put on, either with white in a liquid state, or with white Chalk; and the Paper being left for such objects as are not in themselves white, some notion of the local colour is gained. As the colour of the Paper is even, the lines of the Chalk or Pencil, are quite as distinctly seen as on white Paper, while the contrast is not so harsh. White, whether liquid or dry, should never be used but on such objects as are either in Nature actually white, or very light; and the white on them should be more solid and bright, according to their degree of brilliancy.

White is to be had in metal tubes, in a moist state, and may be either diluted with water, or used as it is. It always appears somewhat brighter when dry, than wet, and for this allowance must be made. The best is called Chinese White.

The coloured Paper which I think best adapted for the Lead Pencil, is a rather warm Grey, as it harmonises best with the colour of the Pencil. It should be of a depth of colour sufficient to give brilliancy to the Lights. If it be too dark, it overpowers the Pencil, and makes the Lights look crude; and if it be too light, it is scarcely better than white paper. For a long time it was difficult to obtain this, or indeed, any other tinted paper, of right depth of colour, from the extreme uncertainty in making it, the grey tints being often of a blue, green, or red cast. Latterly, however, great improvement has been made in the manufacture of tinted papers, in consequence of the increased demand for them. Amongst those who have succeeded best, Messrs. Smith and Allnut seem entitled to especial mention. Their tinted papers, of different colours and various tones, are of a quality which allows of the Chalk being used with greater facility and power,—a much more efficient instrument than the Pencil, when employed on tinted papers. These papers also receive colour tolerably well.

I by no means recommend the use of coloured papers to a beginner; the effects produced on them are, indeed, more captivating than on white paper; but they have a tendency to encourage his natural inclination to rely too much on his materials, and to render him indifferent to the acquisition of a knowledge of the principles of Art. White paper is the best, at first, because it exhibits more distinctly the faults of the Student. I, therefore, earnestly recommend him to use it at first; and when he afterwards uses coloured paper, he will know precisely what means it affords him of producing additional likeness to Nature, and will not expect more from it than it will afford.

All the Skies and Distances should be drawn with long lines; and if afterwards they appear too coarse, either the finger, or a soft leather Stump, passed over them, will reduce their harshness. A still better thing, for this purpose, is a Hair Pencil, used dry. The Stump, when used with judgment, is a most serviceable instrument; with it Skies may be admirably done, charging it with a sufficient quantity of Chalk or Lead, obtained by rubbing soft Chalk or a soft Pencil on a coarse piece of paper. The tones it produces are very aerial; a quantity of colour is speedily obtained; the fleeting forms of Clouds are rapidly secured with it; it subdues the distances of Landscapes to any required degree, according to the distance or nature of the object, and overcomes the superabundant evidence of the markings of the Chalk or Pencil in the Shades. To the Figure it may be applied with the best effect. The tone of colour produced by the Stump on the Shades and Shadows is often very beautiful, as it seems to partake of the very nature of Shade, and succeeds admirably in such parts as are smooth, or comparatively so; for example, the Shades on the Trees and Distance in Plate 10; and the Shadows over the Ground, or the Shaded parts of the Stems of the Beech Trees, in Plate 16; or the Shades on the Buildings, and the Shadow over the Water and Cows, in Plate 21. Whenever such tones of colour are required, it may be advantageously employed; and also whenever the too great evidence of the lines on the Shades or Shadows have a tendency to make them appear too attractive, and to come forward instead of retiring. It must be understood that I speak of the Stump only as another and more ready means of carrying out just principles, as with its speed greater truth is gained, a fact which establishes the best reason for using it. There can be no advantage in taking the more dilatory and weaker means, when the more speedy are the more effective.

Indian Rubber is of little use, except to obliterate entirely. From the force required in the application of it, it spreads the particles of the Lead Pencil, and thus smears the Paper: for removing Chalk it is useless. Any small portions of bright light amidst a mass of colour, such as the small lights on the Trunks of the

Trees in Plate 10, or such as are under the Arch, may be obtained in the following manner:—First, having cut a small hole in a clean piece of paper, lay it gently on the Drawing, leaving that portion of it which is to be removed to be seen through the hole; this may now be rubbed out fearlessly, as the surrounding paper, if held firmly, protects the surrounding portions of the Drawing.

Bread is the better material, and may be used in two ways; first, by rolling it between the thumb and finger into pellets, to subtract the too great depth of colour from small parts; this is done by simply pressing a pellet down perpendicularly on the paper, rather hard, and raising it again in the same way, the superabundant particles of the Lead adhering to it: for this purpose, the bread must be sufficiently new to retain some of its moisture. In the second way, by rubbing it into crumbs, the excess of colour in the first sketch, or any large portion of the Drawing, may be very delicately removed, passing these crumbs gently over the Drawing, with the inner surface of the four fingers.

Bread is the only means of removing Black Chalk; and in drawing the Figure, the nicety required on most of the shades is principally to be obtained by it.

There are many modes recommended of fixing Pencil Drawings. I generally fix mine by first pouring scalding water over them from a jug, or other vessel, when the drawing is laid flat on a board, and inclined. The loose particles of the Pencil are, in this way, instantly removed by the body of water, and carried off before they have time to settle, as they do with some other methods, to the injury of the Drawing. By this means the size in the paper is softened; and this, when the paper dries, is sufficient to hold both the light tints and the darker so firmly, that the Drawing may be passed, without danger, through Gum-water or Isinglass, to fix them. The Gum-water, or Isinglass—which ought never to be so strong as to display shining particles when dry—should be laid in a flat dish, and the Drawing passed through it. Even if the Drawing should be on coloured paper, with white lights put on, the white will not be in the least degree injured or removed by this operation.

One word on the Art which alone could enable me to do this work,—Lithography.

Many persons dislike to receive from their Tutor, Lithographic Drawings as Examples for practice: they expect always to receive from him his own Drawings, not considering that if he have many pupils, his life-time would not be sufficient to supply them all. It is not required that the individual who gives lessons in Language should be the author of the Grammar from which he teaches, nor that the Musician should be the composer of every piece he places before his pupils for their practice. Why then should more be required of the Artist who gives instruction in Drawing?

Some there are who, admitting the merits of an impression from a Lithographic Drawing, still prefer, for practice, a copy of it in Chalk or Pencil. This is like preferring a fac-simile to an autograph; for an impression from a Lithographic Drawing is as completely an autograph—a Drawing made by the original designer's own hand—as anything can be that is not so in the strictest sense of the word. I have many Lithographic Drawings by English and French Artists. In these Drawings we have all the beauty and power peculiar to their authors; but which would be in vain looked for in the best translation or copy. Thus, by means of Lithography, the public have the advantage of being able to study what would otherwise be either wholly unattainable, or only to be procured at so high a price as to be within the reach of very few. Though Lithography may have also contributed to the dissemination of much that is worthless; yet that does not affect the merit of the Art. Sir Walter Scott did not reject the use of type, because that type which gave to the public his inestimable works might have printed " trifles light as air;" nor do the public feel the pleasure of perusing them alloyed, nor their value the less, from any consideration of the utter worthlessness of what is by the same means placed before them.

Within the last few years great improvements have been made in Lithography. In consequence of these improvements, Lithographic Drawings can now be executed with greater vigour and precision, as well as with greater clearness and delicacy; while from the capital improvement of printing a tint over them with the lights preserved, the expression of space in the distance and of substance in the more prominent objects is greatly augmented,—the lights being thus rendered more brilliant, the middle tint more delicate, and the shades more retiring.

Having said thus much of Lithography—an Art of whose ready means and appliances I have availed myself on many occasions—I shall conclude by rendering a willing testimony to the merits of Mr. Hullmandel, who, as a Printer, has contributed so much to its improvement, as well as to its extension, in this country.

THE END.

Supplementary Plates

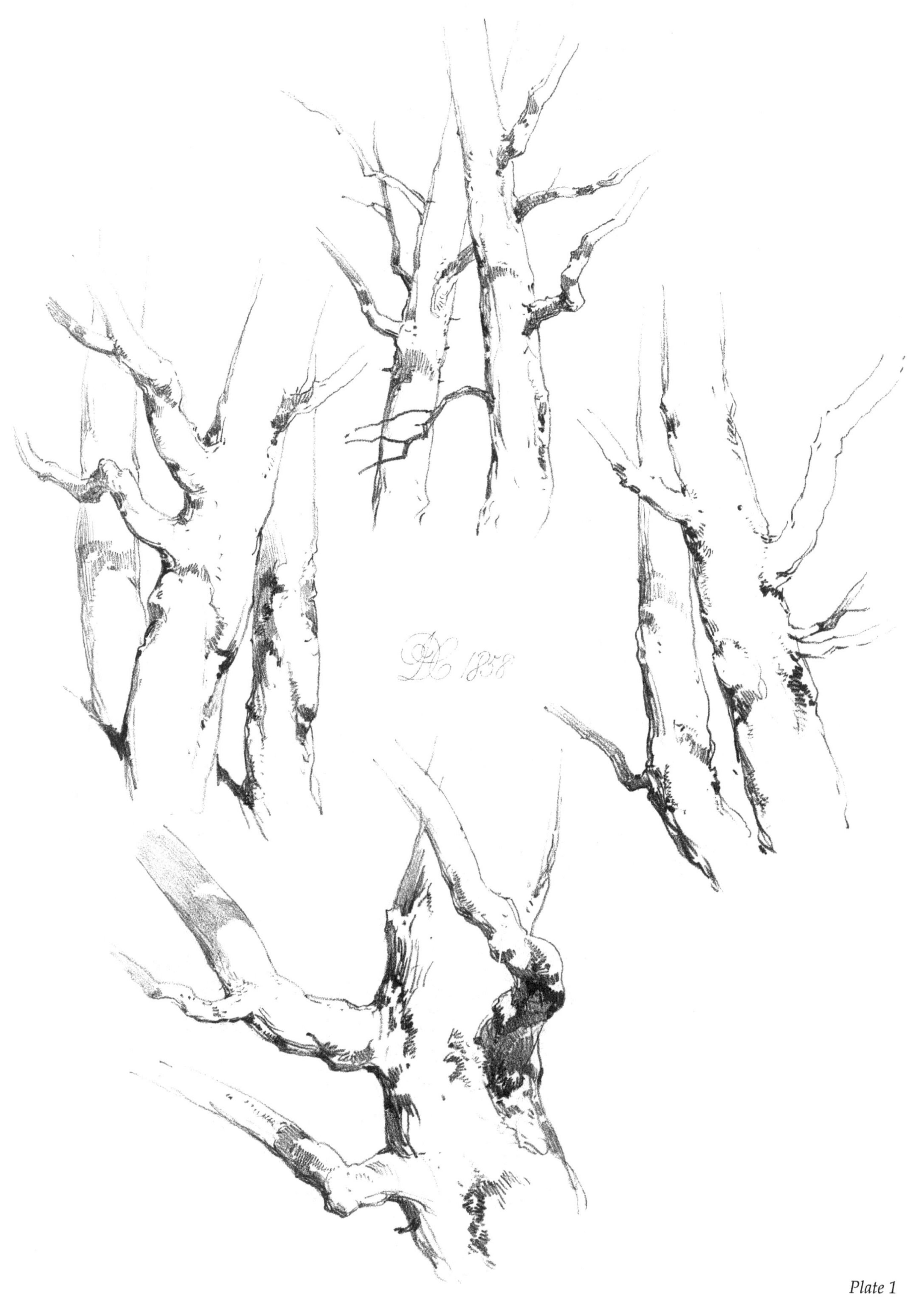

Plate 1

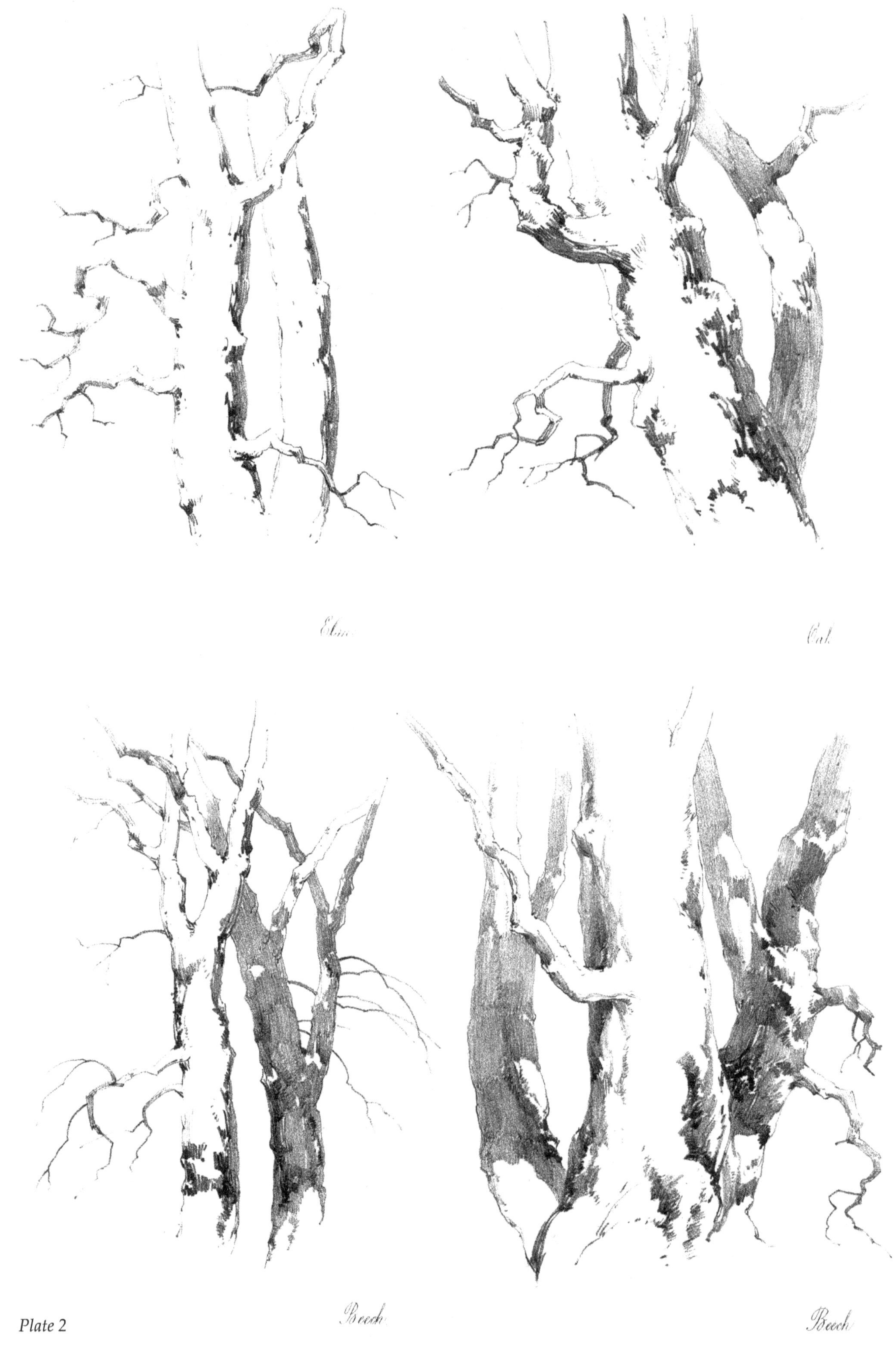

Plate 2

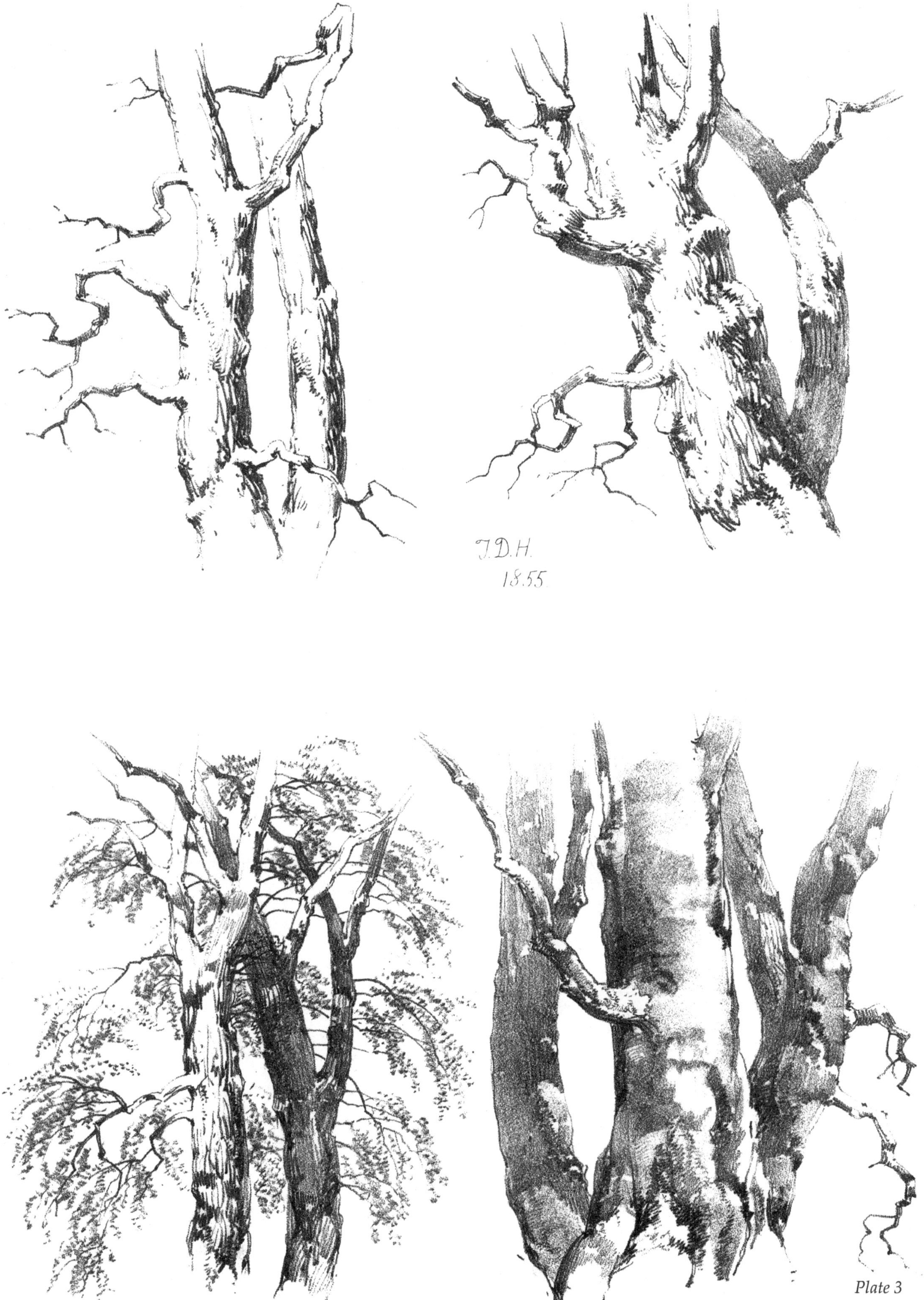

Plate 3

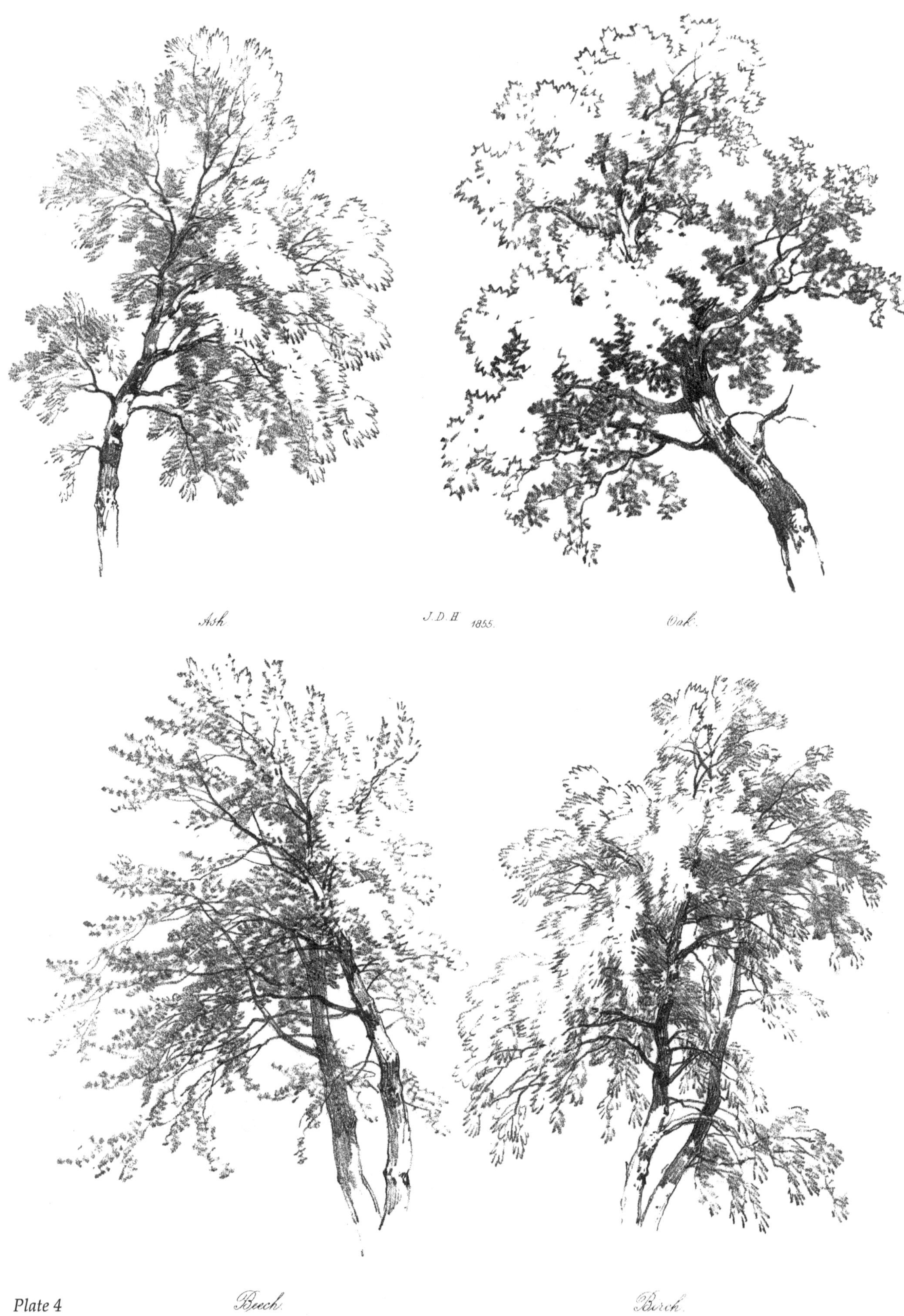

Plate 4

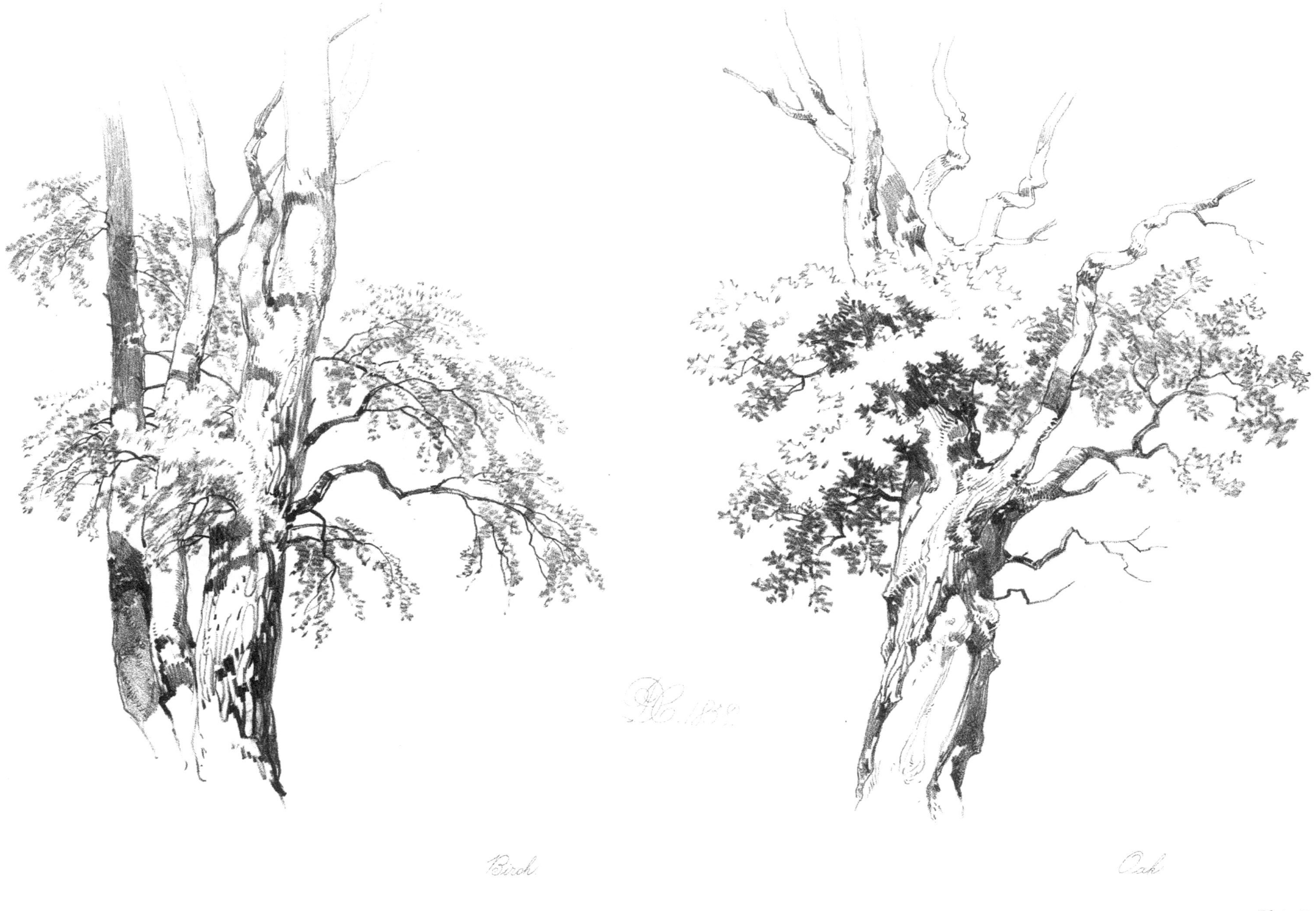

Birch
Oak

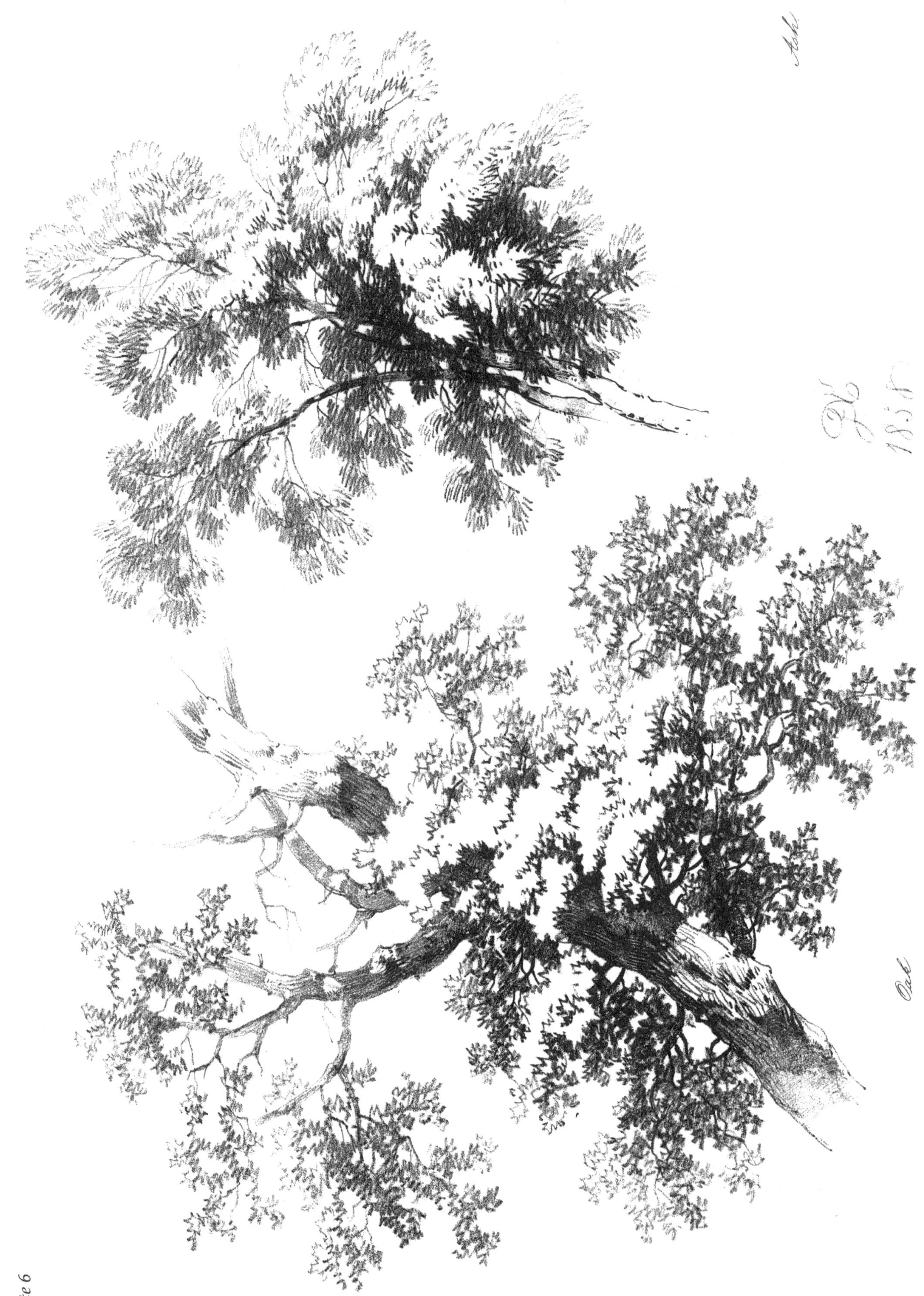
Ash.
1857
Oak

J·D·H·
1850
Beech and Oak.
Ash.

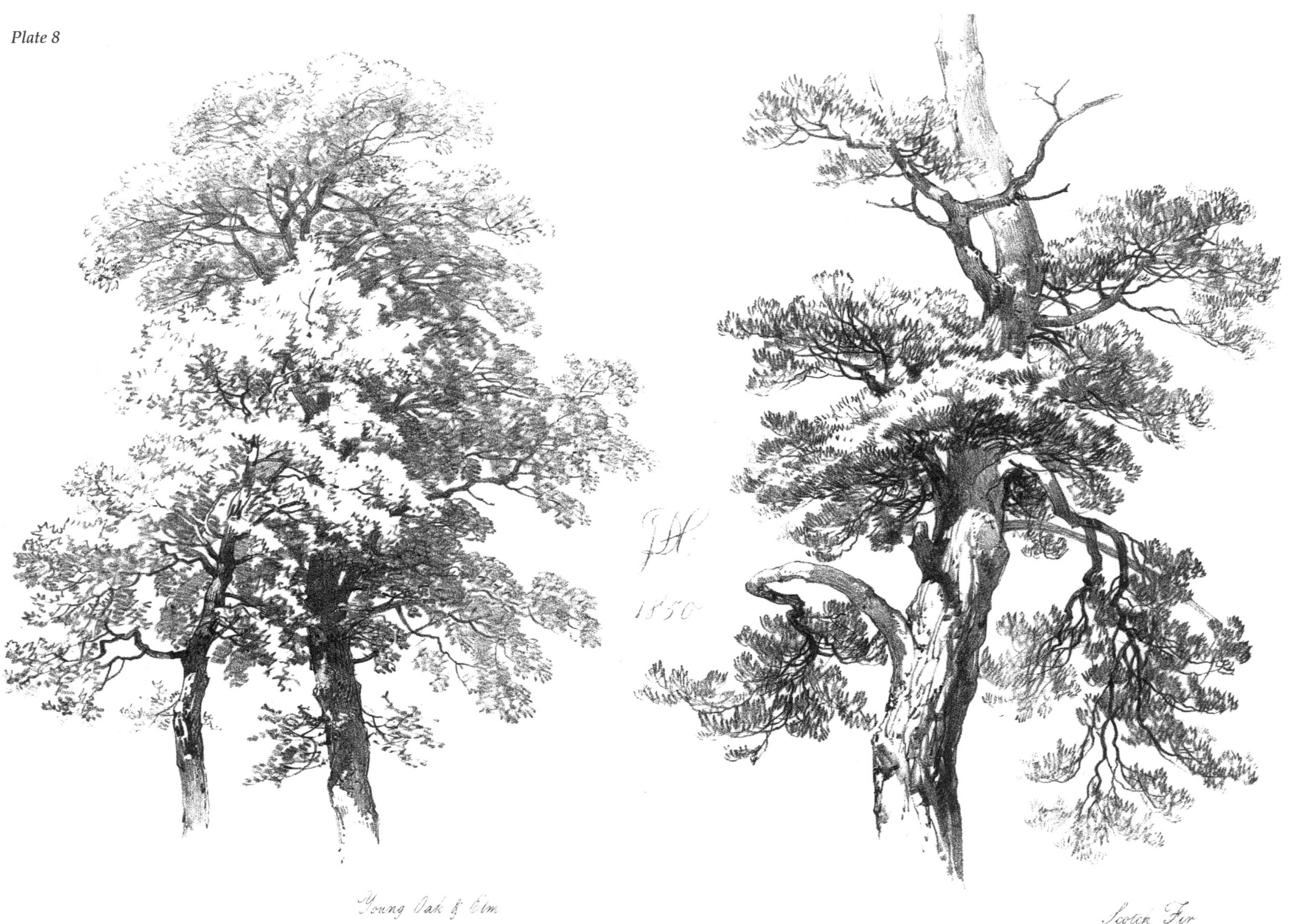

Young Oak & Elm
Scotch Fir

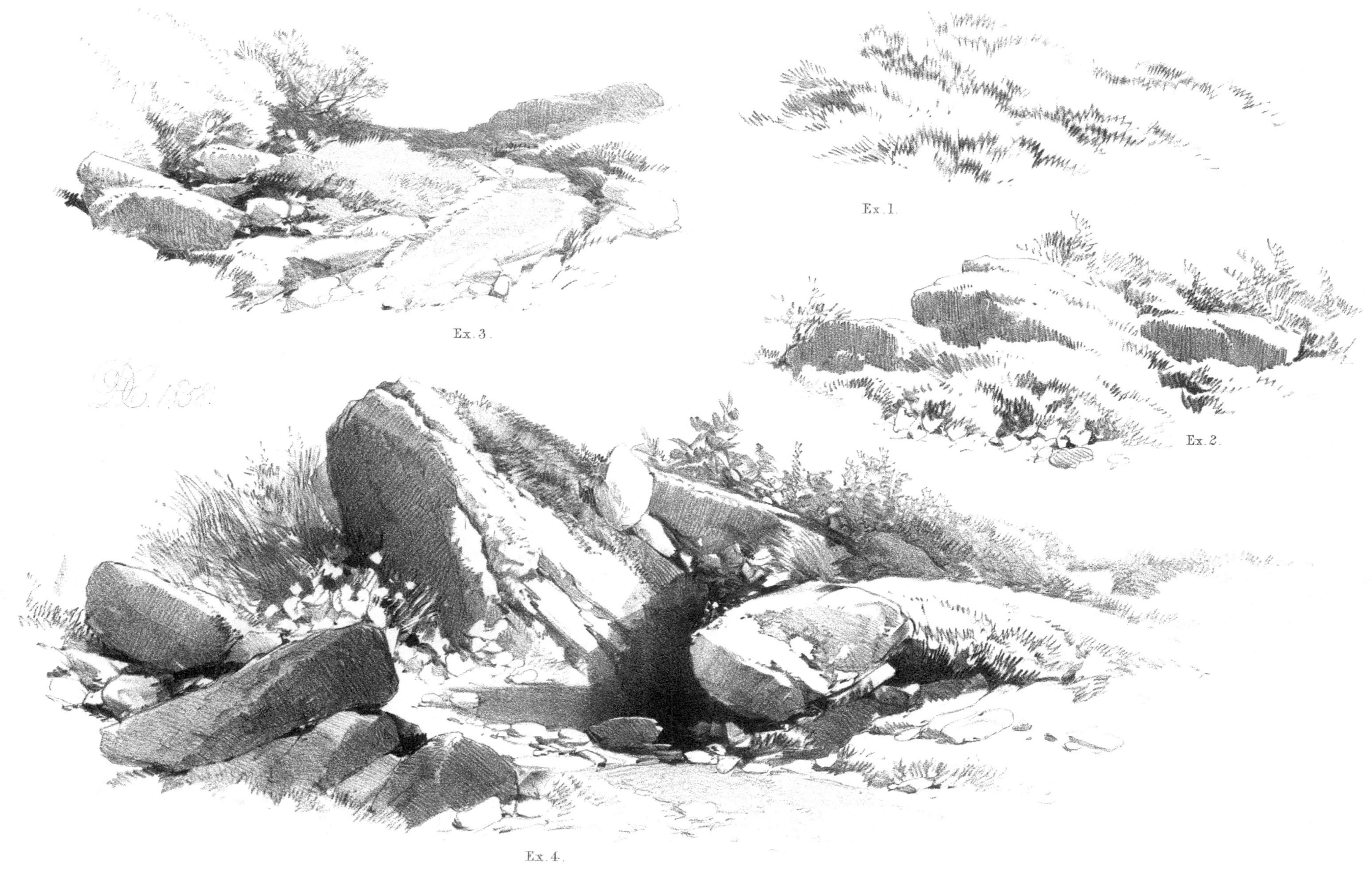
Ex. 1.
Ex. 2.
Ex. 3.
Ex. 4.

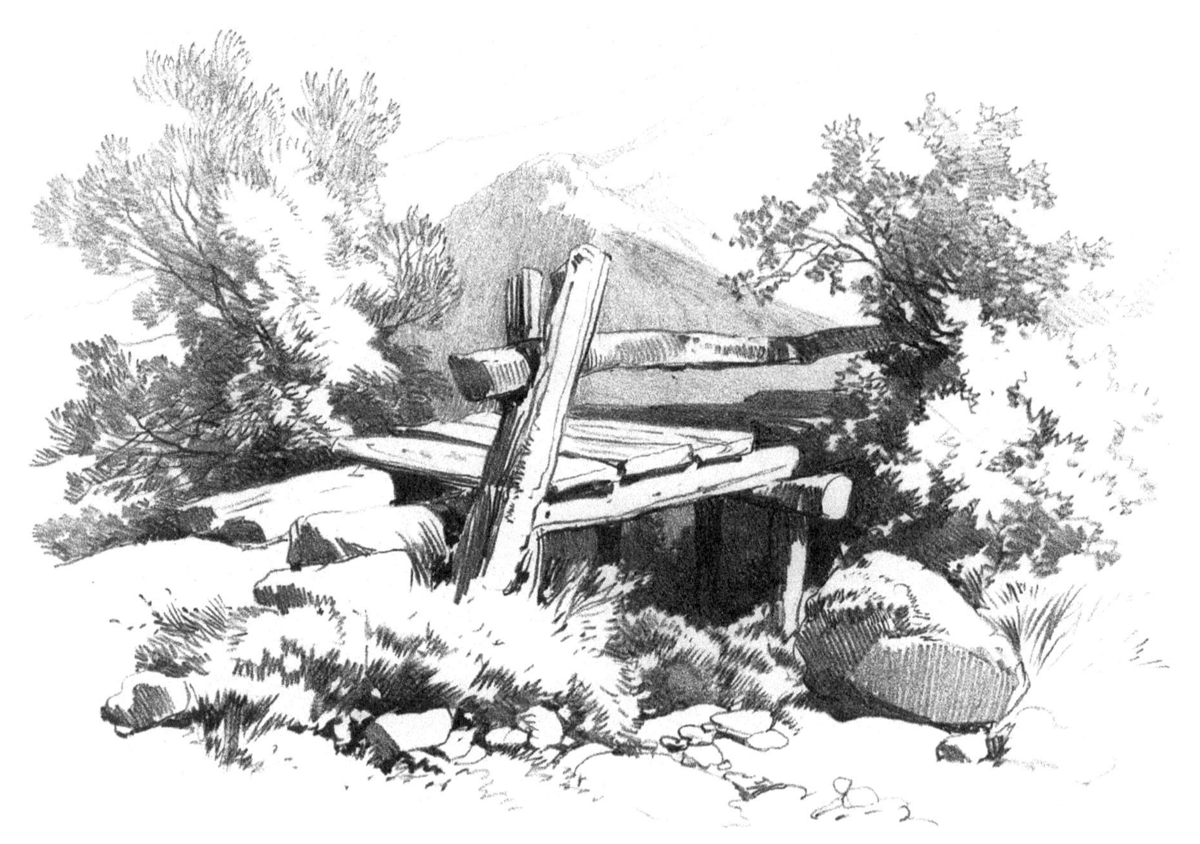

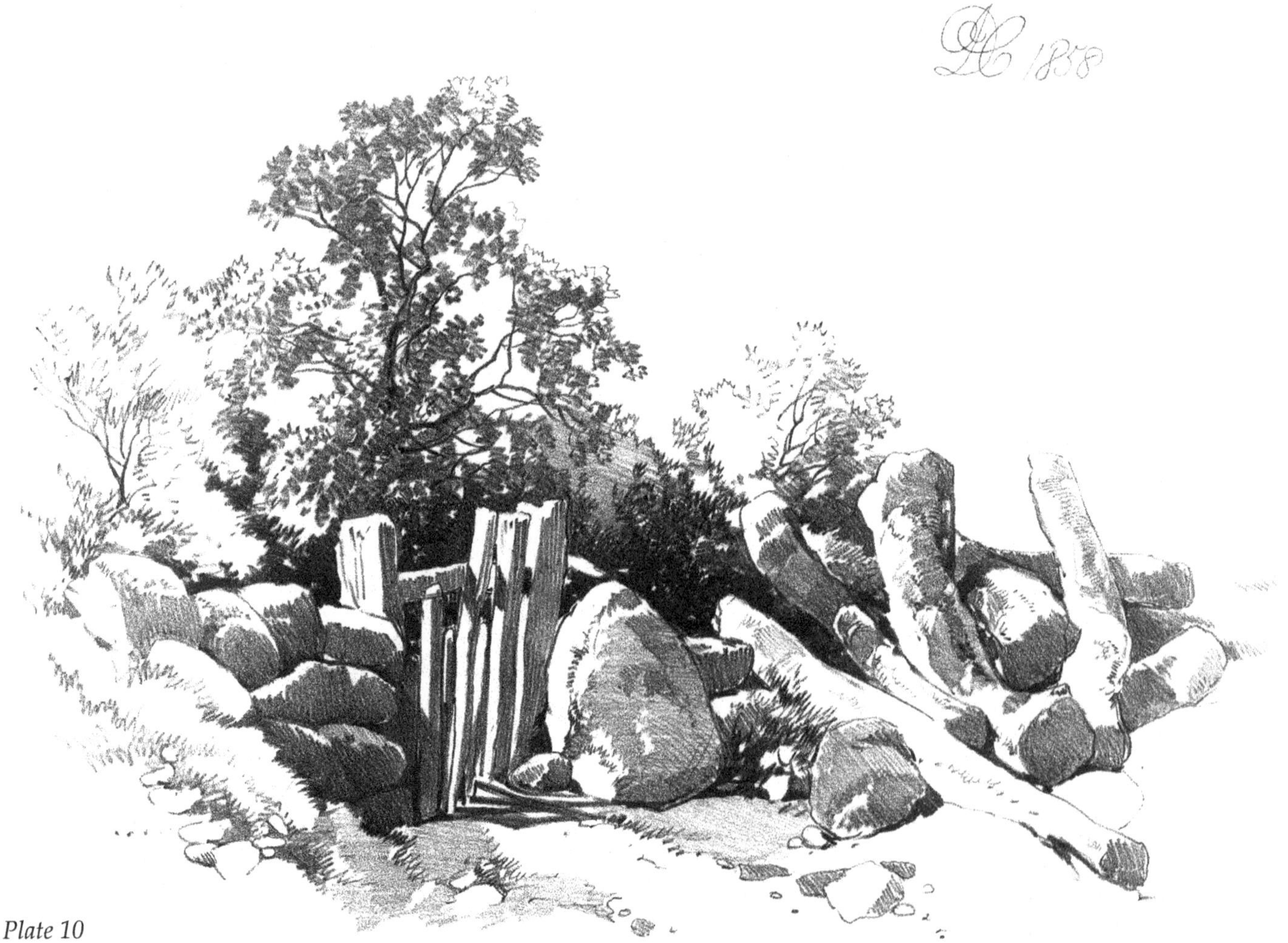

Plate 10

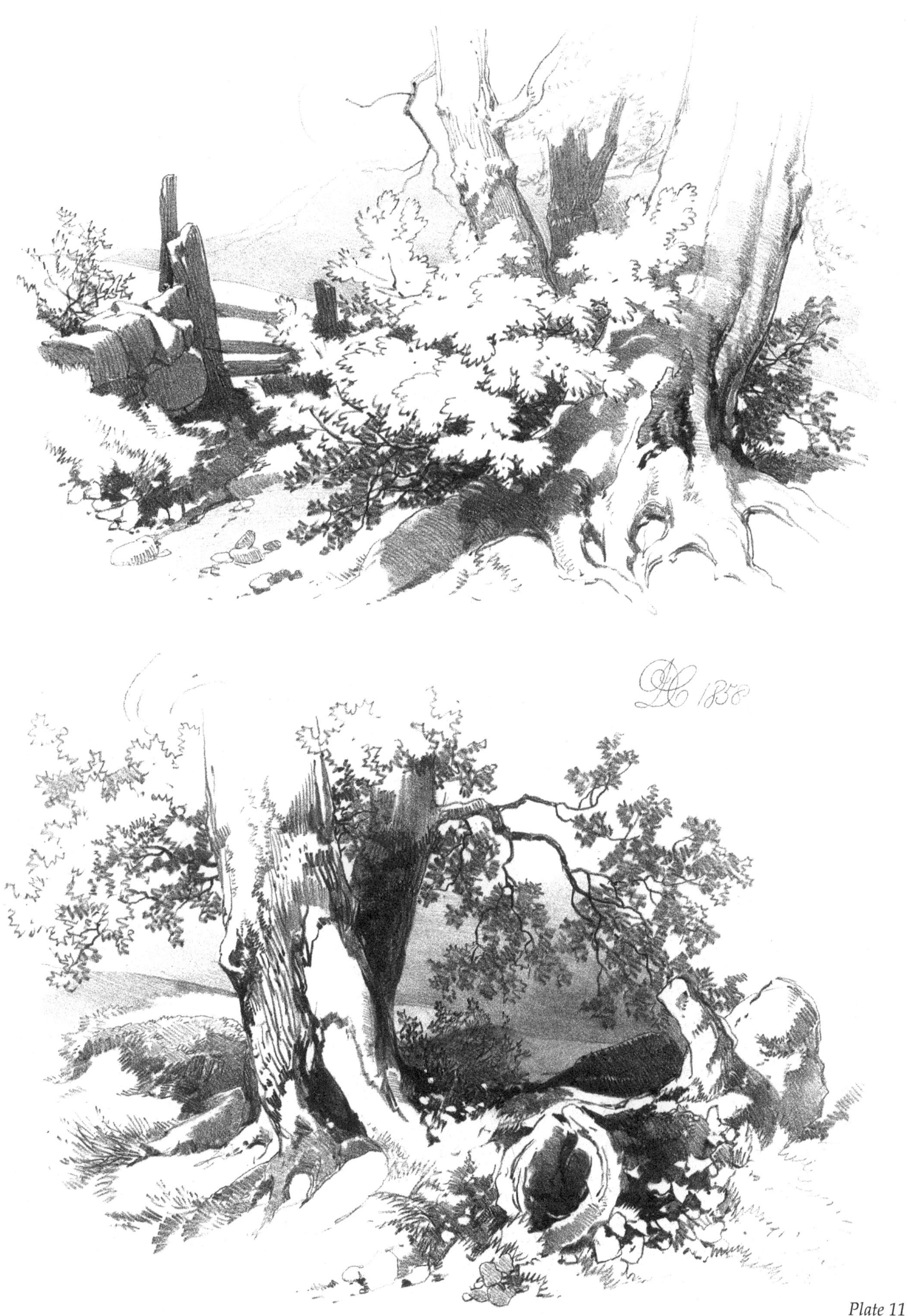

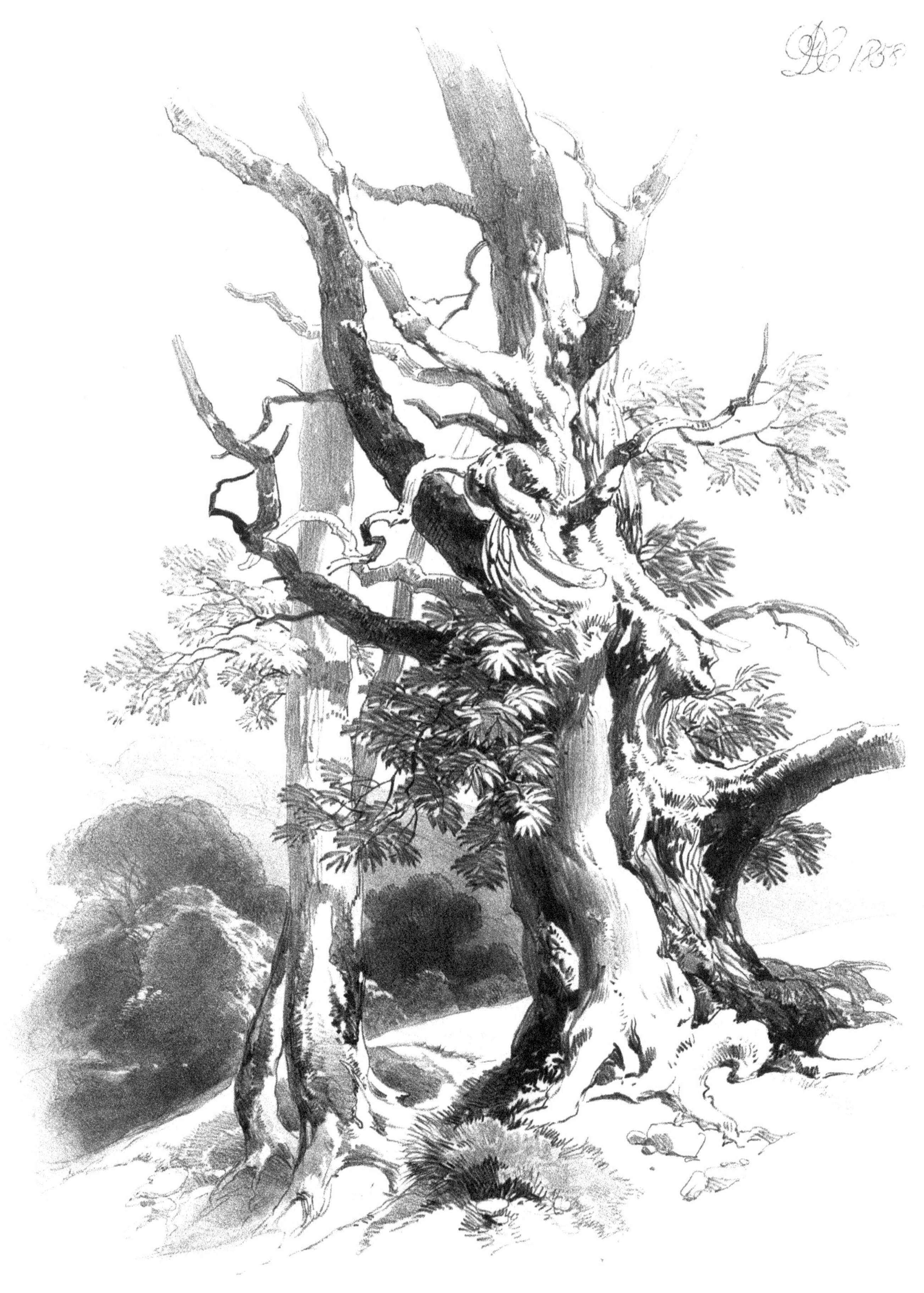

Plate 12

Chestnut and Ash.

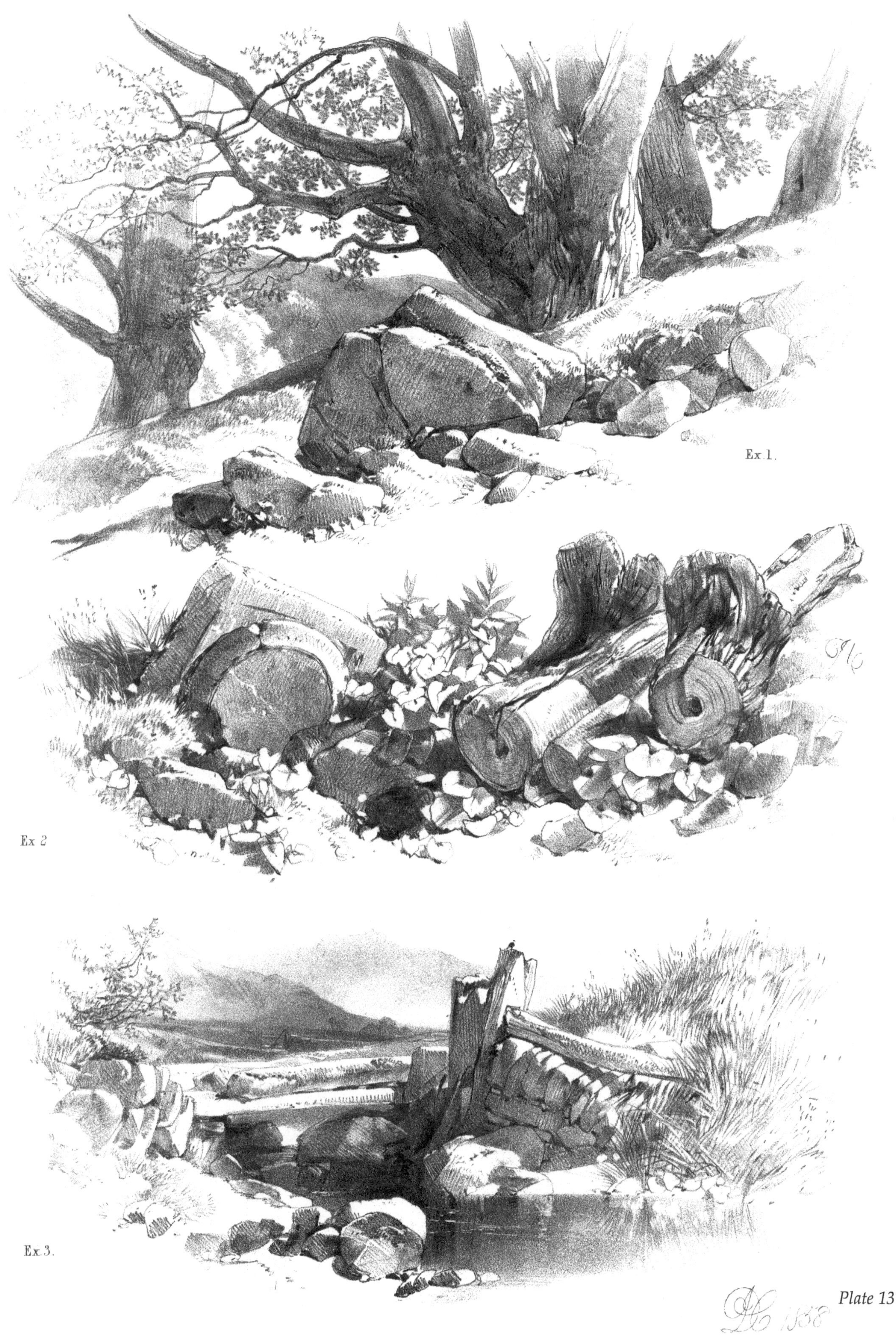

Ex.1.
Ex 2
Ex.3.
Plate 13

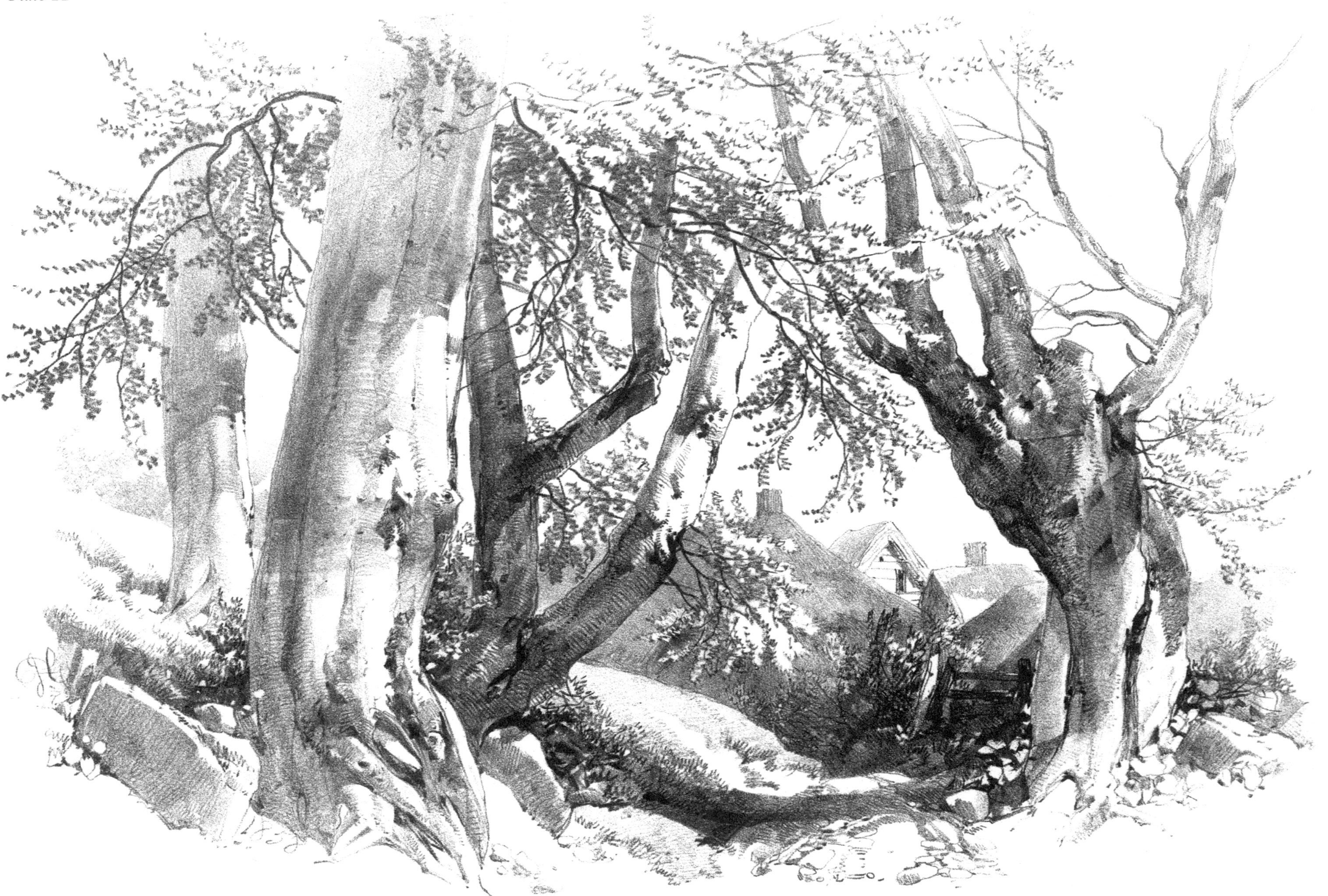

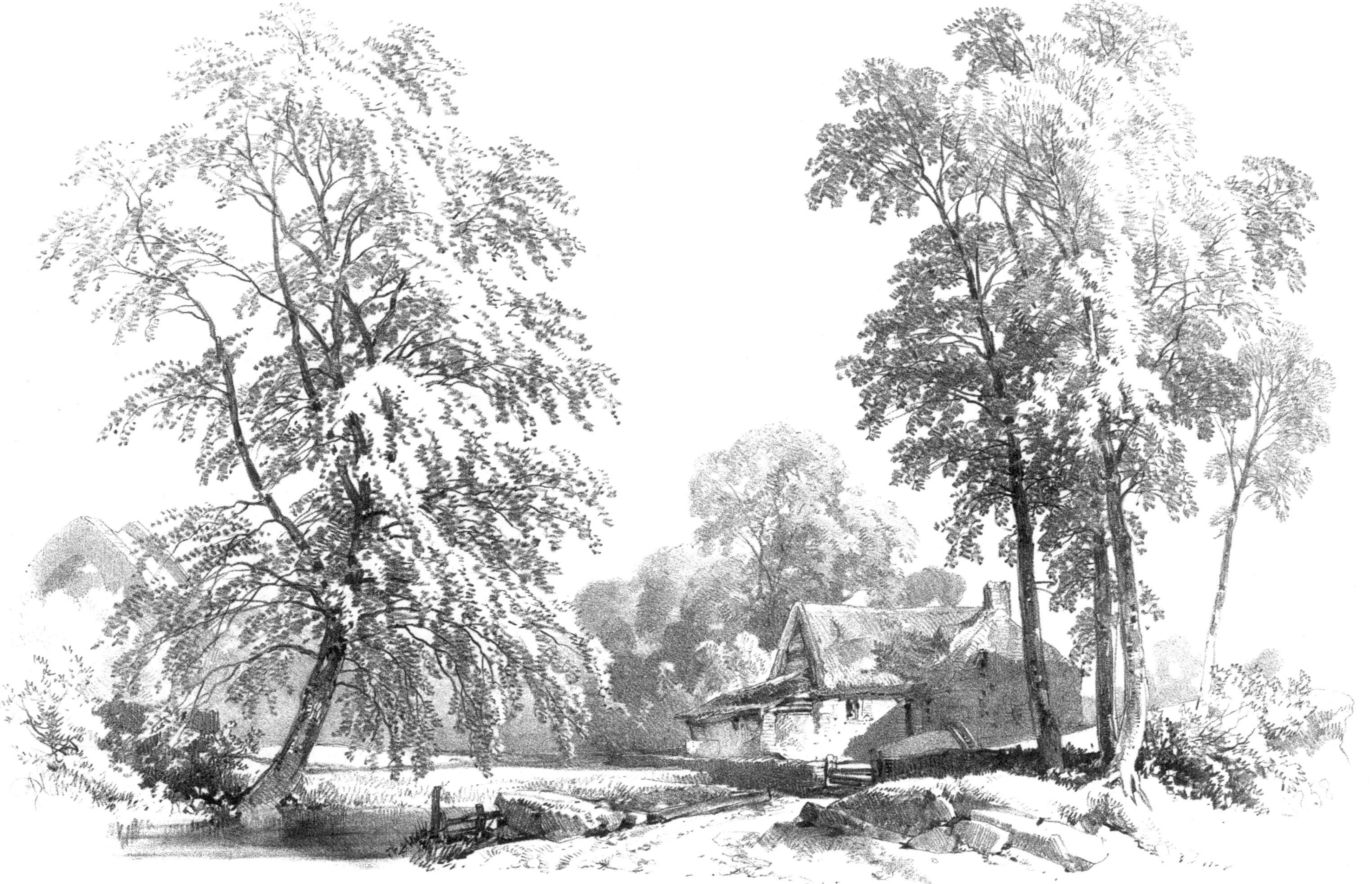

Plate 15

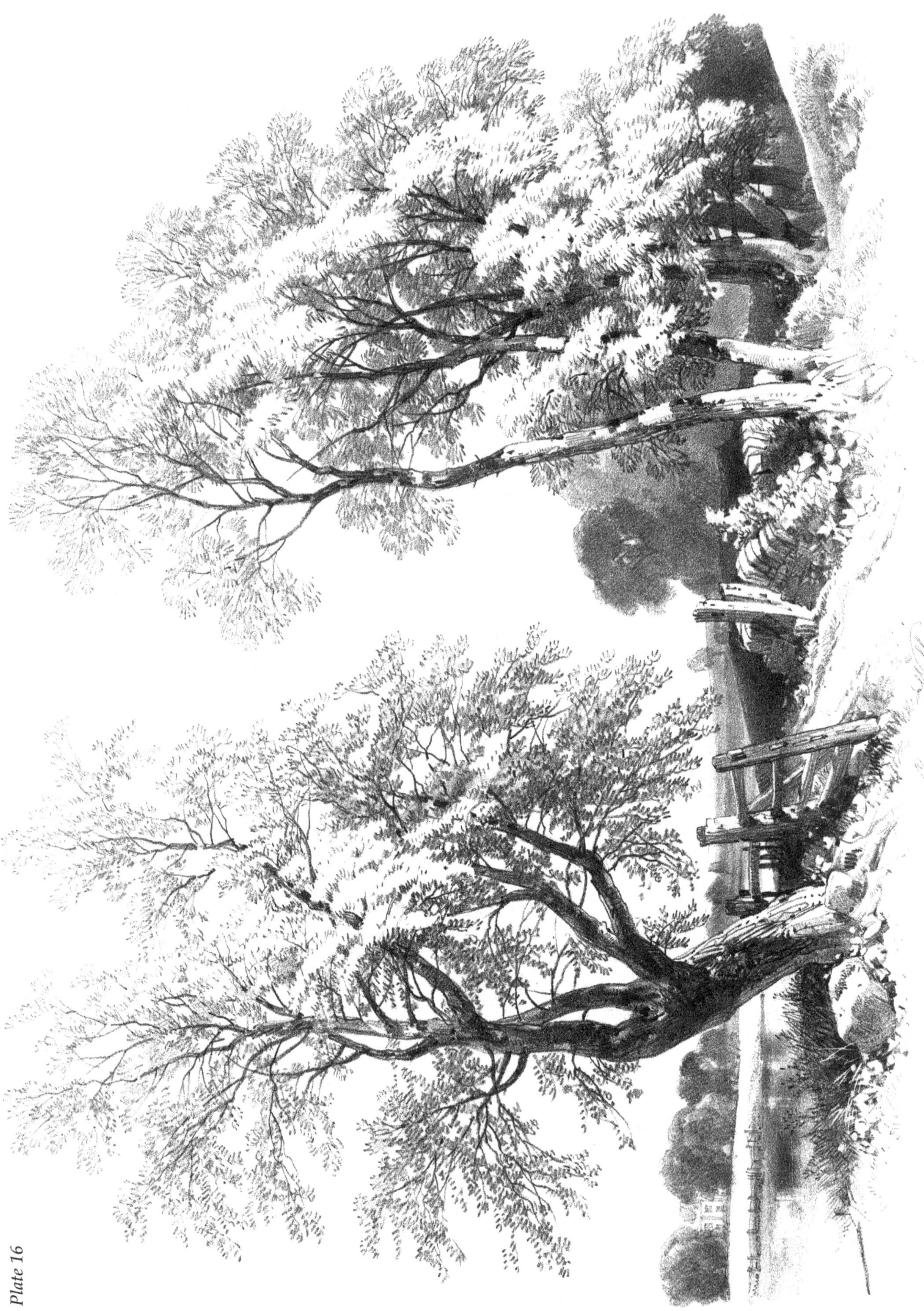

Plate 16

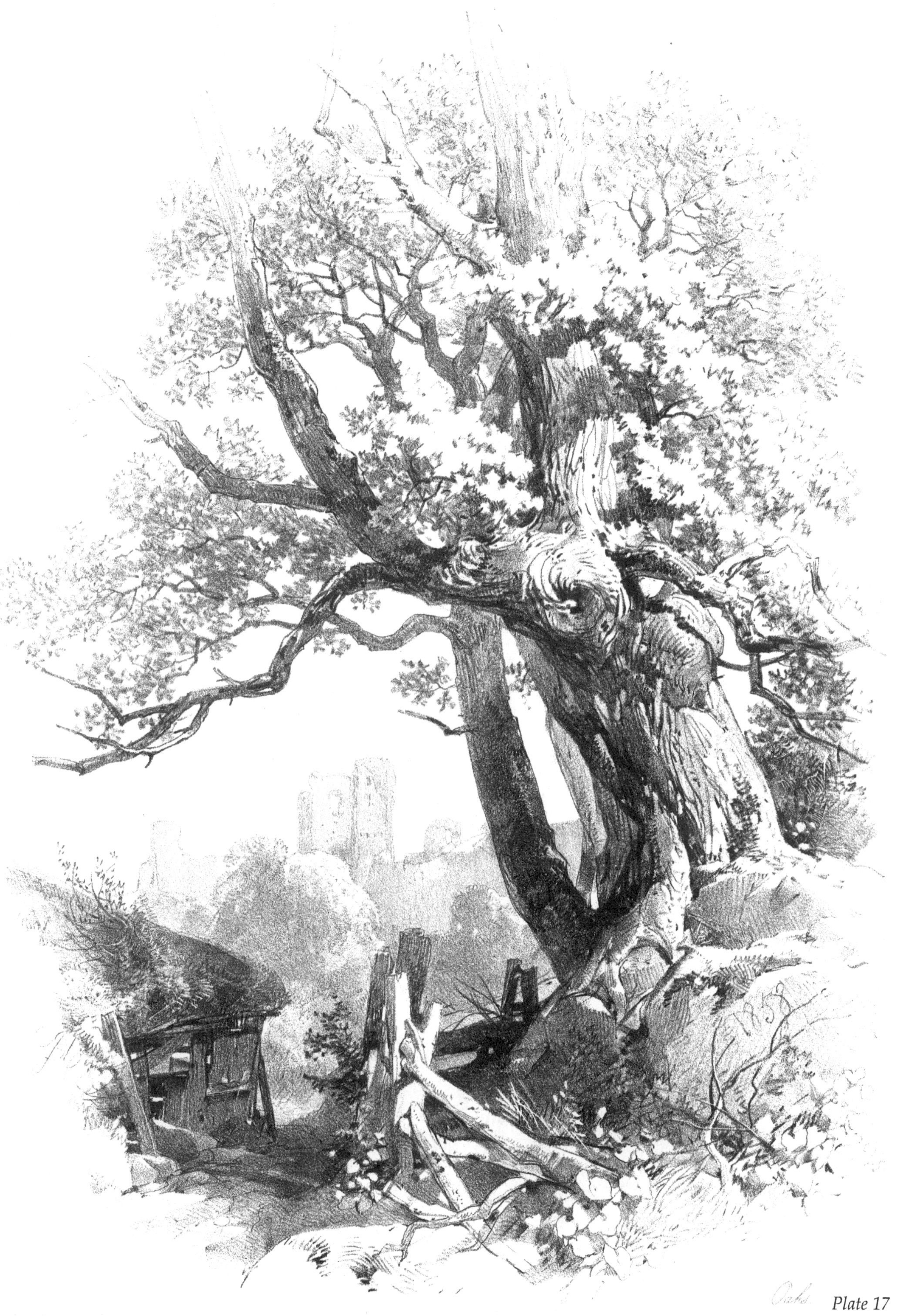

Oaks   Plate 17

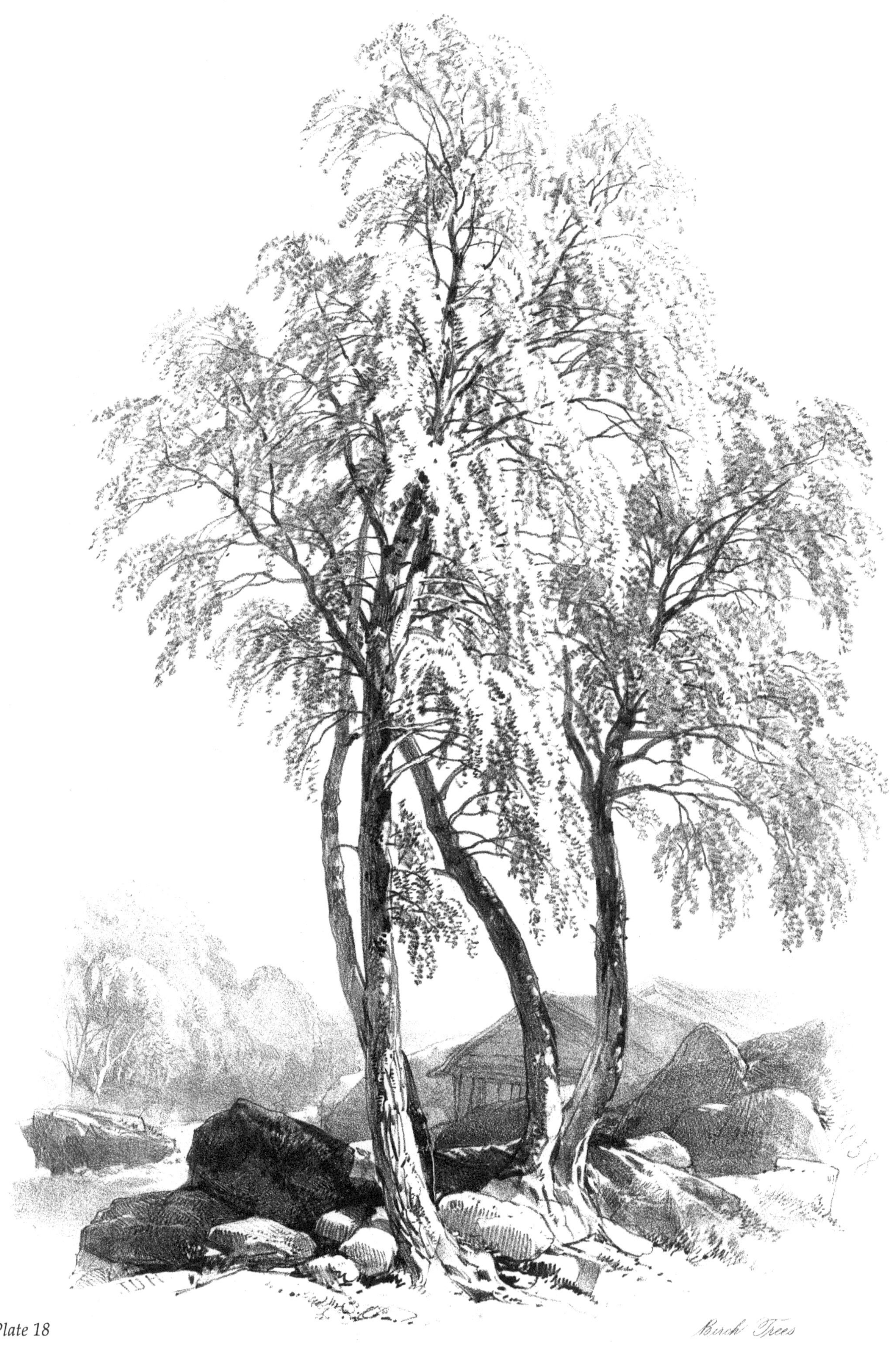

Plate 18

Birch Trees

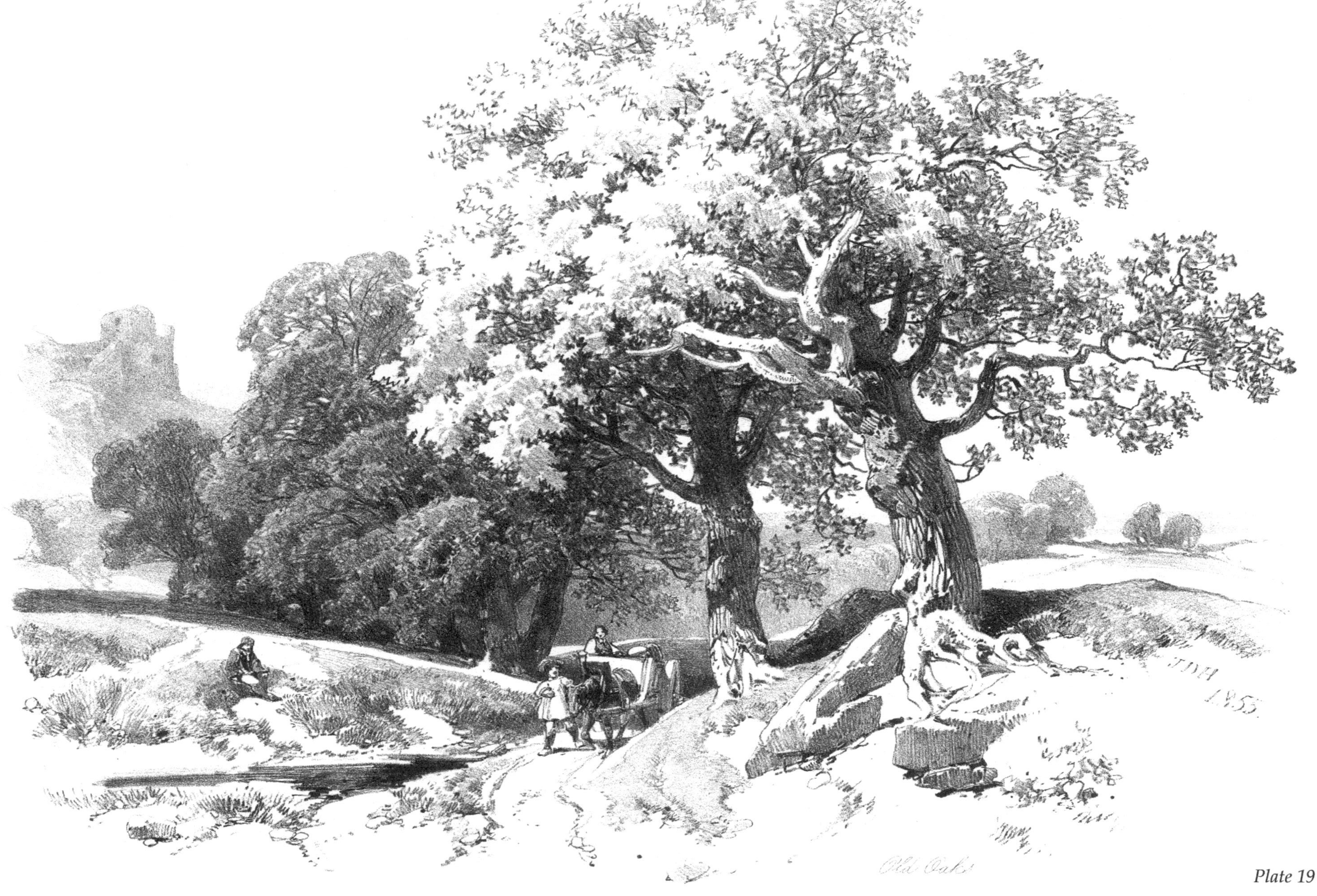

Old Oaks

Plate 20

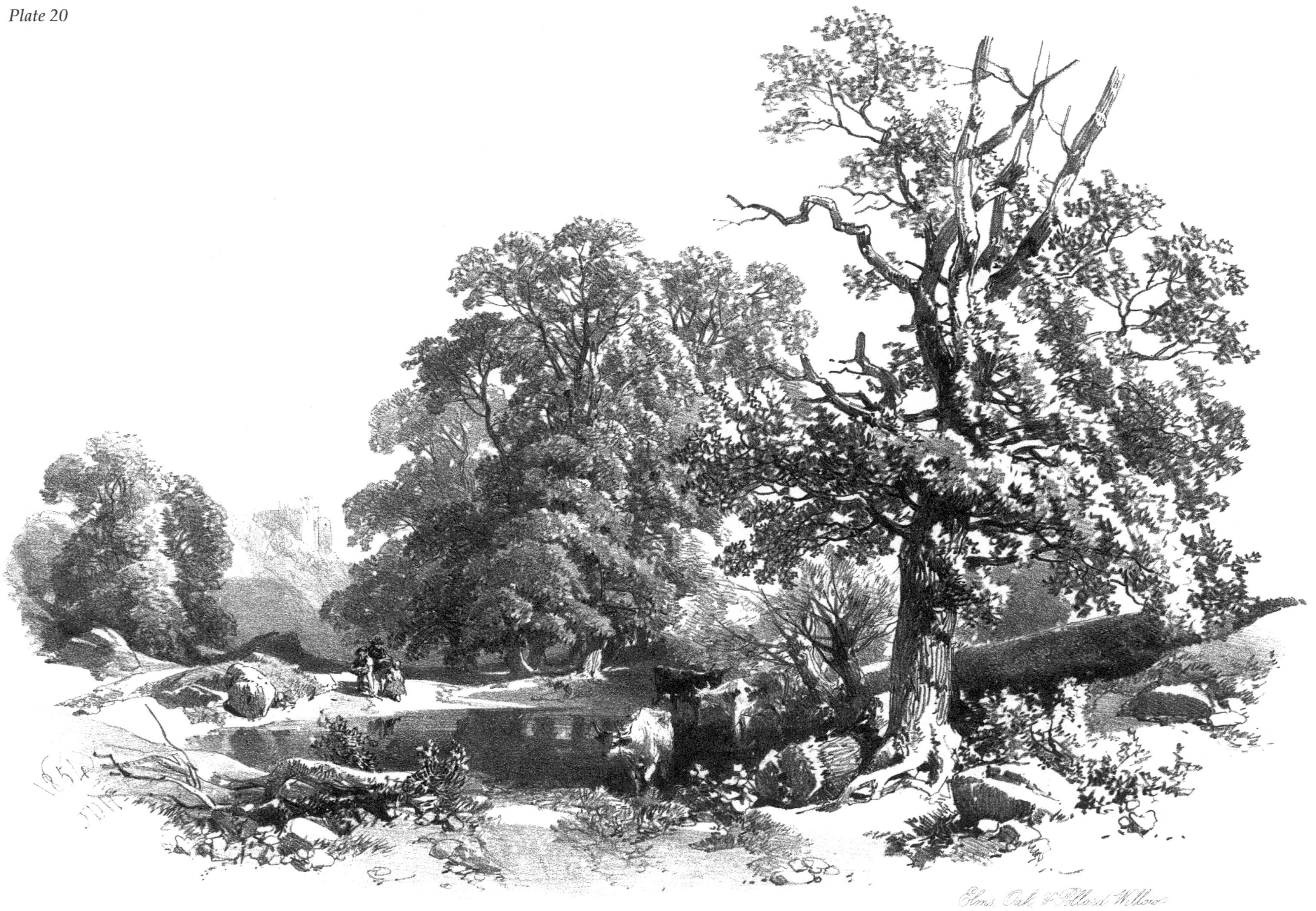

Elms, Oak & Pollard Willow

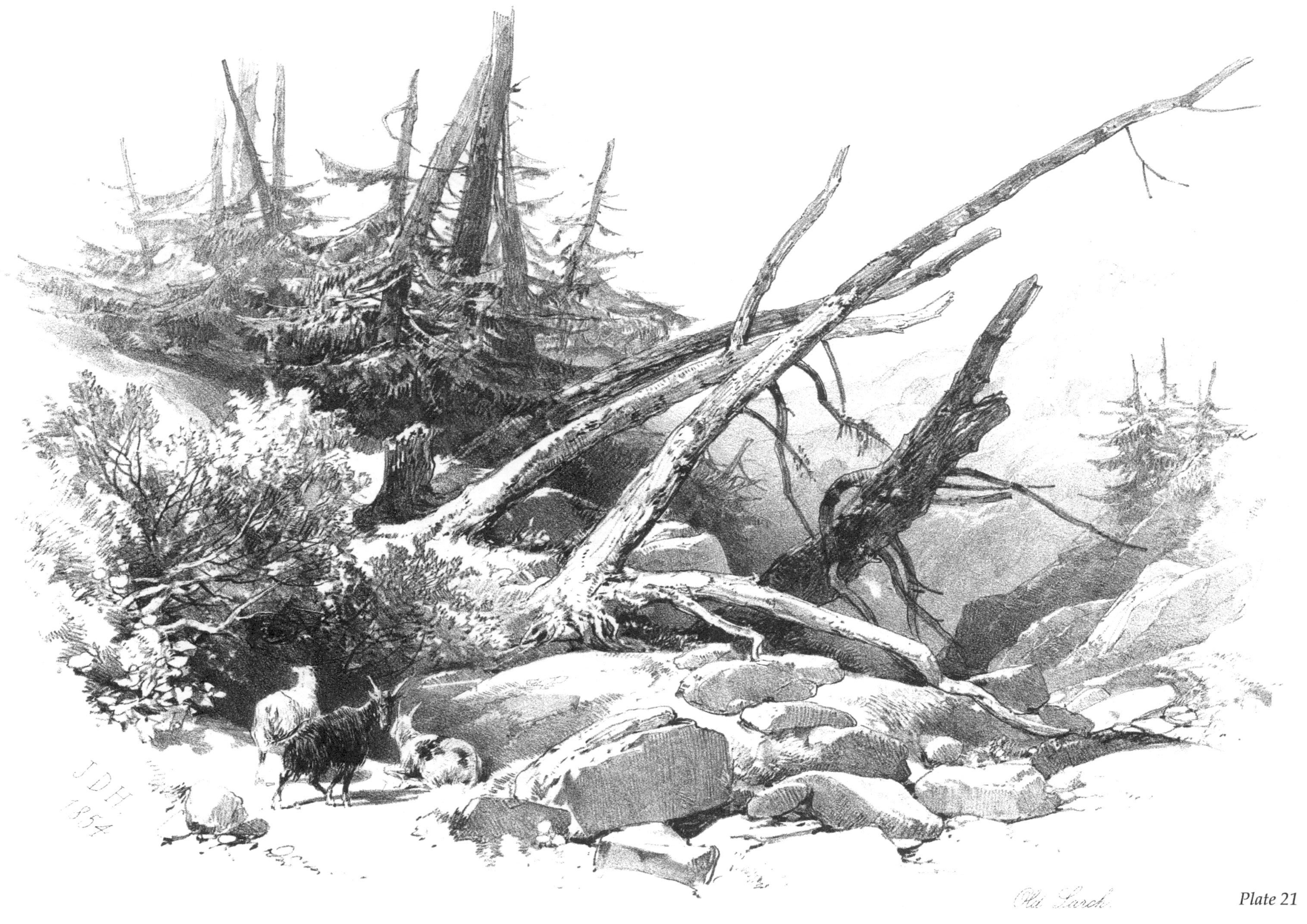

Plate 21

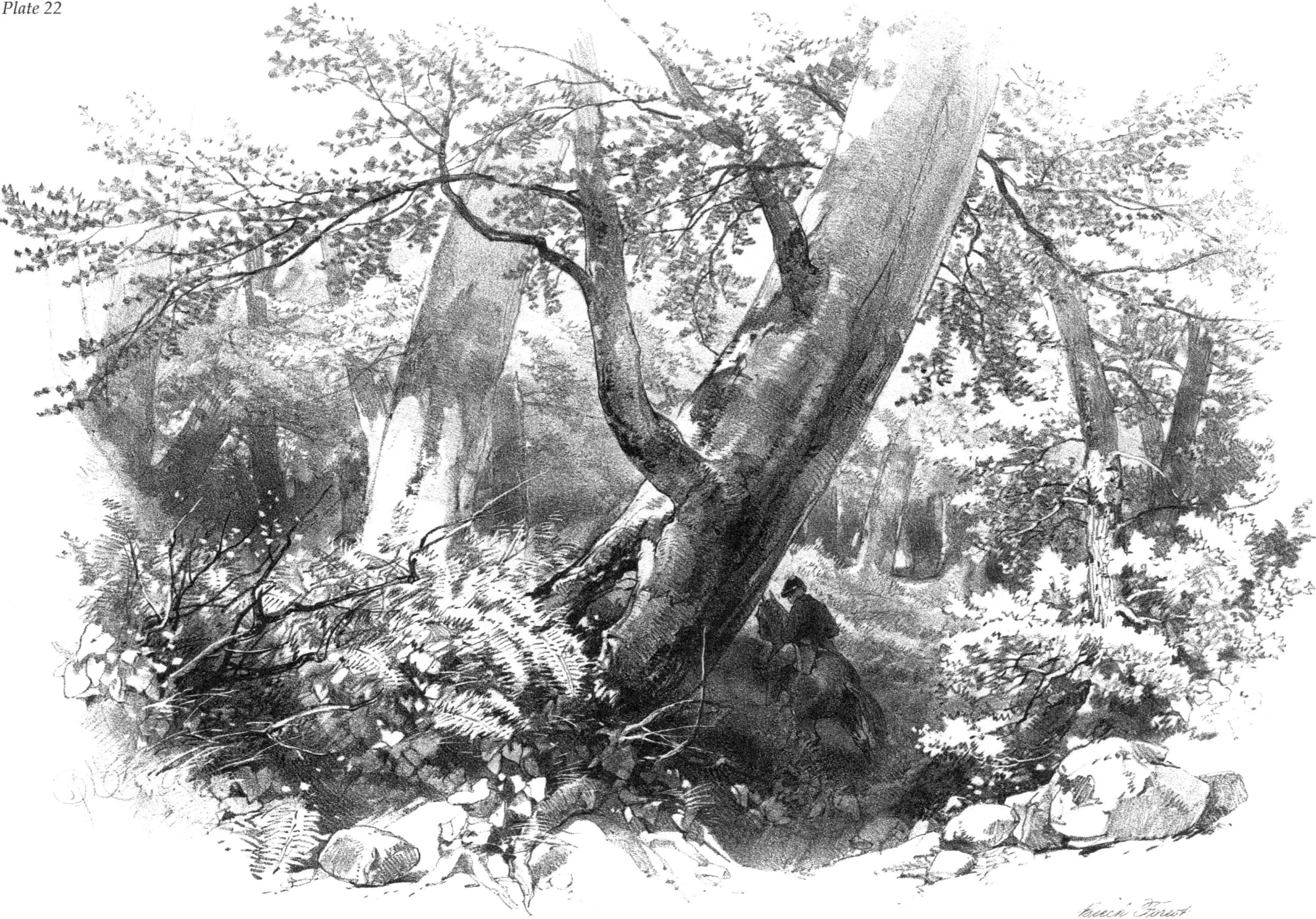

Plate 22
Beech Forest

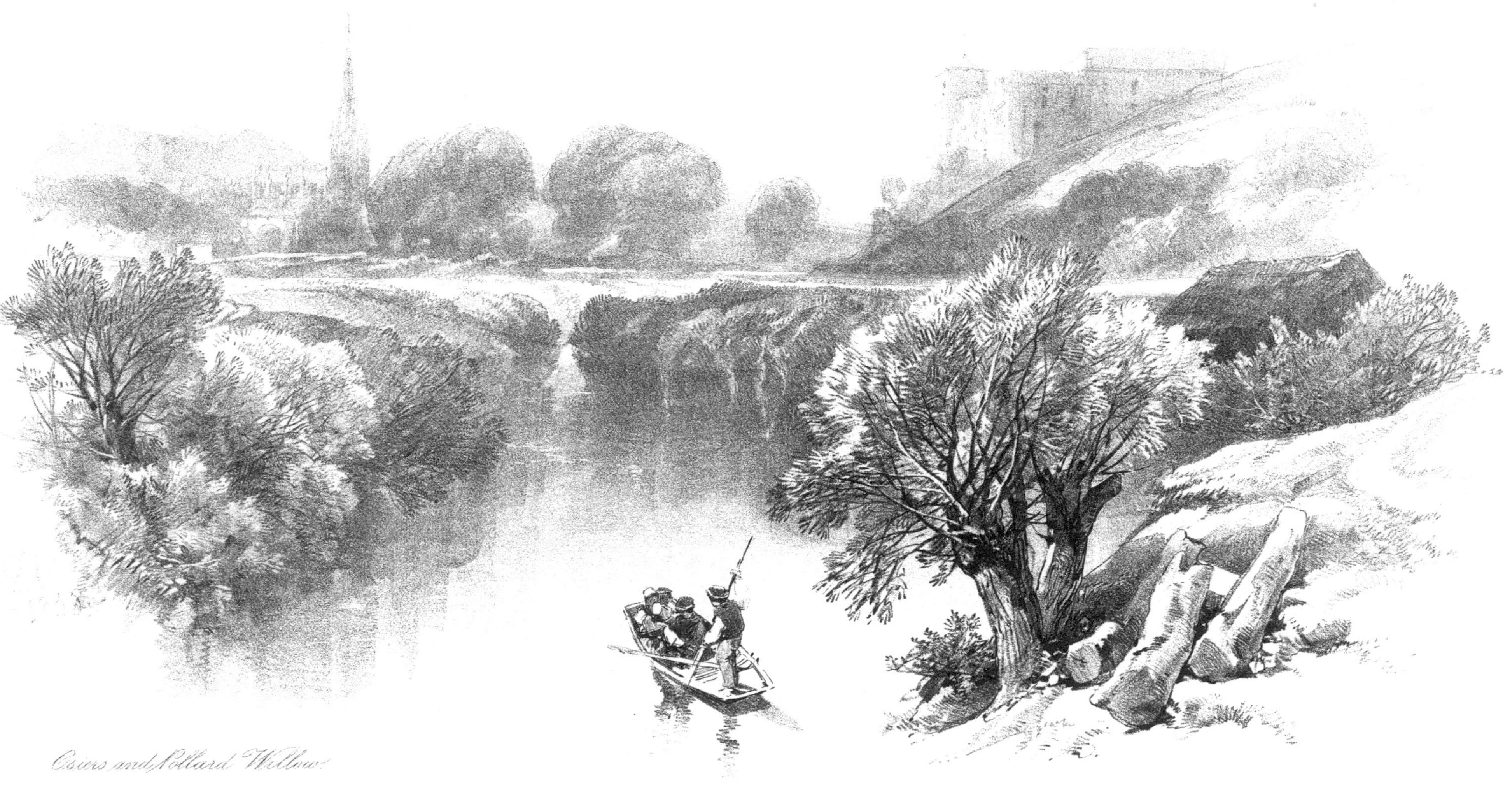

Osiers and Pollard Willow